Introduction to Personal Computers

SELF-TEACHING GUIDE

Wiley SELF-TEACHING GUIDES (STGs) are designed for first-time users of computer applications and programming languages. They feature concept-reinforcing drills, exercises, and illustrations that enable you to measure your progress, and learn at your own pace.

Other Wiley Self-Teaching Guides:

QUATTRO PRO 3.0 STG, Jennifer Meyer

PARADOX 2.5 STG, Gloria Wheeler

Q&A STG, David Angell and Brent Heslop

FOXPRO 2.0 STG, Ellen Sander

ALDUS PERSUASION FOR IMM PC AND COMPATIBLES STG, Karen Brown and Diane Stielstra

PERFORM STG, Peter Stephenson

QUARK Xpress STG, Paul Kaitz and Luther Sperberg

MICROSOFT WORD 5.5 FOR THE PC STG, Ruth Ashley and Judi Fernandez

WORDPERFECT 5.0/5.1 STG, Neil Salkind

WORDPERFECT FOR WINDOWS STG, Neil Salkind

MICROSOFT WINDOWS 3.0 STG, Keith Weiskamp and Saul Aguiar

PC DOS 4 STG, Ruth Ashely and Judi Fernandez

PC DOS 3.3 STG, Ruth Ashely and Judi Fernandez

MASTERING MICROSOFT WORKS STG, David Sachs, Babette Kronstadt, Judith Van Wormer, and Barbara Farrell

QUICKPASCAL STG, Keith Weiskamp and Saul Aguiar

GW BASIC STG, Ruth Ashley and Judi Fernandez

TURBO C++ STG, Bryan Flamig

SQL STG, Peter Stephenson

QUICKEN STG, Peter Aitken

COREL DRAW 2 STG, Robert Bixby

HARVARD GRAPHICS STG, David Harrison and John W. Yu

EXCEL 3.0 STG, Ruth Witken

To order our STGs, you can call Wiley directly at (201) 469-4400, or check your local bookstores.

"Mastering computers was never this easy, rewarding, and fun!"

Introduction to Personal Computers

SELF-TEACHING GUIDE

Peter Stephenson

John Wiley & Sons, Inc.
New York ▲ Chichester ▲ Brisbane ▲ Toronto ▲ Singapore

Publisher: Therese A. Zak
Editor: Laura Lewin
Managing Editor: Nana D. Prior

In recognition of the importance of preserving what has been written, it is a policy of John Wiley & Sons, Inc. to have books of enduring value published in the United States printed on acid-free paper, and we exert our best efforts to that end.

Library of Congress Cataloging-in-Publication Data

Introduction to personal computers: self-teaching guide/Peter Stephenson.
        p.   cm.
Includes Index

ISBN 0-471-54714-x (ppr)

Printed in the United States of America

10 9 8 7 6 5 4 3 2 1

For Michael and Michelle, my favorite PC users

Trademarks

IBM and PS/2 are trademarks of International Business Machines
  Corporation
1-2-3 is a trademark of Lotus Development Corporation
PostScript is a trademark of Adobe Corporation
3Share is a trademark of 3Com Corporation
Microsoft Windows 3.0 and Microsoft Word are trademarks of
  Microsoft Corporation
WordPerfect is a trademark of WordPerfect Corporation
WordStar is a trademark of MicroPro International
dBase is a trademark of Ashton-Tate
Dynacomm is a trademark of FutureSoft Engineering, Inc.
Fastback is a trademark of Fifth Generation Systems, Inc.
Fasttrax is a trademark of Bridgeway Publishing Company
Formworx is a trademark of Formworx, Inc.
Hercules is a trademark of Hercules Computer Technology
LaserJet is a trademark of Hewlett-Packard Corporation
Laserwriter and Macintosh are trademarks of Apple Computer
  Corporation
Perform is a trademark of Delrina Technology, Inc.
Quicken is a trademark of Intuit
SideKick is a trademark of Borland International
Ventura Publisher is a trademark of Xerox Corporation
Viruscan is a trademark of McAfee and Associates
All other trademarks and service marks are acknowledged as the
  property of their respective owners.

Acknowledgments

- Laura Lewin, for promoting the new look of this book and providing her usual editorial guidance, and putting up with my frequent frustration
- Prodigy users, too numerous to mention, who offered advice on what should be in a book like this
- Deborah Stephenson, for advice during the development of the book outline
- John Aitken, for being exactly the kind of person to whom this book is targeted and for responding to the techniques presented here for learning to use PCs
- Nan Poulios, for sharing her beginning PC teaching experiences with me
- Everyone with whom I have ever worked who wanted to throw their PC in front of a passing freight train and took the time to tell me why

Preface

We have no choice. Young, old, male, female, worker, professional, businessperson, all of us will eventually be faced with computers. Actually, we all run into them daily, where we work, where we shop, or where we bank. But what I'm talking about is the inevitable day when we walk into our school or workplace and there, sitting on our desk, is a personal computer. And, chances are, there will be nobody standing there beside it to teach us what to do with it.

Or, perhaps, we haven't bought a PC yet, but we know, sure as the sun will rise tomorrow, that the day is coming. What should we buy? How will we use it? How do we decide? If this sounds familiar (and I'm betting that it does), this book is dedicated to helping you overcome the frustrations you might otherwise have to endure on the road to PC mastery.

This book is a collection of guideposts on that road. It's written in a light-hearted style, that is, at times, as irreverent as is appropriate to the task of becoming "computer literate." What a term! *computer literate*. It actually sounds like you need a course of advanced study just to use a PC. And, of course, if you don't take that course, the implication is that you're "illiterate."

Well, you can relax. The whole idea of this book is that you don't need all that fancy training. You don't need to be a rocket scientist to use a PC. PCs are, simply, tools. They work for us. We don't work for them. With that radical premise in mind, we begin an odyssey that is intended to entertain, teach, and place the use of a very important tool in its proper perspective. The PC will shape how people work (and play) in the twenty-first century.

In the pages that follow you will learn how to select a PC, select the accessories that attach to it, and select the programs you will run on it. After selecting a PC, you will receive detailed instructions on its care and feeding. In fact, by the time you finish this book, you'll have learned everything you need to know to make productive use of a personal computer, even if programming your microwave oven or VCR is a world-class challenge for you.

In addition to the style and content of this book, we have provided a variety of additional aids to quick and easy PC mastery.

Scattered throughout the chapters you'll find axioms of PC use that will give you tidbits of insight in ways that are easy to remember. For example, you'll learn that there are only two kinds of PC users: those who back up their data and those who wish they had.

Also, you'll find many helpful hints. These hints or tips are specific "how-to" instructions that take a concept and compress it into a simple piece of advice. You'll avoid the learning by trial and error that often comes so painfully when you must embrace a new technology.

Finally, you'll be able to check your mastery of the concepts presented in each chapter with questions and exercises at the end of the chapter. By the time you finish you'll know about your new PC, its software, how to connect it to the outside world over telephone lines, how to avoid computer viruses, and a host of other topics that are not only important but interesting.

Writing this book has been a pleasure. After many years of watching novice users and users who didn't want to be users grapple with the task of learning a new personal computer, I've been able to offer an antidote for the pain of achieving "computer literacy."

Yes, I fear we are stuck with that ignominious term. However, don't be too concerned. As you will learn early in this book, the computer world is filled with jargon and buzzwords, many of which have limited usefulness. For example, if your PC is not "integrated," does that mean that it is "dis-integrated"? Of course not. So, in that irreverent spirit, let us proceed to banish the demons of computer literacy and get down to learning and enjoying this most pervasive of twentieth-century gimmicks: the personal computer.

Peter Stephenson

Contents Overview

1   **A Little Background to Help You Get Started**

2   **The Parts of Your PC**

3   **Your PC's Nervous System**

4   **Your PC's Built-In Library of Information**

5   **Printing**

6   **Can We Talk?: Using Your PC to Telecommunicate**

7   **My PC's All GUI!: Using Graphic Interfaces**

8   **Pssst. . .Wanna Buy Some Cheap Programs?**

9   **I Think There's a Virus Going Around**

10 **Now, Let's Get Some Work Done**

Contents

1 A Little Background to Help You Get Started, 1

A Preamble	2
So, You Think You Want a PC	3
What Kinds of PCs Are There?	5
Apples and Oranges	11
Send in the Clones	12
Selecting the "Extras" That Go with Your New PC	14
Software "Musts"	17
Where Do I Go for Believable Information?	18
Buying Information	18
Where to Get Help	21
Thirty-One Essential PC Buzzwords and What They Mean in English	22
Summary	38
Practice What You've Learned	39

2 The Parts of Your PC, 41

The Brain of Your PC—The Processor	42
What Makes Your PC Go?	43
Get on the Bus	44
286, 386, 486—What's That?	45
Keyboards 47	
What Makes the PC Keyboard Different?	48
Displays 50	
It's All There in Black (or Orange, or Green) and White	50
Color Your World	51
CGA	51

EGA	52
VGA	52
Disk Drives	53
Hard Drives—Lots of Storage Space	55
Getting Ready to Use the Hard Disk	56
How Fast Does It Go?	57
Ports—Connecting to the Outside World	58
What We Have Here Is No Failure to Communicate	58
Memory	61
Mice and Other Critters	62
Driving a Mouse	63
Scanners, Games, and Conflicts	63
Summary	64
Practice What You've Learned	66

3 Your PC's Nervous System, 69

Your PC's Autonomic Nervous System	70
CMOS and Setup	71
BIOS	72
DOS	73
What's in DOS?	74
Talking to Your PC— Simple Commands	76
Backup	77
Chdir or cd	78
Chkdsk	78
Cls	79
Copy	79
Date	80
Del	80
Dir	81
Diskcomp	82

Diskcopy 83

Fdisk 83

Format 84

Mkdir or md 85

Ren 85

Restore 85

Rmdir or rd 86

Time 86

Type 87

Ver 87

Xcopy 87

Teaching Your PC New Skills 88

Batching It 89

Special Files You Can Build 90

The Autoexec.bat File 92

Helping Your PC Remember—How Much
Memory Is Enough? 94

Expanding Your Tower 95

Some Hidden Floors 96

Summary 97

Practice What You've Learned 99

4 Your PC's Built-in Library of Information, 101

Your PC'S File Cabinet 102

Preparing the Cabinet to Receive Its Library of Files 104

On Your Mark—Low-Level Format 104

Get Set—Define the File Cabinet 106

Go—Format the Hard Drive 106

Organizing the Library into Logical Areas 107

Begin at the Beginning—The Key Directories 108

Other Directories 109

Putting Files in the Cabinet 109

Keeping Your Hard Drive Running
Efficiently 110

Keeping the File Cabinet Organized 111

What Do You Do If the Library Burns Down? 112

Backing Up 112

Grandfathering: Another Way to Back Up
Your Data 113

Summary 115

Practice What You've Learned 116

5 Printing, 119

A Printer by Any Other Name 120

Basics 120

Theory 121

Simple Pleasures—Printing the Easy Way 123

Any Port in a Storm 124

Seeing Dots 125

The Ultimate in Sophistication—The Laser Printer 126

Standards 127

What Else Do You Need? 128

Paper and Toner 129

PS: What Is It? 131

Keeping Your Printer Under Control 133

Driving Your Printer 134

Summary 135

Practice What You've Learned 137

6 Can We Talk?: Using Your PC to Telecommunicate, 139

Hey, PC—The Phone's for You! 140

How Do PCs Communicate? 140

And Now, the Details   141

COMM Ports Revisited—What Are IRQs
and I/Os?   142

What Is a Modem?   143

Speeds   145

Keeping It All Together   145

This Program's Terminal   146

Setting Up Term Programs   148

File Transfers   150

Stringing Along with Your Modem   151

BBSing—The Most Fun You Can Have with a
Phone and a PC   154

Different Strokes   155

What's an ANSI?   156

Summary   157

Practice What You've Learne   158d

7 My PC's All GUI !: Using Graphic Interfaces, 161

What's on the Menu?   162

Making Your Selection   163

Types of Menus   164

Should You Shell Out for a Menu?   167

How They Work   168

Down the Right Path   168

A Gem of a Desktop   169

So, What's It All Mean?   171

Do You Do Windows?   172

In the Mode   173

Getting It Going   173

One GUI Fits All   174

The Windows System Files   175

Simplifying   181

Summary   183

Practice What You've Learned   184

8   Psssst. . .Wanna Buy Some Cheap Programs?, 187

The Bargain Basement   188

Pricing Games   189

Try It, You'll Like It. If You Don't, Don't Pay for It   191

Where to Buy 'Em   192

Safety   192

Why Buy Shareware?   193

Absolutely Free!   194

What's Available?   195

This Is an Act of Piracy, Captain Bligh!   196

Licensing   196

Summary   198

Practice What You've Learned   199

9   I Think There's a Virus Going Around, 201

Can Your PC Get Sick?   202

More Buzzwords   202

How They Work   202

Worms   203

Typical Viri   204

Is It a Virus, or Just One of Those 24-Hour Bugs?   208

Safety First   210

Shareware   210

We're Scanning the Alien, Captain Kirk   212

Scanners   212

Validating Good Programs 213

Containment 213

Summary 214

Practice What You've Learned 215

10 Now, Let's Get Some Work Done, 217

Applications—Your PC's Working Tools 218

Word Processing 219

Spreadsheets 223

Database Management 225

Contact Management 227

Desktop Publishing 228

Drawing Software 230

Business Forms Management 230

Accounting 232

Personal Applications 233

Utility Programs 235

File Recovery 236

Defragmenters 236

File Transfer 237

Zippers 237

Summary 239

Practice What You've Learned 240

List of Figures

Figure 1.1. A Typical "AT" Class Personal Computer
Figure 1.2. An IBM PS/2
Figure 1.3. A Typical Laptop Computer
Figure 1.4. An Apple Macintosh
Figure 1.5. A Typical Monitor for Your PC
Figure 1.6. A Low-cost Dot Matrix Printer
Figure 1.7. A LaserJet Printer
Figure 1.8. A Three-button Mouse
Figure 1.9. A CPU
Figure 2.1. The Parts of a Typical PC
Figure 2.2. Two Styles of PC Keyboards
Figure 2.3. 3 1/2" and 5 1/4" Floppy Disks
Figure 2.4. A Hard Disk Drive Removed from the PC
Figure 2.5. An Add-in Card that Plugs onto the Mother Board
Figure 2.6. A PC-mounted 9-pin RS232 Connector
Figure 2.7. A PC-mounted 25-pin RS232 Connector
Figure 2.8. A Centronics Connector (Printer End)
Figure 2.9. A Joystick for Use in the PC's Game Port
Figure 3.1. A Typical Listing of a Root Directory
Figure 3.2. A Typical Directory Display Using the /w Switch
Figure 3.3. A Config.sys File
Figure 3.4. An Autoexec.bat File
Figure 4.1. A Directory Tree
Figure 5.1. A High-end Dot Matrix Printer
Figure 5.2. A Laser Printer with Paper Trays for Two Sizes of Paper
Figure 6.1. A Modem
Figure 7.1. A Moving Bar Menu
Figure 7.2. The Lotus Menu
Figure 7.3. Windows 3.0—A GUI Screen
Figure 7.4. A Typical Win.ini File Screen
Figure 7.5. A Typical System.ini File Screen
Figure 9.1. Typical Viri, Courtesy of McAfee and Associates
Figure 10.1. A Typical Word Processing Screen (WordPerfect 5.1)
Figure 10.2. A Spreadsheet Screen (Lotus 1-2-3)
Figure 10. 3. A Database Management Program Screen (dBASE IV)

Figure 10.4. A DTP Program Screen (Ventura Publisher)

Figure 10.5. A Drawing Program Screen (Corel Draw)

Figure 10.6. A Forms Management Program Screen (PerFORM Pro)

Figure 10.7. A Very Simple Accounting Program Screen (Quicken)

Figure 10.8. A Simple PIM Screen (InfoSelect)

Figure 10.9. A File Transfer Software Screen (LapLink)

A Little Background to Help You Get Started

This chapter, as an introduction to your PC, will lay the foundation for the rest of the book. You'll learn the basics of what a PC is and what should go into your buying decision. You'll get a general introduction to the parts of the PC and a tour of the most important PC buzzwords, just so we'll all be speaking the same language. In this chapter you will learn about:

▲ **What a PC is and what types are available**

▲ **The benefits of PC clones**

▲ **The difference between hardware and software and how much of each you will need**

▲ **How to get good advice on buying, learning, and using your PC**

▲ **The thirty-one essential PC buzzwords**

A Preamble

It's no secret that personal computers (PCs) are becoming a key part of our business, personal, and cultural life. Considered toys or business tools just a few years ago, PCs now sit on virtually every business desk and in many homes. And the push by manufacturers like IBM, Compaq, and Apple to start a revolution in *home* computing is just beginning to bear fruit.

Although many small businesses either don't have PCs yet or aren't using the ones they have, increasingly, employees who were working without PCs are coming to work and finding them on their desks. Where is the future of personal computing headed? How do you make the right selection when you choose a PC and everything that goes with it? What does go with it? This book will answer these questions and many more.

When you finish, you'll know everything you need to know to select and use your PC. You won't need to become technically oriented to get the most out of your PC in day-to-day work, so we won't concentrate on technical detail. It's one thing to understand and use personal computers successfully. It's quite another to become a guru. Leave the mysteries of personal computing to the experts. All you need is a special, nontechnical guide to living in harmony with your PC.

Throughout this book you'll find PC concepts in the most nontechnical terms possible. You'll find hands-on exercises to reinforce the information in the book as well as handy tips. Later on in this chapter you'll find a glossary to the only buzzwords you'll ever need to know to communicate effectively about your PC. In the chapters that follow I'll stick pretty closely to those buzzwords.

Occasionally it will be necessary to step outside our own boundaries. When that happens, I'll stop, explain carefully, and proceed with caution. Along the way, I hope to entertain as well as inform you. Now, on with the show!

So, You Think You Want a PC

Everybody needs a PC. All you have to do is turn on your TV and watch the commercials for IBM ("How you gonna do it? PS/2 it!"), Compaq ("It simply works better"), Tandy, or Apple to realize that your life can hardly be complete without at least one of these things on your kitchen table. And small business folks have no chance in this competitive world without a battery of PCs and the incomprehensible hardware, software, and accessories to go with them. The local radio ads exhort you to buy this or that PC—an 80286 or 80386 or 80386SX or goodness knows what else—and you, gentle reader, are befuddled and bewildered.

You are just about convinced that your continued personal, spiritual, and professional existence depends on buying that PC and especially, and this is the hardest part, getting the right one. Everyone has heard at least one horror story of a friend/neighbor/relative who didn't buy right and not only spent a lot of money but never even got the thing to work. So it sits on the shelf. The big problem for many potential users is they not only don't know what to buy, they don't know what they're going to use their PC for when they get it out of the box.

Well, here's a news flash for you! You may not need, or even want, a PC. Unless you are simply fascinated by computers or want an expensive game machine, if you don't have a specific, preplanned purpose for your new computer, don't buy one. Personal computers are very good for some things, and very bad for others.

For example, if you are just looking for a way to balance your checkbook, buy a $19.95 calculator and forget the PC. The TV commercials may show happy families clustered around their home PCs, chatting ecstatically about all of the wonderful things they can do with them right out of the box. But what they don't show are the hours it takes to enter all of the personal information into the computer to make those wonderful programs work. (No,

Virginia, PCs don't come with your checkbook entered already—
you have to do that.)

On the other hand, if you keep several bank accounts and manage a personal investment portfolio or run a small home or hobby business, or would enjoy communicating with other computer users all over the world, perhaps a home PC *is* for you. And if you have a business of almost any kind, you can probably benefit from putting a lot of the "grunt work" on a PC.

TIP

You must know how you plan to use your business computer. There is a firm rule for buying business PCs. Select the software for your job first. Then select the hardware to run the software. Never select a PC the other way around. If you ever walk into a computer store to buy a PC and the first question the salesperson asks *isn't* "What are you going to use it for?"— run, don't walk, to the nearest exit.

If you plan to publish a newsletter or produce your own brochures, you'll need far different hardware than if you want to keep the books or, perhaps, control inventory for your business. Can one PC do both? Certainly. But it would be a costly mistake for you to buy for both applications if you wanted to do only the simpler application. For bookkeeping you wouldn't need the extensive graphics and publishing capabilities required for desktop publishing.

Today's PCs are very powerful computers, indeed. There is as much power in some of the more sophisticated personal computers as there was in the huge mainframes of yesteryear that took up entire rooms. And this power sits on (or beside) your desk. That sophistication, usually, comes at a price. And it isn't always needed. So here is the first axiom for buying and using PCs.

AXIOM

If you don't match hardware power to the software power you need for the job you want your PC to do, you'll either spend too much or get too little.

That, of course, reiterates the rule of software first, hardware to match. There are as many different types and configurations of PCs as there are reasons to use them. In most cases, however, you won't buy a PC for a single task. If you are buying that way, you might want to explore your requirements a bit further. I can think of only a few, very sophisticated, types of applications that would, by themselves, justify a special PC.

And, what about the rapid pace of change within the PC industry? You might take one look at the dizzying rate of advancement in PC technology and decide that as soon as you buy a PC, it will be obsolete. That brings us to the second axiom.

AXIOM

Sometimes "good enough" is good enough. It is not engraved in stone that you need to chase technology to get your personal computing job done right.

If you have a job to do, select the right software (programs) to do it. Then match the correct hardware to support the software. Then, do the job. If you're satisfied that the job is getting done, why chase technology? If you buy right the first time, you will not need to change your PC configuration once a year.

What Kinds of PCs Are There?

PCs come in a large variety of shapes, sizes, and configurations (Figure 1.1). They also come in a couple of different *operating systems*. Don't let that term throw you. We'll explain operating systems shortly. Again, you should select hardware according to the software that matches your application. As this book progresses, you'll get a much better idea of what that means.

For the moment, let's explore some of the possibilities. There are several ways of categorizing PCs. One is by speed. Another is by the types of additional equipment, such as color displays or communications equipment, that the PC supports. A third way of

▼ *Figure 1.1. A Typical "AT" Class Personal Computer*

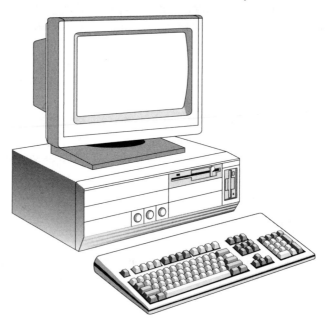

describing a PC is according to the amount of memory or by disk storage available. Usually all of these aspects go together to define a particular PC. And that definition grows out of the needs of your application software. Here's what I mean.

Suppose you wanted to buy a car. You wouldn't go to the nearest dealer and say, simply, "I want to buy a car." You would describe the kinds of options you wanted. You would explain that you wanted a small car or, perhaps, a station wagon. You would probably even have a favorite color or two. Buying a PC is not much different. The salesperson at your store is very wise in the ways of PC neophytes and asks all the right questions. If your first visit to a computer store doesn't go something like this, you may be in the wrong store.

Salesperson: Good morning. May I help you?

You: I'm looking for a PC. It's my first.

Salesperson: Will you be using your PC for business or pleasure?

You: I have a small business. I'm a sales rep for widgets.

Salesperson: What do you plan to use your PC for?

You: I'd like to keep my books. Nothing much, you know. I want to keep that part simple. Oh, and I need to write a lot of letters and proposals. And I'd like to make some of my own brochures and direct mail pieces. Can I get one PC to do all that?

Salesperson: Of course. How much did you plan to spend?

You: I really don't know. I've never bought one of these things before, so I don't what they cost.

Salesperson: Well, your first two requirements, a simple accounting package and a word processor, don't require a very big machine. You could get by with a system for under $1,000. But the brochures and mailers will require somewhat more sophistication. The extra software, memory, laser printer, and high-resolution monitor could actually double the price. Are you sure you want to do desktop publishing at this point?

You: Could I start small and expand?

Salesperson: Yes, if you start carefully with a good, expandable PC. It will be a little more than you really need now, but it will be easy to expand later.

And so on. Notice that our hypothetical salesperson is asking questions that relate to how you are going to use your new PC, what you want to do with it in the future, and how much you want to spend on it. The next step, after you decide whether you want the cheapie, the expandable, or the whole shebang, would probably be to select the software that fits the categories you've decided you need today. Then would come the PC, the monitor and, finally, a printer.

If, for example, you decide to shoot the works, you'll probably get (don't run away, now…you don't need to know what all this means yet) a 386, color monitor, laser printer, and several software packages. If that sounds expensive, it is. The salesperson's estimate of around $2,000 could just about cover the hardware. You haven't even bought any software yet. Worse, if you are a real beginner, you may not know enough about using the more sophisticated software to make it particularly useful to you. Remember, in this little scenario you are running a small business. It's a lot more important for you to sell a lot of widgets (so you can pay the bills) than it is to play with a computer. Computers are supposed to make life *easier*. That's a concept a lot of people, including those who make computers and software, tend to forget.

Here's the point. There are many types of PCs (see Figures 1.2 and 1.3). They have varying amounts of power, are sold at different

▼ *Figure 1.2. An IBM PS/2*

▼ *Figure 1.3. A Typical Laptop Computer*

prices, and support different accessories. Which one you select will depend on how you plan to use it. There are some simple guidelines to help you, though. The easiest way to show you those guidelines is in chart form (see Table 1.1). This chart will, of necessity, have some entries you won't completely understand. But look at it anyway and refer back to it as you read on and gain more understanding.

Notice that I have left out applications like communications and games. Also, I have avoided the subject of printers altogether. These issues will surface a bit later. Jumping ahead of our buzzwords, suffice it to say that in general if the CPU (that's the computer's main processor—the engine that makes the PC go) is a *386*, this implies bigger, faster, more, than if the CPU is a *286*. As a rule, the bigger numbers have more oomph than the smaller ones.

One last point. For the moment, you have learned that you should match your hardware to your software, which is matched to your application (the work you want to do). But the salesperson in our scenario was astute. The last suggestion was that you might want to get something *a little bit more* than you really need now so you can expand easily later. This is good advice indeed, and it proceeds from another axiom:

▼ *Table 1.1. Typical Small Business PC Setups*

TYPICAL APPLICATIONS	TYPICAL SOFTWARE	CPU	DISK DRIVES	MONITOR
Word Processing	WordPerfect, Microsoft, Word	286	1 HD 1 FD	Mono
Accounting (Small business)	Quicken, any of several small accounting packages	286	1 HD 1 FD	Mono
Database	dBASE, Paradox	286 or 386	1 HD 1 FD	Mono or Color
Desktop Publishing	Ventura Publisher, Pagemaker	386	1 HD 1 FD	High res Color
Spreadsheet	Lotus 1-2-3	286	1 HD 1 FD	Mono or Color
	Excel	386	1 HD 1 FD	High res Color
Key:	HD = Hard Disk FD = Floppy Disk Mono = Monochrome monitor High res Color = High resolution Color Monitor			

AXIOM

Data expands to fill the available storage space and new applications always need just a little more computer power.

What that means is that you can continue to upgrade to meet your expanding needs (if they do, indeed, expand) without having to trade in your PC for next year's model. Sometimes this little extra power can prevent you from bumping up against limits you didn't know would be a problem when you first bought your computer.

Apples and Oranges

One of the chief differences between PCs is in the *operating system*. This is another term you don't really need yet. But you need to know what it implies. For most new computer users it means just one thing: Apple or IBM. And what that boils down to is, if you have an Apple computer, including Macintosh, you won't be able to run any programs designed for use on IBM or IBM-compatible computers. That goes both ways, of course. You can't take your IBM programs and run them on your neighbor's Macintosh (Figure 1.4).

The reason is that Apple and IBM have different operating systems. That means that the way the two kinds of computers run a program, store data, and arrange disk storage is significantly

▼ *Figure 1.4. An Apple Macintosh*

different, and the two schemes are not compatible. There are other types of operating systems that you might encounter, but at this point in your emerging computer career they are unimportant.

Send in the Clones

OK, you know the difference between IBM and Apple. But what about all of those non-IBM PCs that claim to be IBM *compatible*? There are more of them than there are true-blue IBM PCs, and they cost a whole lot less. Can you use—*should* you use—one of these? These PCs are generically referred to as *clones*. With a little care you can certainly select a clone, save a lot of money, and run every program ever written for IBM PCs or IBM PS/2s (IBM's lines of personal computers). The question, aside from money, is "Why buy a clone?" That's closely followed by "What's the risk in buying a clone?" Let's take them one at a time.

Why Buy a Clone?

Cost is the obvious answer. Clones cost, in many cases, half of what an IBM PS/2 costs. But there is more. For your money you can often get a lot more performance. For example, I just specified a large clone PC for a very critical application for one of my clients. Later, I chanced to discuss a similar application with another consultant. She had used a less powerful IBM PS/2 for a similar application. Her PS/2 cost twice what my clone did, and I got decidedly more machine. But these are murky waters and danger lurks for the uninitiated buyer.

What's the Risk?

In most cases, your risk is limited to how well your supplier will support the clone. However, you should be aware that there are clones and there are clones. Within the clone community there are well-known manufacturers and there are no-names. Some of the well-known companies, such as Compaq, produce PCs every bit as expensive as IBM. There are also some well-known companies that produce very low-cost PCs of rather high quality.

But, as I said, there is danger here. Many computer stores have their own house brands. Now it is basically true that there is a limited number of manufacturers making the parts for these clones. So, for the most part, most of the no-name PCs you'll find are assembled from a range of pretty standard components. However, the store is often not really equipped to maintain these no-names properly. Also, if you should ever want to sell your PC and buy another, the resale value is very limited. Finally, if the store goes out of business, and a great many of them do with frustrating regularity, you've got yourself a really terrific boat anchor, but not much in the way of a PC.

So how do you know? One way is to read up on PCs from the newsstand computer magazines and make sure you recognize the brand your store is trying to sell you. Another possibility is to buy only from the larger chains. Not only are they more reliable, they also have more buying power. Buying power usually means better prices. The PC sales game is quite competitive; you *can* get good prices.

As to choosing a clone over a real IBM PS/2, I recommend it. That, by the way, brings out another point. In the early days of PCs, the term *clone* referred to a copy, model by model, of IBM's product line. Today, it simply means IBM compatibility. Most good clone makers have extraordinarily complete product lines with PCs for almost every need.

TIP

If your clone maker doesn't have a complete line of PCs for a variety of uses, stay away from them. The manufacturer that produces only one or two different PCs is not serious about the business and probably won't be around long.

So are clones a good bet? Yes, if you stick with the majors. Just be sure that there is someone who can support (maintain) your PC and that there is an aftermarket if you want to sell it some day. It's true that you can save money if you buy through mail order. But at this point you aren't quite ready to take that step, because you have to know exactly what you're buying. Most mail-order PCs have, as the toy makers say, "some assembly required." Also you'll have to be the one to support your new PC. Mail order, for the moment anyway, is not recommended.

Selecting the "Extras" That Go with Your New PC

It's probably obvious to you by now that you don't just go out and buy a PC, complete and ready to run. There are a lot of other pieces to the personal computing puzzle, and most of those pieces are as puzzling as the PC itself. To get you started, though, there are some broad categories of things that go with the main box (the part I called the *CPU* earlier).

The first group of accessories really aren't accessories in the sense that you can get along without them. This group includes disk drives. As you will learn later, there are all kinds of disk drives. You will, at minimum, need a floppy disk drive. Fortunately, virtually all PCs come equipped with at least one of those. Of course there are several kinds and sizes, but for the moment, add "one or two floppy drives" to your shopping list.

Also in this category are the hard or *fixed* drives (or *hard disks*, if you prefer). These are used for mass storage and, in most cases, you'll want one of those too. Like the floppies, hard disk drives come in several sizes and types. There are a lot more choices, though, than there are in the floppy bunch. Once you know which one to select, you should probably consider adding a hard drive to your purchase right from the start.

Next comes the monitor, or display (Figure 1.5). Obviously, you can't get along without one of these. They come in two broad types: color and monochrome. Color monitors range from a little more expensive than monochrome, to a whole lot more costly. Like everything else in the PC world, there are lots of choices here. Wait until we discuss monitors in more depth to make your choice.

▼ *Figure 1.5. A Typical Monitor for Your PC*

Selecting the "Extras" That Go with Your New PC

Now we get to the options. At the top of the list is a printer (Figures 1.6 and 1.7). If you thought you had choices for monitors, wait until you look at printers. Prices range from a bit over a hundred dollars, to several thousand dollars. Like the monitor, printer choice depends very heavily on what you plan to do with your PC.

You will also need to shop for a modem. *Modems* are for communicating over telephone lines with other PCs, bulletin boards, and online services (more on this in Chapter 6). Modeming is a lot of fun and it can also be very useful in some types of business. Modems are relatively inexpensive if you keep it simple. You also need some special software, which is not usually included, to make them work. We'll get to those details later on.

Finally, there are a host of other accessories that are truly optional. These accessories are generally referred to as *peripherals*. Generally speaking, peripherals are additional devices that plug into your computer to perform some function under your PC's control. The printer, for example, is a peripheral.

▼ *Figure 1.6. A Low-cost Dot Matrix Printer*

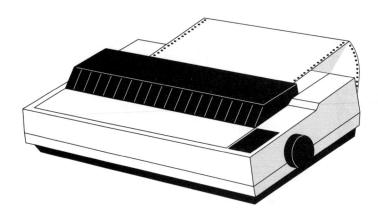

▼ *Figure 1.7. A LaserJet Printer*

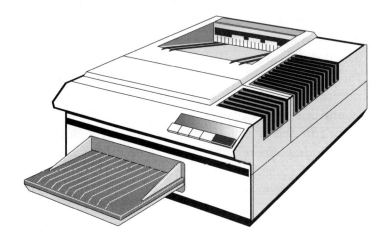

Software "Musts"

I'm not going to get into the specifics of individual software packages at this point because the information wouldn't be of much use to you yet. Starting with Chapter 7 we'll begin to explore the various kinds of software programs that are available for your PC. For now, it's important only that you become familiar with the kinds of software you're likely to need.

Let's begin by defining *software*. In simple terms, it's the stuff you buy at your local computer store that consists of one or more floppy disks and a user's manual packaged in shrinkwrap. What is on those disks, however, is what really makes your PC useful. If we were to compare loading a software program into your PC with some form of human endeavor, the simile would be learning a new process or operation. You *teach* the computer a new skill by loading the software to perform the task.

Software can be dedicated to a specific task (*application software*). It can provide menus or some other *operating environment* for the user. Or it might be special *programming language* software, intended for use by programmers. There are several categories of application software in which you, as an average user, are likely to be interested. Those basic categories are *word processing*, *database management*, *spreadsheet*, *communications*, and *desktop publishing*. In addition, you may be interested in accounting software if you are using your PC to help you run a small business.

Utilities

There is also a variety of specialized little programs to help you manage your PC itself. These small applications are called *utilities*. Finally, you will find a large number of very specialized programs that don't seem to fit into any category. Which ones will you need? By now you know that depends on what you're going to do with your PC. For most users the basic application in their PC is word processing. If you keep mail lists or other lists of people or things you might need a database management system.

Databases

There are a wide variety of database management systems (or *DBMS* as they are sometimes called). Some are "roll your own" programs that you will use to create your own custom application program. Some are prebuilt, such as any of the hundreds of mail list or rotary-card file programs. Chances are you'll find a use for at least one of these. I recommend that you stick to the premade products for the moment. If you do much financial calculating, you might also want a spreadsheet program, which makes the job of managing finances much easier. Then, of course, you'll pick up a collection of utilities along the way to becoming a PC power user.

Games

If you like games, you now can buy a wide variety of games every bit as sophisticated as those found on your kid's Nintendo or in any video arcade. Add a joystick to your PC and you've got a powerful (if somewhat expensive) game machine.

In short, those useful tools that make your PC worth having are the software programs. Since you use the software for specific tasks, you can begin to see why you should begin by selecting the software that you will use most. Remember, the PC itself is just metal, plastic, and circuitry that allows you to run that software. So put the emphasis where it belongs—on the tasks you need to accomplish and the software required to accomplish them.

Where Do I Go for Believable Information?

For new PC users, getting reliable, useful information is a bit like searching for the leprechaun's pot of gold, or winning big in Las Vegas. There's an awful lot of information available, but most of it is narrowly focused, self-serving, or just plain wrong. There are basically three things you need to know about a computer: buying it, learning it, and using it.

Buying Information

If you thought that this heading meant that you had to *buy* information, you were about half right. For the most part, reliable information about PCs is going to cost you something. It might be nothing more than the cost of a computing magazine or a book on some aspect of PCs. Or it might be the services of a professional consultant. It's a sad fact of computing life that all of those well-meaning folks handing out free advice will usually end up costing you in the long run. So, unfortunately, here's another of axiom.

Where Do I Go for Believable Information?

AXIOM

Just as there's no such thing as a free lunch, there's no such thing as free advice.

And even if you pay for help with your computing, that doesn't mean that you're going to get the best advice. You still have to pick your sources. All of which brings us to the other way to read this section's heading: *advice for buying a PC*. That may be the hardest kind of good advice to get. One good source of reasonably free, reasonably sound advice is users groups. There are a great many groups that specialize in the various personal computers and the programs that run on them. For example, there may be an IBM or Macintosh group in your area that can provide you with the advice born of experience. For the names of these groups ask your dealer.

Magazines and Handbooks

The next best place to start is with a book like this and recent copies of computer magazines from your newsstand. There are several types of these publications, so you have to be a little careful about which ones you buy. For example, *Byte Magazine* and *PC Magazine*, probably the best-known of all personal computer magazines, may have limited usefulness for you unless they focus specifically on the type of machine you think you want to buy. Why? Both publications tend to cater to the more technical reader, usually in a business environment.

On the other hand, *Computer Buyers Guide and Handbook* and its sister publications for printers and desktop publishing are written at a much simpler level and cater to first-time buyers. They provide solid information on products and prices. And when it comes to reviews, remember, most reviewers are power users and may not have the knack of viewing the products they review from the perspective of the novice. There is one thing of which you can be certain, though. If you find most publications have awarded Editor's Choice or other kudos to a product, you can bank on it being a safe bet in terms of quality and performance. Whether you need that particular product for your application is another issue entirely.

Salespeople

It is a dangerous thing to ask the salespeople in a computer store what you should buy because they generally only want one thing: for you to buy from *them*. However, it's worth the time to go to several well-known stores in your area and ask the same questions. If you get a consensus, then you're on the right track. What constitutes a well-known store? Usually you can count on the larger chains, but remember, no store is any better than its staff. Here is my general evaluation of some of the larger chains.

Tandy (Radio Shack) Generally staffed by young sales staff. They have a limited range of products, with fair to good pricing on hardware. Know what you want in advance if you go here.

Egghead Discount Software Excellent choice of software at good to very good prices. Sales staff reasonably knowledgeable about packages in general, but little real application depth. It helps to know what you want first, but sales staff can probably help if you don't.

SoftWareHouse The price leader in most cities. If you know what you want you'll usually get the best price here. Mostly software, but getting more and more involved with hardware and peripherals.

BusinessLand Just as the name says—targets businesses, especially smaller ones. They generally have knowledgeable staff and can often provide consulting services. Don't come here if you're price shopping. Service isn't (and shouldn't be) cheap. The emphasis here is on systems. They can get just about anything that fits your application and can support it after the sale.

ComputerLand Their main thrust is moving product, so if you know what you want, and it falls within the fairly narrow range of what the store has available, you can get a pretty good price.

There are also a multitude of small local stores and some of the smaller or regional chains. There is a whole bag of stores that are OK but, as a group, really have little to distinguish them. These are the ones you have to look at very carefully in your local area. They can often be excellent. The key to early success, if you need help buying, is to find a store that caters to small businesses. You'll pay a bit more, but the advice is more likely to be accurate and the after-sale service is more likely to be reliable.

Where to Get Help

Once you buy your new system, you have two tasks. You have to learn it and you have to continue to use it. Let's start with the learning part. If you're one of those folks who likes formal training, you can usually find several personal computer training centers in just about any town. The trouble is, those that offer entry-level, generalized PC training are few and far between. If there are some in your town, you will usually find them quite expensive. Fortunately, there's an alternative if you bought smart in the first place.

The different dealers (called *resellers* in PC lingo) that provide good advice and support after the sale usually have some means of helping you learn to use your new PC. That might be through formal training or just by being there to answer your questions as they arise. Don't take that "consulting" lightly. In terms of getting you up and running in a hurry, and reducing your frustration level, they can be a big plus. Now here's a hint.

TIP

Never buy a PC on a Friday or weekend. If you need help getting started it won't be available. Buy early in the week if you think you're going to need help.

Another good source of startup information is your local bookstore.

If you have no prior experience with PCs, don't count on the tech manuals or user guides that come with your PC or application software. Most are written by technical writers who are underpaid, undertrained and, often, can't write. The exception is in very large companies. The problem there, however, is that the manuals are all written by committee. Everybody from the president to the janitor feels that they need to add to the documentation. Unfortunately, the committee approach pops up in smaller companies too. The end result is, usually, user guides of minimal usefulness. The moral? Get a good third-party "how-to" book at your local bookstore. You'll be miles ahead.

Thirty-One Essential PC Buzzwords and What They Mean in English

This may be the most important part of this book for some readers. I can tell you without fear of contradiction that it is the most fun for me to write. Why? The PC world is so full of jargon it's a wonder anyone can understand anyone else. However (here's a Catch 22), if you don't have specific ways of expressing certain concepts or describing the pieces that make up the personal computing environment, you'll end up using inconsistent gobbledygook to communicate essential ideas. For example, you'll have a hard time getting any useful technical support for your PC if you tell the tech support engineer that "the gizmo under the top front of the PC doesn't seem to work right." What the engineer really needs to hear is, "The A floppy drive won't start up."

So, in the interest of giving you what you need to talk computerese, and not one bit more, here is the essential PC glossary. Actually, it's a lot more than a glossary, which is why it's here, in the front of the book where you can actually use it. I'll try to stick pretty closely to this list of terms as the book progresses. The advantage is that once you read this section you probably won't need a glossary. You'll have the required lingo down pat. Here we go.

Application

An application is any program that you run to perform a specific task. An application might be generic, such as a database, word processor, spreadsheet, or something more specific like an accounting package or a mail list manager. Applications are the workhorse software of personal computing in that they do the specific work. Other types of software, such as programming languages or environments (like Microsoft's Windows), are not considered applications. The software containing the applications is called *applications software*.

ASCII

ASCII is the acronym for *American Standard Code for Information Interchange*. It's a format for representing the characters of the alphabet, numbers, and certain symbols in a code that the computer understands. But the term ASCII has a broader meaning in some contexts. For example, when most word processors produce text, they add special characters that you can't see, called *control characters*. (These are sometimes called *unprintable* characters because they don't cause a printer to place them on the page.)

Unprintable control characters are important to the word processor because they contain information such as "make the text that follows bold," or "underline the following text." However, if you were to try to read the text produced by the word processor without the help of the word processing application, you would not be able to.

If, on the other hand, you produce the text with a special kind of word processor called a *text editor*, there would be no control characters (and no bold, underline, or other special effects, either) and you could read the text simply by using the DOS TYPE command (more about DOS and the DOS commands later). That clean, no-control-character text is called *ASCII* text because it contains only those characters in the ASCII character set. The file containing the ASCII text is often called a text file or ASCII file. Some word processors have a special mode for producing ASCII text called a DOS text or nondocument mode.

Backup and Recovery

This refers to the process of making a special copy of the data on your hard disk (*backup*) for use in the event that you experience a failure that destroys the data on your disk. You are actually making a compressed copy you can use to replace (*recover* or *restore*) the lost or damaged data. There are several backup and recovery programs (these fall into the generic category of *utilities*) including BACKUP and RESTORE commands as part of DOS, the PC's internal operating system. (We'll discuss DOS and operating systems in much more detail later.)

In most cases, you'll find that third-party backup utilities are faster and every bit as safe as the DOS versions. In any event, you should never fail to perform periodic backups. There will come a time when you will lose the data on your hard drive. If you have a recent backup you will be able to recover your lost data up to the point of your last backup. If you don't, you can count on losing your data. Time for another axiom.

AXIOM

There are only two kinds of personal computer users: those who perform frequent backups, and those who wish they had. It's not a case of *if* your hard disk will fail. It's *when*.

BATch File

A batch file is a simple DOS (there's that word again—you'll have to wait for the Ds to learn more about it) file that contains a series of simple commands for performing elementary tasks. For example, you might use a batch file to start a word processing application using a particular document. Suppose you are an attorney and the document is a will. What you want to do is start your word processor, call the document (so the will form shows on your PC screen), fill it in, and print it. You could do it all in one step by putting the commands in a batch file called *Will.bat*. (See the "bat" ending? That's called a *filename extension*.) All you would do is type *will* and the word processor would load with the will form all ready for you to fill in and print.

There's a special batch file called *Autoexec.bat*. This is a file that contains much of the information your PC uses to get started when you turn it on. You create the Autoexec.bat file with the various features and functions you want in your PC's *environment*. There is another file that affects the environment on startup called *Config.sys*. We'll discuss these special files and the meaning of your PC's environment later on in much more detail. You don't need these two special files, but most PC users create them so that they can customize their PC to the special needs of the applications they run and their own preferences.

BIOS

BIOS (pronounced "Bye-Os") is another one of those PC acronyms. This one means *Basic Input/Output System*. That's tech-talk for some software that resides deep in the bowels of your PC. Actually, BIOS (also sometimes called ROM BIOS because it resides in *ROM*—Read Only Memory, or, in simpler terms, a computer chip) is considered to be *firmware* instead of software because it resides in a chip instead of on a disk and you can't do anything with it yourself. The computer uses BIOS to control its own innermost actions. It's important to know about because, although IBM created the first "official" BIOS, there are now many companies that produce BIOS ROMs.

You must be sure that you have an IBM-compatible BIOS in your PC or you won't be able to run IBM-compatible software. Besides giving the computer its compatibility (it's the BIOS, among other things, that determines the difference between an IBM compatible and an Apple Macintosh), the BIOS does such things as perform the cold start routine when you turn on your computer.

Byte

Strictly speaking a byte is 8 bits. A bit (short for *binary digit*) is the smallest unit of computer information. It must be either a 1 or a 0. Eight of these binary digits makes one byte. However, in popular terminology, a byte is also the same as a character. So if you have a hard disk that stores 40,000 bytes, it is safe to say that it can also hold 40,000 characters. Now it starts to get a little more convoluted.

Application programs, unlike text files or word processing documents, don't really contain characters. But they do contain bytes—some of those unprintable things we discussed earlier. So PC tech-types settled into the terminology by referring to just about everything in terms of bytes instead of characters. That works all of the time.

Now that we have that under control, users rarely talk about a disk having 40 million bytes of space on it. They say it has 40 *Megabytes* or, in writing, *40MB*. That's because the prefix *Mega* means the same thing as *million*. 40 *Million* bytes = 40 *Megabytes* = *40MB*. They're all the same.

You can do the same thing with *thousands* too. One thousand is the same as the prefix *Kilo*. So 1,000 bytes is really 1 *Kilobyte*. You abbreviate kilobyte as *KB*. So, 1 *Thousand* bytes = 1 *Kilobyte* = 1KB.

Sometimes PC users just reduce the whole thing to the letter *K* and say 1*K* for 1,000 bytes. It's all pretty straightforward. You use these byte quantities to describe the space on a disk, the amount of memory available, or the size of a file.

Command.com

This is a very special file that must exist at the computer's startup time. It's the first thing the BIOS looks for. Command.com (pronounced "command-dot-kawm") is a software file on an IBM PC or clone that is also sometimes referred to as the computer's *command interpreter*. That's actually a pretty good description of the file's function. Command.com reads every command in a program or typed in by you at the keyboard and tells BIOS what to do with it. It also contains a great many special commands of its own.

There are three files that must be present in order for your computer to start or, in computerese, *boot*. Two of those files are special hidden files (you can't see them if you use the DIRectory command to list the files on your disk, but they're there). The third is Command.com. Command.com must be the same version as certain other important files (the hidden ones and some other DOS files) or your computer won't work correctly. When you buy a copy of DOS, it contains the Command.com and the other important files. Most PCs are delivered by the dealer with DOS, so Command.com is already installed.

Cursor

This is the little flashing line (or box) that shows up on your screen to tell you where the next character you type will be located. Cursors appear in many applications as well as at the DOS prompt when you start your PC. There's not a lot more to say about this term. When you see it, you'll know it.

Desktop Publishing

This is a rather broad term that refers to something more than word processing and short of full press publishing. It includes the production, using your PC, of original materials containing a variety of different type styles, page layouts, and illustrations. There are a couple of aspects to desktop publishing, also called *DTP*, that make it, well, desktop publishing.

First, DTP uses both text and graphics, or illustrations. Second, your screen display must be exactly the same as you will see on the printed page. That has a couple of implications for those of you who want to do DTP. First, you'll need a screen capable of displaying graphics and different type styles in detail. Second, you'll need a printer capable of printing in the same amount of detail. This is an excellent example of the application dictating the hardware you'll need to perform it.

In addition to the specialized hardware, there are, of course, several types of specialized DTP software applications. Some of these are actual DTP packages. Their job is to let you mix graphics and text in a variety of type styles. They are sort of supercharged word processors with graphics capabilities. But there are other types of applications such as drawing software for creating illustrations.

Disk Drive

Disk drives are the mechanisms that hold disks. The disks are the *media* that you use to store your data. There are two basic types of disks: floppy disks, and fixed or hard disks. That means, of course, that there are the same two types of disk drives. The differences between the two types are significant. Floppy disks are flexible—they can be bent—so they are encased inside vinyl or plastic jackets to protect them. They don't hold a lot of data, usually little more than a megabyte. And you can remove them from the floppy disk drive and store them away. Programs come on floppy disks. You insert the floppy disk with the program in one of the two possible floppy disk drives (IBM systems support the A and B drives as floppies) and either run it (*execute* it) or install it on the hard drive if your PC has one.

Hard drives, on the other hand, contain hard disks. But you can't remove them like you can the floppies. The actual disks (there may be several stacked on top of each other like records on a record changer) are installed inside the sealed disk drive. These disks hold a lot more data (often hundreds of megabytes) than floppies. The mechanism used to read and write the data is a lot more precise than the mechanism used for floppy drives.

There are several kinds of hard drives, and we'll discuss them later in the book. You should consider your hard drives as your PC's *mass storage*. In fact, most PC users simply refer to the PC's storage capacity in terms of the size of the installed hard drives. Most PCs can have more than one fixed drive. How many depends on the manufacturer. A typical hard drive for a home or small business may be 40MB. That will hold several medium-sized applications and a fair amount of data. Large, specialized PCs might have as much as 360MB on a single drive.

Display

The display, or monitor, on your PC is the screen you use to see what's going on in your application or in the computer. It's your window into the computer. Obviously, there are lots of different types of displays. As I said earlier in this chapter, the two broad categories are color and monochrome. But beyond those two global classifications, there are special versions of each.

PCs treat all monochrome displays the same, with two exceptions. There are two special kinds of mono displays: the first is the Hercules graphics type and the second is the paper-white graphics display. As their names imply these special screens are for graphics use. The rest of the mono screens are for text only. The paper-white displays are usually larger than most screens. For this reason they are sometimes called *full page* monitors. They can display a full page (as if printed on an $8\frac{1}{2}$" x 11" piece of paper) of text and graphics as black on a white background. These displays are often used for DTP.

In the color department, there are three common types. These types are defined in terms of *resolution* or the amount of fine detail they can display. The types are CGA (Color Graphics Adapter), EGA (Enhanced Graphics Adapter), and VGA (Video Graphics Array). The CGA is the oldest and has the worst resolution. EGA is the intermediate while VGA is the best. There is also a very high-resolution version of the VGA called a Super VGA. The different types of color displays are *downward compatible*. That means that you can get CGA resolution (required on some older programs not written to take advantage of EGA or VGA) on a VGA screen but not the other way around.

Every monitor needs a special printed circuit card placed inside the PC, called a *display adapter*, in order to function. The display adapter must be compatible with the monitor. That means that if you have a VGA monitor you need a VGA display adapter card to make it work. You can't mix adapters and monitors.

DOS

Well, here it is. You've been seeing this term for the last several pages. It really is a pretty simple term. Technically, DOS (pronounced "dawss") means *Disk Operating System*. In practical terms, DOS refers to the special *operating system* in IBM PCs and compatibles. There are only two real versions of DOS: PC-DOS and MS-DOS. PC-DOS is the DOS created by IBM. MS-DOS is created by Microsoft Corp. Any other PC manufacturer must use a version of one of these two implementations. For example, Zenith Data Systems has a version called Zenith DOS. Actually, it is a special version of MS-DOS, customized for use with Zenith PCs.

DOS is the part of your PC that defines how it processes information. It is characterized, at least in part, by Command.com and the two hidden files we discussed earlier. But it also contains several special utility programs such as backup and restore. In short, DOS is a complete set of programs that let your PC operate and perform the most basic of computing tasks. It is the prerequisite for running any other application. And the version of DOS you are running may determine what applications you can execute.

Apple has a version of DOS as well for its older Apple II series. So, from that perspective, DOS can be thought of generically. But when we refer to DOS in general PC conversation, we almost always mean either PC-DOS or MS-DOS and we almost always mean IBM PCs or compatibles. The newer Macintosh models use an entirely different system. So one of the major incompatibilities between the Macintosh and IBM-type PCs is their operating systems.

Dot Matrix Printer

This is a type of low-cost, low-performance, low-resolution printer used to produce rough or draft text quality printing. It is called dot matrix because the characters are created using a pattern of dots consisting of from 7 to 24 points. Obviously, the *24-pin* dot matrix printers give the clearest, sharpest characters. These printers are often called *near letter quality* or *NLQ* printers.

The advantage to dot matrix printers (DMPs) is that they are rather fast in their printing and are very inexpensive to buy and operate. They have two basic styles in terms of how they handle paper. One style, sheet feed, lets you insert paper to be printed on a single sheet at a time. The other style, tractor feed, requires paper

Thirty-One Essential PC Buzzwords and What They Mean in English

that has small holes on the edges and is in a continuous sheet. Individual sheets are separated from the continuous sheet by tearing at periodic perforations. Thus these tractor feed printers are also called continuous sheet printers. Most DMPs can't print graphics very well if at all.

Font

A font is a combination of characteristics that determines how characters look on your screen or on a printed page. A font is made up of typeface (or type style), size, spacing, pitch, orientation, style, and weight. Fonts are referred to (incorrectly, it turns out) by the name associated with the typeface, such as Times Roman, Courier, or Palatino, with the addition of such other descriptive words as italic or bold.

Actually, there is a lot more to font definition than typeface and weighting. You should at least indicate the size, usually specified in *points,* in addition to the other information. So the minimum conversational terminology might be *24-point Times Roman, Bold.* Technically, you should specify all of the other information in order to clearly define a font.

Graphics

Graphics refers to the use of pictures or images. That's just about all there is to it, at least for the purpose of describing the term. The implications, however, are a bit more complex. If you plan to use graphics in your PC system, you will need to be sure that you include certain pieces of hardware. You'll need a graphics monitor and display adapter. If you want to print graphics, you'll need a graphics printer. Both printer and display should have the resolution appropriate to your needs.

If you plan on processing graphic images, you'll probably need a good deal of software. This might include a DTP package, a paint or drawing package and, perhaps, a scanner software package if you choose to use a scanner. Scanners are devices that view a printed page and translate the image into something the computer can use. In other words, a scanner turns a visual picture into an electronic image.

LAN

LAN (pronounced as a word: "lan") is an acronym for *Local Area*

Network. You could write whole books on LANs, and, in fact, I have. LANs are networks of PCs, connected together for the purpose of sharing programs and data. They are usually contained within a single building and they can include hundreds of individual PCs. There are many ways to connect PCs together in LANs, but they all have a few things in common.

First, LANs let all the users share the same files and programs. Second, they allow users to communicate with each other using a mechanism such as electronic mail. Finally, all users on the LAN share network *resources* such as printers and modems. That means that each user no longer needs his or her own private printer. Several people can share the same printer "over the network."

Laser Printer

Remember when I said earlier that if you want to do graphics you may need a higher-resolution printer to print them accurately and with fine detail? Well, that printer is called a *laser printer*. There are many kinds of laser printers, but *LaserJet*, the proprietary trademark of Hewlett-Packard Company, has become the generic term for laser printer, just as Kleenex has become the generic term for facial tissue.

Laser printers are, in simplest terms, computer controlled photocopiers. In fact, laser printers actually use some of the same parts that photocopiers do. They work by means of a beam of laser light controlled by the PC that deposits toner, directly or indirectly, on the paper. The toner is heated by passing through hot rollers to fix it to the paper. Typical laser printers provide a resolution of 300 x 300 dots-per-inch. Needless to say, you need a magnifier to see the dots. The appearance is very nearly that of a typeset page. Laser printers are used in DTP and other graphics applications.

There are two basic kinds of laser printers, defined by the type of *character generation* the printer uses. The printers compatible with the Hewlett-Packard (HP) LaserJets require that fonts be transferred to the printer before the printer can print. That means that you must have a software program or a special plug-in cartridge for every font you want to use (programs and cartridges contain several fonts each, so you don't really need one for each font). The fonts that are created in software are called *soft fonts*. The cartridge fonts simply plug into the outside of the laser printer.

Laser printers also use a *page definition language* called PostScript. I'll tell you more about that presently, but for now you need to know that PostScript printers are not the same and are not compatible with HP-type printers. There are, however, cartridges that allow the HP printers to accept PostScript.

Finally, laser printers need memory, just like PCs (you'll learn about memory a little later). In laser printers, the amount of graphical information or the number of fonts your printer can handle depends to a great extent on the amount of memory. Laser printers with less than 1MB of memory are worse than useless.

Letter Quality Printer

The last type of printer fits between the DMP and the laser printer. It is called a *letter quality* or *daisy wheel* printer. It is usually capable only of printing text since it works much like a typewriter. The printer has, usually, a daisy wheel printhead (a round printhead with the characters around the edge like the petals of a daisy) that prints by impacting the paper through a ribbon. Obviously, only the characters that are on the daisy wheel can print. Because of this limitation, and the relatively slow speed and high cost, these printers are no longer very popular. Their place has been taken by low-cost lasers and 24-pin DMPs.

Mass Storage

I said earlier that hard disks are generally considered to be mass storage devices. But there are others. For example, you can store data on magnetic tape. Some types of magnetic tape storage are used with PCs to provide backup storage for large hard disks. There is also *optical storage*, which you'll learn about shortly. The important thing is that mass storage refers to methods of permanently or semipermanently storing large amounts of data so that when you turn off your PC, your data isn't lost.

Memory

This is the other kind of storage you'll find in a PC. Memory, also called RAM (Random Access Memory, pronounced as a word: "ram"), is temporary by nature. It is only active when the computer is turned on. But RAM is very important because it's where your program actually executes. When you store or install your applications, you usually put them into mass storage, probably on your hard disk. But when you go to *execute* (run) them, DOS places them in RAM. The reason is that RAM is many times faster than your hard disk. When you exit the application, it is removed from memory to make room for other applications. There are a few programs that stay in memory so that you can use them whenever you want. More about them later.

There are three ways to characterize a PC in general discussions. One is by mass storage (how big, in MB, is the hard disk), the second is by memory (how many MB of RAM), and the third is by processor type (you'll learn about processors in a moment). Many novice users get mass storage and memory capacity confused. When you say "how much storage does it have?" you have asked an ambiguous question. You need to ask specifically about either hard drive (mass storage) or memory.

Menu

Menus are simple ways of calling the applications you want to be able to run. They are also used within applications to define and execute the functions of the applications. Here's what I mean. We might have a main menu that is displayed when we turn on the PC. That would be our PC's *operating environment*. It might have selections of all of the programs we would like to be able to run. We could make a simple choice without having to type in a lot of commands.

Once the application is loaded, we might need another menu to select the various things the application can do. Menus, in general, are just lists that we can select from to simplify the performance of some task. There are many types of menus. The simplest are those asking you to type the letter or number associated with your selection. There are menus that let you move a bar of light from choice to choice and then select the highlighted choice by pressing the ENTER key. And there are special graphical menus called graphical user interfaces that further simplify the process.

Mouse

A mouse is a special *pointing device* that lets you move around the computer screen by moving the puck-shaped device around a surface like a table (Figure 1.8). When you move the mouse, the cursor on your screen moves with it. To select an item on your screen, instead of hitting the ENTER key, you *click* one of the buttons on the mouse. When you are working with graphics, it is

▼ *Figure 1.8. A Three-button Mouse*

much easier to move around on the screen with a mouse than it is using the arrow keys.

Mice come in two styles: serial mice and bus mice. Serial mice just plug into your PC's serial port (ports are explained in a later chapter). Bus mice require a special printed circuit card that goes inside your PC. Mice also require a special software program called a *mouse driver* to make them work.

Optical Disk

Optical disks are a form of mass storage that uses light to read and/or write information on a special disk. On other mass storage devices, the usual method is reading and writing data magnetically on a tape or disk surface coated with a magnetic material, much like a common audio tape recorder. There is a big advantage to optical storage. It can store huge amounts of data on a fairly small surface. For example, it is not uncommon to store 600 to 800MB of data on a single 5 $\frac{1}{4}$"-diameter optical disk.

Optical disks come in three varieties. CD-ROMs (pronounced "See-Dee-Rawm") are like the familiar audio compact disks (CDs). The information on them cannot be removed and you cannot add (store) any more to them. They are used, primarily, as a publishing method for very large collections of data.

WORMs (Write Once Read Many, pronounced as a word: "worm") are a special type of optical disk that lets you store information once and then, like a CD-ROM, continue to read it. Once you have stored data on a WORM you can't erase it. You can use WORMs for small publishing (in terms of the number of disks you need to distribute) and archiving.

The last type is called the *erasable optical disk*. As the name implies you can read, write, and erase this large-capacity disk. Optical disk drives are rather expensive, but the disks, considering the amount of data they hold, are not.

Peripheral

Peripheral is the generic term for everything you connect to your PC. It includes things like monitors, printers, optical disk drives, tape backup units, and the like. The only requirement for a peripheral is that it be hardware and it not be part of the CPU (central processor unit, or the main part of the PC).

PostScript

PostScript is two things, really. First, it is a tradename for a software product from Adobe Software. Second, it is the language that makes up that product. PostScript is a page definition language used for printing on PostScript laser printers. Earlier, in our discussion of laser printers, I drew the distinction between the HP-type laser printer and the PostScript printer. I told you that the HP-type printer handles fonts individually. PostScript, on the other hand, creates fonts *on the fly* as it defines the total contents and layout of a page to be printed. PostScript is, actually, a programming language that sends its commands directly to the printer, which then, like a PC, executes them in order to print the page.

PostScript allows more precise definition of fonts than simply loading the fonts into the printer. The result is that PostScript printed pages have a more finished look. PostScript printers are, as a whole, significantly more expensive than HP-type printers. But they do not require font cartridges and their results are superior. If you happen to have a LaserJet (non-PostScript) you can, for a reasonable amount of money, turn it into a PostScript printer using a PostScript cartridge. The results, from the standpoint of the print quality, are just about as good as any full PostScript printer. However, the performance (printing speed) is not quite as good.

Processor

A PC's processor is its brain. The processor is also called the CPU (Figure 1.9), although CPU has, generically, come to mean the entire main part of the PC—the "box," so to speak. There are

Thirty-One Essential PC Buzzwords and What They Mean in English

▼ *Figure 1.9. A CPU*

several different types of processors. Most processors for IBM-compatible machines are manufactured by Intel. The Macintosh uses processors from Motorola. I told you that one of the ways to characterize a PC was by processor type. I should point out that, like most IBM-compatible users, I generally mean IBM compatible when I speak about PCs. Strictly speaking the Macintosh and, for that matter, the rest of the Apple family are also PCs. I will, for the purposes of this book, continue to use PC to refer to the IBM side of personal computing and call a Mac a Mac. This, by the way, comes from the days when the IBM offering was called a Personal Computer or PC, as opposed to today's generation, which is called a Personal System.

Anyway, there are four processors in general use today. They are the 8088, 80286, 80386, and 80486. The last three are the most popular and are simply called 286, 386, or 486. Going from low number to high number, the processor gets more powerful. You'll learn a lot more about where these types of PCs fit into the scheme of things as we progress, but for now, here are some guidelines.

The 8088 and 80286 cannot easily do more than one thing at a time and have some real restrictions on how you can use their memory. The 80386 and 80486 are designed to multitask (do more than one thing at once) and have very few limits on how you can use their memory. 8088s are relatively slow. The rest are much faster. It is quite possible to have a 286 that is faster than a 386. But the memory capability of the 386 would make it preferable in many cases.

There is a special kind of 80386 called an 80386SX. The 386SX is a watered-down version of the 386. It retains many of the 386's important capabilities for the average user but costs a lot less.

RAM Resident Program

This is the type of program that I mentioned earlier that stays in memory waiting for you to invoke it. These programs, also called TSRs (Terminate and Stay Resident) and pop-ups, are usually small programs that you load and then invoke by pressing a single keyboard combination referred to as *hot keys*. The application pops up, no matter what else you are doing, and then goes back to waiting in memory for the next time you call it when you are finished.

TSRs have the advantage of being ever-present and, therefore, handy for certain applications. They have the disadvantage of using up memory that you might need for other, non-TSR, applications. An example of a RAM resident program is the popular SideKick from Borland. SideKick lets you pop up a notepad, calculator, calendar, or other "desktop accessory" any time you want one.

TSRs are also used to control computer functions in the background (without your help and while you do something else) such as printing or screen capture.

ROM

Read-only memory (pronounced "RAWM"). ROMs are special memory chips into which the manufacturer has placed a program. Your PC can run the program but, unlike RAM, you can't make any changes to the data in the ROM.

RS-232

This is the communication specification that describes one of the classes of *ports* on your PC. A port is a connection point on your computer for peripherals like modems and printers. The kind of port described by RS-232 is the *serial* or *communications* (comm) port. The serial port allows data to pass in and out *serially* or *one bit at a time*. These ports (called COMM1 through COMM4 on some PCs) are for connecting serial mice, modems, and some types of printers (serial printers) to the PC. The other ports are called parallel or printer ports. They carry the designation LPT1 through LPT4 and they pass data in *parallel* or *one byte at a time*. Their purpose is to connect parallel peripherals such as parallel (the most common type) printers to your PC.

System Software

System software is different from *application* software in that it controls the basic operation of the computer. The example of system software to which you have been introduced is DOS. However, there is a gray area between system and application software that covers certain types of large programs, such as database managers, used to run other applications. For example, if you have a copy of a database management system such as dBASE IV and you write an application to run on it, your application is the application software and the dBASE IV package becomes system software for your application.

Just as DOS is system software for the PC itself, so the dBASE IV package becomes the system software used to run the application. So system software is, generally speaking, software used to run something else as opposed to application software, which in and of itself performs a predefined end-task.

WYSIWYG

What You See Is What You Get. This refers to the characteristic of DTP and graphics programs that allows you to see, on screen, exactly what will be printed out on the paper if you print with a high-resolution printer such as a laser printer. Using a WYSIWYG (pronounced Wiz-ee-wig) display, you'll see each font exactly as it will print as well as all graphic images.

Summary

- You may not need a PC. If you don't have a specific reason to buy one, don't.
- Get the right PC for the job. First select the software (programs) you will need to do your job right, then select the hardware (PC, printer, etc.) to match the software.
- There are two classes of PCs: IBM PCs and PS/2s and their clones, and Apple computers. They are not the same and programs for one won't run on the other.
- You can save serious money by buying a clone. Clones are PCs

that are manufactured by a company other than IBM but are 100 percent compatible with the IBM computer.

- At minimum, besides your PC, you'll need a floppy disk drive and a monitor. For most applications, you should also have a hard disk drive. You'll probably also want a printer of some sort.

- Users groups, computer magazines, books, and consultants are good sources of information on buying and using PCs.

- Software falls into the basic categories of application, operating system, and programming.

- Backing up your PC's hard drive is probably the most important aspect of your day-to-day computing.

PRACTICE WHAT YOU'VE LEARNED

1. What is the difference between system and application software?

2. What type of color monitor or display has the best resolution?

3. Name two types of ports.

4. Name four types of processors.

5. What are the three types of optical disks?

6. What is the difference between desktop publishing and word processing?

7. Can you use Macintosh software on an IBM or IBM compatible?

8. What is the most important factor in selecting a PC?

ANSWERS

1. System software operates something, such as DOS, which operates the basic functions of the computer itself. Application software performs a specific standalone end-task, such as word processing or mailing list management.

2. The Super VGA has the best resolution of any color monitor.

3. Serial and parallel

4. 8088, 80286, 80386, and 80486

5. CD-ROM, WORM, and Erasable

6. Desktop publishing includes far greater use of graphics than does word processing.

7. No. The operating systems of the two computers are not compatible.

8. The single most important factor in selecting a PC is how you plan to use it.

The Parts of
Your PC

Now that we have the language down pat, it's time to take the cover off your new PC and explore under the hood. In this chapter you will learn about:

- ▲ What the terms *processor, 286, 386,* and *486* mean
- ▲ Your keyboard and the different types of keyboards
- ▲ What the different kinds of *displays* (or *monitors*) are and what that means to you
- ▲ Disk drives
- ▲ What *ports* are and how you use them
- ▲ The different kinds of memory
- ▲ *Pointing devices* such as mice

This is a hardware chapter intended to familiarize you with the pieces that fit together to make your PC work (Figure 2.1). Along the way you'll also learn how to match up the right pieces for your particular PC requirements. We'll start with the thing that makes your PC work: the computer's *processor*.

The Brain of Your PC—The Processor

Every living thing has a brain. One of the functions of a brain is to direct the basic operations of the body to which it is attached. That means that the brain governs, for example, the organism's heartbeat, breathing, and other automatic functions. While I would never go so far as to suggest that a computer is a living being, it does have some things in common.

First, there are functions in a computer that must be carried out automatically. In the next chapter you'll learn more about those

▼ *Figure 2.1. The Parts of a Typical PC*

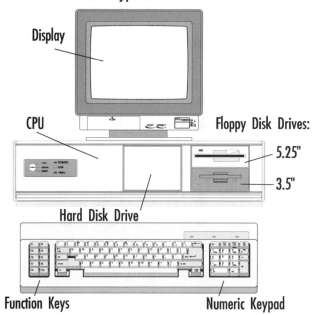

functions and how the computer performs them. At this point, however, we need to explore the device in the computer that, like a living brain, is responsible for keeping the basic functions of your PC running. That device is called the *processor*. Strictly speaking, the processor is called the *central processing unit (CPU)*. However, as you learned in Chapter 1, CPU has become a sort of generic reference to the PC as a whole—in other words, the "box" that contains all of the other parts.

As long as you realize that CPU can have either the strictly correct meaning or the rather broad conversational meaning, you will be right on target. In this discussion we'll be sticking to the strict interpretation of the term. There are several types of CPUs available in PCs today. Often the CPU type is one of the ways you can categorize a PC.

Physically, the CPU is a "chip" or *integrated circuit*. The chip fits into a socket on the main printed circuit board in your PC. That main board is called the *mother board*. All of the circuitry that surrounds the CPU as well as the connectors into which you will plug other circuit boards are on the mother board. If you look inside your PC, the mother board is the one lying on the bottom of the PC with all of the other boards plugged onto it.

On IBM PCs and clones, the CPU is usually made by Intel. The Intel CPU chips in today's PCs usually carry the model or part numbers 80286, 80386, or 80486. As I explained in the last chapter, the higher the part number, generally, the more power the CPU has. But what does the term *power* mean in this context? Does it refer to processor speed? Or size? What about memory management? To a greater or lesser extent, it is a combination of all of those aspects, because the CPU controls all of those functions. Let's get a little more specific.

The Brain of Your PC—The Processor

What Makes Your PC Go?

There are several basic functions that make up the operation of a PC. These functions are memory use, processing speed, and the instruction set the computer uses for its own internal language. Let's take these one at a time. Memory use, also called memory management, refers to how much memory your PC can use and the ways in which it can use it. Later, we'll get into that in more depth. However, it is the CPU that determines memory management in your PC. In order for your programs to use memory, something has to tell them where the memory is, how much is available, and how to access or *address* it. The CPU performs those functions and the results vary depending on which processor your PC uses.

Processing speed is controlled, but not determined, by the CPU. The *system clock*, the heart of the PC, is a combination of a crystal oscillator and some other circuitry, and sets the actual speed of the computer. That speed means, in practical terms, how fast your programs will run. But, unfortunately, just because the PC's clock is fast doesn't mean that the computer is fast. Something has to control how the programs use the clock. That something is the CPU. Strangely enough, CPU speed is not a function of which CPU you select. Simply buying a PC with an 80386 processor won't guarantee you a faster processor. It is quite possible to have an 80286 with a faster CPU speed than an 80386. However, because of other features in the CPU the actual speed with which a program can execute in an 80386 may be faster than in an 80286 with a faster clock.

Get on the Bus

One of those features is called *bus width*. Physically, the bus is several wires (actually copper tracks on the printed circuit board that take the place of wires) on which the data being processed by the CPU travels in and out of the CPU chip. It stands to reason that the more of these wires there are, the faster the data can pass because individual bytes don't have to wait as long for their turn on the bus.

Think of this process in terms of a real bus. If the bus has one door, ten passengers waiting in line to get on will have to wait one behind the other for their individual turns. If the bus has four doors, however, the ten passengers can split up into shorter lines and use all four doors to board the bus faster. This is also true of the CPU bus. There is a catch, though. In order for a program to automatically take advantage of the wider bus it must have been written with that capability in mind. Many of today's business programs are, in fact, written for use with the wider bus of the 80386 if the program is running on an 80386 computer.

There are other aspects to the size of the bus and, in fact, there is more than one bus. However, that discussion is beyond the scope of this book. The important thing to remember is that there is more to CPU performance than raw speed. Now let's take a look at the differences between the three most popular PC CPUs.

The Brain of Your PC—The Processor

286, 386, 486—What's That?

Before we discuss the differences between these three CPUs, we need a few more definitions. As I said, there are other aspects to CPU performance besides raw speed. One of those aspects is the *internal word size* of the CPU. That means how many bits of data the CPU can process at one time. The earliest microprocessors (another name for the CPU chip) could process only 4 bits of data at a time. They weren't particularly useful for personal computers, but those primitive chips were often part of industrial machine controllers that didn't need to process huge amounts of data.

The first serious personal computers used CPUs with 8-bit processing capability. That is the same as saying that they had an internal word size of 8 bits. Today's microprocessors, depending on which one you choose, have either a 16-bit or 32-bit internal word size. This larger size, coupled with bus size on both of the CPU's two buses (I told you above that there was more to buses than we discussed at the time) and the clock speed determine the processor's performance.

The 80286 CPU, usually referred to simply as a *286*, is a microprocessor with a 16-bit internal word size, clock speeds from around 12Mhz to around 20Mhz, and the ability to access or *address* 16MB of RAM memory. It is, on a somewhat primitive level, multitasking, which means that it can perform more than one task at a time. A 286 is an excellent home PC and, for a great many small business applications, a fast 286 will work just fine. They have the drawback that the memory above the 640K of DOS application memory is difficult to use. We'll discuss memory usage later, but for now you should know that your programs run in the first 640KB of memory on your PC. The rest of your RAM, if you install extra memory, may be used for other tasks we'll discuss later.

80386 CPUs, or 386s, offer much higher performance than 286s. They have an internal word size of 32 bits and can access two different types of memory: physical and virtual. We will discuss memory toward the end of this chapter. However, for the moment, physical memory is real memory that you install in your PC. It consists of physical memory chips and the 386 can access up to 4 Gigabytes (1GB = 1 Billion bytes). Virtual memory is memory that, although it doesn't exist physically, can be used by certain types of CPUs including the 386. The CPU does this by fooling the existing physical memory into allowing itself to be used more than once at a time. The 386 can address up to 4 Terabytes (1TB = 1 Trillion bytes) of virtual memory.

Clock speeds for 386s vary between 16Mhz and 33Mhz or higher. As you can imagine, one of the great strengths of the 386 is its ability to manage huge amounts of memory in a variety of ways. The 386 is multitasking and, with the wider bus structure, the 386 offers very high performance. If you have demanding applications such as desktop publishing, you'll benefit by the muscle of a 386.

There is a smaller version of the 386 called the 386SX. There are two differences between the 386 and 386SX. First, the 386SX is slower than the 386, usually limited to 16Mhz. Second, the SX does not use the 32-bit data bus as does the 386. However, both the 386 and the 386SX have the same 32-bit internal word size. For most programs, however, the 386SX provides performance that appears to equal its larger sibling. The real benefit to users is that the 386SX is usually much less expensive than the 386, which means that for about the price of a good 286 PC, you can have a 386SX.

Finally, the brute of the PC CPU world is the 80486, or 486. The 486 is a higher performance version of the 386. It has all of the features of the 386 plus it runs at higher clock speeds. For almost all home applications and most small business applications the 486 is really overkill. Currently, the major use for 486s is heavy graphics processing, scientific and engineering programs, and as servers for local area networks.

Keyboards

Every PC needs a keyboard. The keyboard is the way that you as a user type your instructions into the computer, respond to the programs your computer runs, and enter data into your PC's programs. It is, at first blush, a typewriter keyboard with some extra keys. How many extra keys your keyboard has and what they do depends on a number of things. Let's start with a look at a typical PC keyboard (Figure 2.2).

The main part of the keyboard is the same "QWERTY" key layout you see on typewriters. However, there are a few additions to the typing portion of the PC's keyboard—four to be exact. Those additional keys are the *Control* (abbreviated *[Ctrl]*), *Alternate* (*[Alt]*), *Escape* (*[Esc]*), and *Enter* keys. You use the first three of these keys in combination with other keys to allow a wider variety of optional *control characters*. Control characters are nonprinting characters that, by themselves, perform some special function within a program.

▼ *Figure 2.2. Two Styles of PC Keyboards*

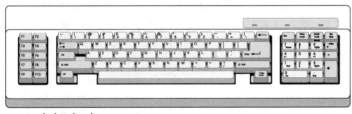

Standard Keyboard

Extended Keyboard

For example, in a word processing program you might place your cursor at the beginning of a line of text and type *[Ctrl]Y* (the Control key held down while typing the Y at the same time) to "Yank" or delete that line of text. The control code (in this case *[Ctrl]Y*) is a shortcut for deleting an entire line of text.

What Makes the PC Keyboard Different?

The *Enter* key, sometimes called the *Return* key, is the key you use after you have entered some piece of data or a command. Enter tells your PC, "do it!" For example, suppose you want to load your word processor. To do that, if your word processor happens to be WordPerfect, you might type *WP51*. However, just typing WP51 at the DOS prompt doesn't do anything. You have to tell your PC "do it!" So, you press Enter after the WP51 and your PC dutifully starts WordPerfect for you. In most word processors, the Enter key also serves as the *end of paragraph* key.

The next obvious difference between the typewriter keyboard and your PC's keyboard are the *function keys*. These are the keys along the top or left-hand side of the keyboard labeled *F1, F2, F3*, and so on. If the function keys are across the top, you probably have twelve of them in a single row. If they are along the left side, there are ten in two rows of five keys each. In either case they serve the same purpose. The function keys are used by programs to provide shortcuts to program functions. That means that the program designates some of the functions or commands that would normally require several keystrokes as functions to be performed by the function keys. In that regard, the function keys are a lot like the *control codes* I described a bit earlier.

The F-keys are selected in place of the control codes, however, because the functions they represent are so repetitive that it is more convenient to remember a function key than a control code combination. However, you can also combine the [Ctrl], [Alt], or Shift keys with F-keys. When you use these additional keys, you hold down the [Ctrl], [Alt], or Shift key while you depress the appropriate F-key. So if you wanted to use the [Alt]F4 key, you would hold down the [Alt] key and press the F4 key.

The next departure from the standard typewriter keyboard is the *numeric keypad*. The numeric keypad is two keypads in one. It is a number pad very much like a traditional ten-key adding machine or calculator, the purpose of which is to provide a way for you to enter numbers quickly. You can use the keypad with a calculator or other numeric programs for rapid number entry. Around the outside of the numeric pad you'll see several gray-colored keys. These keys are the arithmetic functions add (+), subtract (–), multiply (*), and divide (/), plus an Enter key and another key called *Num Lock*.

Num Lock is a special key that makes your numeric pad a numbers-only keypad. Why would you need this key? Remember I told you that the numeric pad is two keypads in one? It turns out that there are eight keys in the numeric pad that control your cursor location. Of course, they can't do both functions at once, so when the Num Lock is on, the numeric pad is for numbers only. When it is off, the cursor controls are active and the numbers no longer work.

The cursor controls are four arrows (pointing right, left, up, and down), *Home* (which relocates the cursor to the upper-left corner of the screen), *End* (which has various functions depending on the program you are running), *PgUp* (Page Up), and *PgDn* (Page Down). Also, under the numeric pad are two additional keys. In the Num Lock on position they are the number 0 (zero) and the decimal point. With Num Lock off the zero is the *Insert* key and the decimal point is the *Delete* (Del) key. Insert and delete are used in word processors and some other types of programs that allow you to either insert characters in a line or type over them (the insert key), and delete characters in lines of text or numbers (the delete key).

On some keyboards, the cursor control keys also appear in two separate keypads. One keypad contains the four cursor arrows. Just like on the numeric pad, the cursor arrows move the cursor in the direction of the arrow. The other keypad contains the Insert, Delete, Page Up, Page Down, Home, and End keys. Again, these keys duplicate their functions on the numeric pad when the Num Lock is off. The benefit of these extra keypads is that you can leave the Num Lock on at all times designating the numeric pad as just that: a numeric pad only. The cursor control keys are then available separately on their own keypads.

These extra keypads are available only on the "enhanced" keyboards (the so-called *101 Key* boards) intended for use on 386 and 486 machines. If you intend to use this fancier keyboard on a

Keyboards

286, especially an older one, you may need special drivers. Drivers are specialized control software that tells your PC what kind of keyboard you have attached. Drivers are usually required only for third-party keyboards (keyboards manufactured by companies that build add-on products for your PC).

Displays

Displays are also called monitors. That term comes from the days when workers using mainframe computers had a "monitor" and a "keyboard" to connect to the mainframe. Of course, mainframe connections are still done the same way, but in the world of personal computing we generally speak of the screen as a display or VDT (video display terminal). Displays are either monochrome or color. But within those two broad categories there are a lot of variations. Without getting into excruciating detail, we'll peruse the various types of displays.

It's All There in Black (or Orange, or Green) and White

Let's start off with the monochrome displays. These come in two types. There are monochrome text-only monitors and monochrome graphics monitors. The graphics monitors are also available in a variety of types. The most popular of the monochrome graphics monitors is the Hercules. The Hercules is, actually, a display adapter or "driver card" that goes inside your PC. It is a printed circuit board that plugs onto the mother board in your PC and provides the correct signals to make your graphics adapter work. The actual monitor plugs into a connector on the adapter card that sticks out of the back of the PC. All displays are a combination of the screen and the driver card.

Another popular type of monochrome display is the full-page paper-white monitor. These displays are used in desktop publishing applications and show black printing on a white background. The shape of the screen is vertically oblong instead of the usual horizontal so that it can display a full 8 $\frac{1}{2}$" x 11" page of information. These displays are of very high resolution.

Monochrome displays intended for graphics must actually be graphics monitors (except in the case of the paper-white displays). The Hercules and other monochrome graphics adapter cards translate colors into various shades of gray plus black and white. These displays are sometimes called *gray-scale displays*. You won't save a lot of money by using a monochrome graphics display. Although many users of desktop publishing and other text-based applications prefer the colorless displays, they still need the graphics ability from time to time. Monochrome displays intended for text-only applications do not require a graphics adapter card or a graphics monitor. These monitors are not capable of displaying graphics. They are used exclusively in text applications. They are also very inexpensive.

Color Your World

Color graphics displays come in three basic varieties. For these displays you will need an appropriate color monitor as well as a matching adapter card. Most good color graphics adapter cards can be set up to serve virtually any monitor attached to them. The three basic types of color monitors in use today are *CGA* (Color Graphics Adapter), *EGA* (Enhanced Graphics Adapter), and *VGA* (Video Graphics Array). There is also a very-high-resolution version of the VGA called the *Super VGA*. Here are the differences between the three basic styles of color graphics displays.

CGA

The CGA or Color Graphics Adapter is the oldest of the three color display schemes. Strictly speaking, all of the graphics "modes" we are discussing here refer to the specification attached to the adapter cards. These specifications are expressed in a variety of ways. For example, the various types of displays (which we will interpret to include both the adapter card and the actual monitor) have a *text mode* specification that expresses how many *lines* of characters of a given *column width* (one column is the same as one character) will fit on a single screen.

They also have a *graphics mode* specification. The graphics mode spec is expressed as screen width and height (W x H) in *pixels*. A pixel, or picture element, is the smallest display element on a screen. If you imagine a picture as being made up of thousands of tiny dots, each dot would be a pixel. The graphics mode also specifies how many colors are available. This spec is expressed in the number of colors that can be displayed simultaneously from a *palette* (collection of available colors) containing a (usually) larger number of colors. Finally, the specification indicates the type of monitor that you will require to display the output of the adapter card.

That all seems pretty confusing so here is the specification of a CGA display. CGA displays have a text mode that can display 25 lines of 80 columns (characters) on a single screen. The graphics mode has a *resolution* of 320 x 200 pixels (the screen is 320 dots wide and 200 dots high). And it can display up to four colors simultaneously from a palette of 16. There is a special medium-resolution mode that allows a resolution of 640 x 200 pixels, but only allows you to select two colors at a time from the palette. The CGA requires a digital display monitor (one that accepts only digital signals from the adapter card).

EGA

The EGA (Enhanced Graphics Adapter) specification demonstrates higher resolution and more available color. The text mode specification for the EGA, like the CGA, is 25 lines of 80 columns. The graphics mode offers a resolution of 640 x 350 pixels. And you can display up to 16 simultaneous colors from a palette of 64 colors. The EGA adapter requires a digital monitor capable of EGA resolution to achieve EGA displays. EGA adapters can, however, provide CGA resolution when used with a CGA monitor.

VGA

The VGA, or Video Graphics Array, was designed for use with IBM PS/2 personal computers. However, it is available for virtually all IBM-compatible PCs. The approach to text is somewhat different from that of the other adapters. Instead of specifying lines by columns as the text spec, the VGA is specked in pixels, just like a graphics spec. For the VGA the specification is 720 x 400 pixels, about double the text resolution of CGA and EGA. It means that a VGA screen can contain 50 lines of text instead of the usual 25.

The graphics mode is 640 x 480 pixels with a typical color complement of 256 colors at any one time. The original IBM VGA displays allowed only 16 colors at a time. The boost in number of available colors came from third-party vendors. The super VGA increases resolution to 800 x 600 pixels. Like the EGA display, the VGA allows *backward compatibility* with EGA and CGA. That means that a VGA adapter card can provide either CGA or EGA resolution for applications that require lower resolution. The VGA requires an *analog* monitor instead of a digital one to achieve its higher resolution.

Disk Drives

For the purposes of our disk drive discussions, we'll ignore the exotic ones such as optical drives and concentrate on two sizes of floppy drives and hard disk drives. We'll start with the floppy drives. These are the drives that take floppy disks. Floppies are the disks that your application programs come on. These disks have two possible physical sizes, each of which has two possible densities. The higher the density on a floppy disk, the more data you can put on it. The physical sizes for floppies are 3 $\frac{1}{2}$" and 5 $\frac{1}{4}$" (Figure 2.3). The size refers to the diameter of the disk.

The larger-diameter floppy disks are the more common size. Virtually every PC today is shipped with at least one 5 $\frac{1}{4}$" floppy. Most of these are high-density drives. The two densities available on 5 $\frac{1}{4}$" disks are 360KB and 1.1MB. These densities refer to the number of bytes you can store on a single floppy disk. The low-density disks can be read and written by high-density drives. The reverse, however, is not true. You cannot read or write a high-density disk in a 360KB drive. The number of bytes available on the disk is the number after *formatting*, but before you transfer the system if you wish to make the disk bootable. Here's what that means.

▼ Figure 2.3. 3 1/2-Inch and 5 1/4-Inch Floppy Disks

5 1/4-Inch Disk   3 1/2-Inch Disk

When you buy a new floppy disk, it is usually not formatted. That means that it has not been prepared for use in the computer. You have to format the disk using the DOS *FORMAT* command. You'll learn more about that command later. When you format a floppy disk, you have the choice of making it bootable. That means that you can boot your PC from the floppy instead of from the internal hard disk. However, when you make a floppy bootable, you use up some space on it. So a 360KB low-density floppy, prepared as a bootable disk, would have somewhat less (about 80KB or so) space on it than one that has not been made bootable.

DOS knows what kind of floppy drive you have in your PC so it knows when you try to put the wrong kind of disk in it. For example, if you try to use a high-density (1.1MB) 5 $\frac{1}{4}$" disk in a 360KB drive, you'll get a message to the effect that track 1 is bad on the floppy. It's not; you just tried to shove ten pounds of potatoes into a five-pound sack. The 1.1MB floppies won't work in 360KB drives. However, you'd have no trouble getting a 360KB floppy to work in a 1.1MB drive. Now you're only putting five pounds in a ten-pound sack. Also, because of the physical makeup of the disk, you can't fool a 360KB floppy into formatting as a 1.1MB disk, even if you have the right drive. It simply won't work.

Now, on to the 3 $\frac{1}{2}$" disks. These little guys are encased inside a plastic envelope, unlike the bigger ones that are inside a mylar casing. That makes the $3\frac{1}{2}$s a bit more rugged. But even the low-density version of the $3\frac{1}{2}$" floppy holds more data than its physically larger low-density sibling. Low-density $3\frac{1}{2}$" floppies hold 720KB of data (formatted) while the high-density minidisks hold 1.41MB. Of course, the same formatting rules apply to the smaller disks as to the $5\frac{1}{4}$" disks.

Floppy disks must always be handled with care. They are adversely affected by magnetic fields, dirt, humidity, moisture, and rough handling. Worse, dirt on a floppy disk can damage the heads on your floppy disk drive.

Disk Drives

TIP

Keep floppies in protective envelopes or disk cases. Never touch the magnetic media inside the disk carrier (the envelope or plastic case that protects the disk inside). Avoid smoking near your PC since small particles of smoke and ash can get inside the drives and damage them.

Hard Drives—Lots of Storage Space

Now for the hard disk drives, also called fixed disk drives (Figure 2.4). As I told you earlier, the hard disk has the advantage of holding far more data than the floppy disk. It also is much faster than the floppies. A typical hard disk can hold anywhere from around 30 or 40MB to several hundred MB. It can locate a specific piece of information several times faster that can a floppy drive. Also, hard drives are usually well sealed so they are less subject to damage from dirt and dust than are floppy disks.

However, they still must be treated with care since they are subject to damage from physical shock. Most hard disks have a *parking* mechanism that places the drive heads in a safe location and locks them down when the PC is turned off. This parking allows you to move the PC safely from place to place without fear of damaging the heads or disks of your hard disk drive.

The hard disks are not removable—as I said, the units are usually sealed—and there may be several individual disks inside the unit. These individual disks are called *platters*. Each platter is

---

▼ *Figure 2.4. A Hard Disk Drive Removed from the PC*

capable of recording data on both sides, and the heads that read the data are, likewise, located on either side of the platters. The heads are attached to arms in much the same way that a phonograph cartridge is attached to the record-player arm.

Information is stored on disks in *sectors*. These sectors are physical areas of the hard disk. Dividing a disk into sectors makes it easier for DOS to tell the heads where to look on the disk for data. Within the sectors there are smaller divisions called *cylinders*. As with a floppy, you must format a hard disk before use. However, there are more steps to formatting a hard disk than there are to formatting a floppy.

Getting Ready to Use the Hard Disk

First, you must perform a *low-level format*. This prepares the disks to receive the segmenting that occurs when you perform the actual format. Because the data is far more densely packed on a hard disk (they tend to be about the same size as floppies, but they hold several times as much data), you must carefully prepare the surface before you can format it. This preparation often includes identifying bad sectors. Once those sectors are identified, most formatting programs do not attempt to prepare them for data, and DOS will usually not attempt to place data on them.

The second step in the hard disk formatting process is to *partition* the disk into large areas. Each of these partitions acts as a separate drive. For example, you could have a single, large hard disk that you partition into two smaller drives that you might call C and D. These two partitions are on the same physical hard disk, even though they act as if they were two separate drives. For clarity, we often refer to these disks within disks as *volumes* or, sometimes, *logical drives*. The larger drive containing the smaller ones is sometimes called the *physical drive*.

The final step in preparing your hard disk for use is to format each of the volumes using the regular *FORMAT* command. This whole process is actually a bit more complex than I've presented it here, so we'll take up the subject of hard disk preparation in more depth in Chapter 4.

There are several types of hard drives. Like displays, disk drives, both fixed and floppy, actually consist of the drive itself and a *controller card*. The controller card, like the display adapter card, is a printed circuit board that plugs onto the PC's mother board. The drives connect to the controller card using wide, flat cables called *ribbon cables*. Most typical drive controller cards can handle more than one single drive. Some control as many as two floppies and two fixed drives on a single card.

How Fast Does It Go?

Like displays, hard drives can be classed by performance. There is no need to go into too much detail regarding the technical differences between these various types of hard drives. I will, however, class them in terms of cost and performance. The first type of hard drive is the *MFM* drive. It is the most common type of hard disk drive. It is usually the lowest-performance type of fixed drive. MFM refers to the method of recording data on the disk itself.

RLL is the other type of disk recording technique used in hard disks. It has a much higher performance than MFM-type drives. You cannot use an MFM controller with an RLL drive, or vice versa. Another way to categorize hard disks is by the way data is transferred between the controller and the drive. The most common method is ESDI (Enhanced Small Device Interface, pronounced "ezzdee"). This connection method allows you to transfer from 1 to 3MB per second to or from the drive and it can handle drives with up to 1 Gigabyte (1GB = 1 Billion bytes) of storage.

The fastest connection method is the SCSI (Small Computer System Interface, pronounced "scuzzy"). SCSI can handle up to seven drives on one controller card at data transfer rates of 4MB per second. In terms of price RLL SCSI drives are the most expensive, and MFM ESDI drives are the least. There are all types of combinations. Generally, however, we refer to drives simply as SCSI or ESDI. We don't become too concerned with the recording technique.

Ports—Connecting to the Outside World

I mentioned earlier that your PC could connect to printers, modems, and a host of other *peripherals*, without going into much detail at that point as to how it might be made to do that. I'm going to introduce you to the means (if not the process) now. On the back of your PC you'll see several (usually) oblong connectors, obviously intended for connection to a plug with a great many pins. These connectors are called *ports*. They are the means by which your PC connects to these peripherals and, thus, to the outside world.

What We Have Here Is No Failure to Communicate

Generally speaking, there are two types of ports (besides the special one that connects to your PC's display) in your PC. One type is called *COMM ports*. The other type is called *printer ports*. Here is the difference between them. COMM ports are the *serial* communications ports on your PC. Physically, they are either 25-pin or 9-pin connectors on the rear of most PCs. Roughly speaking, these ports conform to the RS232C serial communications standard. The COMM ports may be used for connection to modems, some mice, and some printers. Also, many programs, such as LapLink, that allow you to transfer files directly between two PCs use the serial ports.

DOS supports up to four COMM ports if you are using DOS version 3.0 or higher. However, most PCs don't have four COMM ports installed. All ports, including COMM ports, have the following two characteristics: Associated with every port on your PC (regardless of the type of port) there exists an *I/O Address* and an *interrupt request* (also called an *IRQ*). The port I/O is always expressed with a hexadecimal number and the IRQ is always a decimal number between 1 and 9.

Unfortunately, the issues of I/Os and IRQs can become painfully technical. In the spirit of protecting you from the onslaughts of overly technical salespeople, however, I am introducing these two terms without a great deal of in-depth explanation. You need to know a couple of possible problems that can be associated with I/Os and IRQs, even if you don't need to know all of their techy ins and outs. (See Chapter 6 for a more detailed discussion.)

Other devices, such as add-in cards (Figure 2.5), also use I/O addresses and IRQs. The important thing to remember for the moment is that no two devices can simultaneously share the same address or IRQ. One of the biggest problems novices and experts alike run into on PCs is the *interrupt conflict*. This is important now because the four COMM ports actually share two IRQs. Ports 1 and 3 are the same as ports 2 and 4. The I/O addresses, however, are unique for each of the four ports. That means that you can't use ports 1 and 3 or 2 and 4 at the same time. For that reason, among others, PC manufacturers give you only COMM ports 1 and 2 as standard offerings, even though DOS could recognize two more.

Now for a brief word on the difference between serial and parallel. Data is transferred through serial ports one *bit* at a time. The other pins on the connector are for control signals of various types. These control signals are different for *full RS232C implemen-*

▼ *Figure 2.5. An Add-in Card that Plugs onto the Mother Board*

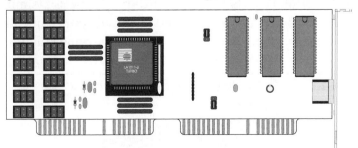

▼ *Figure 2.6. A PC-mounted 9-pin RS232 Connector*

tation than they are for *simple communications*. If all you want to do is use a modem for simple communications, all you need are the 9 pins in the smaller 9-pin connector. This connector is a subset of the larger, more standard, 25-pin connector (Figures 2.6 and 2.7). However, for some applications, such as serial printers, you need all of the RS232C signals. That means that you need to use the 25-pin version. Most serial mice use only the 9 pins, so you will usually need an adapter plug.

Also, many add-in communications boards provide only a 9-pin connector, which might make that board unsuitable for use in some applications, such as serial printers. Since all serial printers are not alike, however, you'll need to read the printer manual to see if it can use a 9-pin plug or if it requires a full 25-pin implementation.

Parallel ports transfer data 1 *byte* at a time. That means that the parallel port can move data faster that the serial port can. Parallel ports are used for most printers. For most novices parallel printers are far easier to configure (set up) because there are virtually no parameters or switches to set. Serial printers can be very difficult to set up since there is a very wide variety of possible parameter settings. As with the COMM ports, there are four possible parallel ports. These are LPT1 through LPT4. However, most PCs have only LPT1 as a standard parallel port. The cables you will use for the parallel (or printer) ports often have a 25-pin connector (similar to the serial connector) on one end and a special connector called a *Centronics* connector on the end that plugs into the printer (Figure 2.8).

▼ *Figure 2.7. A PC-mounted 25-pin RS232 Connector*

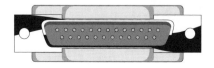

▼ *Figure 2.8. A Centronics Connector (Printer End)*

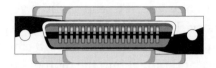

Memory

The next chapter discusses memory in somewhat broader terms than we will here. However, there are some important introductory points for you to know regarding your PC's memory. First, there is a tendency to confuse memory with disk space. Let's review the distinctions. Memory is *volatile storage*. That means that when you turn the PC off, anything stored in its memory will disappear. Also, memory is usually on the order of a few megabytes. Disk, or *mass* storage, can be tens or hundreds of megabytes. Data stored in mass storage is *nonvolatile*, meaning that when you turn the PC off, it remains stored.

You PC executes (runs) its programs in its memory. That memory, sometimes called *RAM* (Random Access Memory) is divided up into 640KB of *DOS Memory* and up to 31MB of additional *exTended* or *exPanded* memory. Some programs can use this exTended or exPanded memory to increase their efficiency and speed. In Chapter 3 you'll get a more detailed description of the difference between exTended and exPanded memory.

The 640K of DOS memory plus an additional 384K of *high memory* make up the first megabyte (1024KB) of memory in your PC. All DOS programs must run in the 640K DOS region. That is why that chunk of memory is referred to as *DOS memory*. The next 384K is used for such things as video memory for your display and a few other things your PC needs to run. When you buy a PC, the salesperson will often tell you that it comes with 640K of memory. The fact is that if it is a 286 or higher, it actually comes with 1MB. You just can't do much at this point with the upper 384KB. Later we'll see how to get some use out of that largely unused block of memory.

Because many programs can take advantage of either exTended or exPanded memory (there is a difference between the two), it is often beneficial to buy your PC, especially if you buy a 386, with additional memory. That additional memory, depending on what brand of PC you buy, usually comes in 2MB chunks. You can buy the extra memory and plug it into the mother board or use it in an add-in memory board, again, depending on the make of your PC. When you add memory you'll need to update your PC's configuration so that it recognizes its new memory. We'll go into that in more detail in the next chapter.

AXIOM

You can never have too much memory, too much disk space, or too fast a processor. But you may not need all of that the day you buy your first PC.

Mice and Other Critters

Going back to our brief definition of the term *peripheral*, we saw that peripherals are add-on devices such as printers or modems that plug into your PC to add additional functionality. For example, the modem adds the functionality of communications. Printers let you print the contents of certain types of files, and so on. There are several other peripherals besides modems and printers. Each of these adds some additional functionality to your PC. The first of these peripherals is a group of *pointing devices*. Pointing devices let you move the cursor on your screen without using the arrow keys.

There are two common types of pointing devices, the mouse and the digitizer puck. We won't concern ourselves with the digitizer since that is a specialized device used with computer-aided drafting (CAD) systems. But the mouse has become one of the most common peripherals for today's PCs. The reason is that a great many applications, such as desktop publishing and drawing programs, essentially require its use.

The mouse is a puck-shaped device that moves the cursor

around the screen as you move the mouse over a surface, usually a foam rubber pad called a *mouse pad*. The mouse can have either two or three buttons, one of which takes the place of the [Enter] key on the PC. How the mouse and its buttons respond to use depends on the individual application program with which you are using it.

There are two types of mice: bus and serial. The *bus mouse* requires a special add-in card for your PC. The most popular bus mouse and the standard in the industry is the Microsoft Mouse. Most programs that require mice are designed primarily for the Microsoft Mouse. The other kind, the *serial mouse,* uses one of the serial (COMM) ports on your PC. It doesn't require a card. This can be useful if you need an extra slot in your PC for some other add-in card and don't have room for the bus mouse.

Driving a Mouse

Mice, like many peripherals, require *driver software*. Driver software is, simply, a program that tells your PC that you are using the mouse and how the mouse is connected to the PC. In the case of mice, there are two kinds of mouse drivers. One, the *Mouse.sys file,* can be loaded as part of your PC's *environment*. That means that when you create your boot files (the autoexec.bat and config.sys files—discussed in Chapter 3) you can easily load the mouse driver. Your mouse will then be operative all of the time.

If you want your mouse active during only some of the programs you are using, you can use the other type of mouse driver, the *Mouse.com file*. Mouse.com is a terminate and stay resident (TSR) program. That means that once you load the driver it will stay in memory until you remove it. You can load mouse.com, load the application program, run the program using the mouse, and then unload the mouse and the application at the same time.

Scanners, Games, and Conflicts

Another type of peripheral is the scanner. Scanners allow you to transfer a drawing, photo, or any other document from paper into your PC. The scanner, like the bus mouse, requires both an add-in card and a driver. For playing computer games, there is a special

▼ *Figure 2.9. A Joystick for Use in the PC's Game Port*

peripheral called a *joystick* (Figure 2.9). The joystick, a common gaming tool, plugs into its own add-in card, called a *game port*, and of course has its own driver.

The important thing to remember about these various devices is that they all require some way to connect to your PC (usually an add-in card) and they all require drivers. Additionally, most of them require an I/O address and IRQ just like the COMM ports we discussed earlier. That brings up an important point. Because of the potential for I/O or IRQ conflicts you may have difficulty installing some of these peripherals.

A symptom of such a conflict is erratic behavior or nonoperation of the newly installed device. If that occurs, you might be better off seeking the help of someone familiar with configuring PCs with add-on peripherals. Clearing these conflicts can be quite tricky. There is not enough room in this book to describe all of the possible solutions to I/O or IRQ conflicts. The best way to learn is through experience and by reading the manual that comes with the device you are adding to your system. However, for most PC users, it's simply easier to get a PC professional to solve the problem for you.

Summary

- The processor, or CPU, is the brain of your PC. It is usually (in IBM PCs and clones) an Intel 80286, 80386, 80386SX, or 80486 chip.

- There are several basic functions that make up the operation of a PC. These functions are memory use, processing speed, and the instruction set the computer uses for its own internal language.

- Actual processing speed of a PC (the speed with which it can run a program) depends on a combination of clock speed, internal word size, bus width, and the CPU's instruction set.

- In general, the higher the model number of the CPU chip, the faster the processing, the wider the bus, and the more memory it can manage.

- PC keyboards differ from typewriter keyboards in the addition of function keys, a numeric pad, and cursor control keys.

- There are two basic kinds of monitors or displays for PCs: monochrome and color.

- Color displays can be (in order of improving resolution) CGA, EGA, VGA, or Super VGA

- You must have a display adapter or driver card in your PC that matches the monitor itself.

- There are four types of floppy disks that come in two sizes: $3\frac{1}{2}$" disks can have a capacity of 720KB or 1.4MB; $5\frac{1}{4}$" floppies can have a capacity of 360KB or 1.2MB.

- There are special DOS commands that allow you to format a high-capacity disk for a low-capacity drive, but you cannot format a low-capacity disk for a high-capacity drive.

- Hard disks (also called fixed disks) have far greater capacity than floppies, are enclosed in a package that includes the disk drives, and require special preparation before formatting for use.

- There are connectors on the back of your PC called ports. They are either serial (communications or COMM) ports or printer ports. If they are COMM ports they may be designated COMM1 through COMM4. If they are printer ports they will be designated LPT1 through LPT4.

- There are two types of memory that are in all AT class (80XXX CPUs) PCs: DOS memory (the first 640KB) and high memory (the next 384KB). DOS memory is where your applications run.

Summary

High memory is where special programs to operate your display (among other things) run.

- You can install additional memory in your PC called exTended or exPanded memory. DOS uses this extension memory to run certain kinds of programs that are designed for it.

- Peripherials are add-on devices such as printers, mice, scanners, etc. that you can use to add additional capabilities to your PC.

PRACTICE WHAT YOU'VE LEARNED

1. What do the terms "286," "386," and "486" refer to?

2. What is a "mother board"?

3. What controls the PC's processing speed?

4. What are the four additional keys on the QWERTY area of a PC keyboard?

5. How many function keys are there on a PC?

6. What are the two functions of the numeric pad and how do you switch between them?

7. What components make up all PC displays?

8. How does a monochrome graphics display handle colors?

9. What are the three main types of color graphics displays?

10. What are the available sizes and densities for floppy disks?

11. What are the three general steps for preparing a hard drive for use?

12. What are the two main types of hard drives and which is faster?

ANSWERS

1. They refer to the type of processor in a PC (Intel 80286, 80386, or 80486). In general, the higher the number, the more powerful the features of the PC.

2. The mother board is the main printed circuit board in a PC. All of the other printed circuit boards (also called "cards" or "add-in cards") plug into connectors mounted on the mother board.

3. The speed itself is controlled by the PC's clock. The CPU determines how fast the clock can go and the bus width helps determine how efficiently the PC processes information.

4. Control, Alternate, Enter, and Escape.

5. Ten or twelve depending on the type of keyboard. There are ten if they are placed along the left-hand side and twelve if placed across the top of the keyboard. The eleventh and twelfth keys are usually assigned special tasks in a program that you can access in other, less simple ways if you have only ten F-keys.

6. The number pad and the cursor arrows. You switch between them with the Num Lock key.

7. A monitor and a display adapter card that plugs onto the PC's mother board.

8. Monochrome graphics displays consist of a monochrome graphics adapter card, such as the Hercules card, and a color graphics monitor or a paper-white monitor that displays colors as a series of shades of gray plus black and white.

9. CGA (Color Graphics Adapter—the lowest resolution), EGA (Enhanced Graphics Adapter—mid-range resolution), and VGA (highest resolution, with the exception of the super VGA).

10. $5\frac{1}{4}$" floppies can have 360KB or 1.1MB densities; $3\frac{1}{2}$" floppies can have 720KB or 1.4MB densities.

11. Low-level format, partition, and format.

12. ESDI and SCSI. SCSI drives are much faster and can control up to seven fixed drives.

Your PC's Nervous System

You've learned the basics, and you've learned the hardware that makes up your PC. Now it's time to turn it on and learn what makes it tick. In this chapter you'll begin to move from theory to practice. But first, just a little more theory. In this chapter you will learn about:

▲ **BIOS, CMOS, and more about DOS**

▲ **Using simple DOS commands**

▲ **Batch files, including the Autoexec.bat file, Config.sys**

▲ **Loading programs and copying files**

▲ **Advanced memory concepts, including the differences between exTended and exPanded memory**

So, fire up your new PC and let's get started.

Your PC's Autonomic Nervous System

We've likened the PC's CPU to the brain of a living creature and the system clock to its heart. Now we'll discuss the PC's autonomic nervous system. In medical terms, the autonomic nervous system is the part of an organism that controls involuntary functions. For example, when the doctor taps your knee with a small hammer, your leg jerks. That's an autonomic reaction. In a PC there are certain functions that could be considered "autonomic."

Those functions have to do with remembering what kind of *system configuration* your PC has—what types of disk drives, ports, CPU, and memory you have installed in the computer. Another aspect of this part of your PC's system describes (to the CPU) various fundamental input/output functions. That means information regarding how to manage ports, keyboard, drives, and so on must be conveyed to the CPU. Finally, at a somewhat higher level, there must be something to control the overall operation of programs running on your PC. There are three *system level* programs that control these "autonomic" functions (Table 3.1).

▼ *Table 3.1. Important System Level Programs*

SYSTEM LEVEL PROGRAM	PURPOSE
BIOS (Basic Input/ Output System)	Instructions for managing the peripheral devices attached to the PC (keyboard, screen, ports, disk drives, etc.)
CMOS	Definitions of the devices attached to the PC
DOS	Operating system that provides instructions for running programs and managing the processing of information entering and leaving the PC

CMOS and Setup

The information indicating such things as your PC's configuration doesn't just appear. It must be learned. In order for your PC to learn what devices are attached to it, you must tell it (or, at least, confirm what the PC *thinks* is its configuration). That means that you must somehow let the PC know what disk drives, memory, display, and similar devices you have attached. The PC must retain that information so that, the next time you turn it on, it can recall how it was set up. You provide the information on most PCs by running a special program called *setup*. Then the PC stores your answers in a special random access memory (RAM) called *CMOS*.

You run the setup program the first time you use your PC (unless your dealer has run it for you) and then you won't need to run it again except in very special circumstances. One of those circumstances is, of course, when (or if) you change your PC's configuration. The other is when the CMOS battery for *nonvolatile memory* goes dead. You'll recall that *random access memory* is volatile. That means that when you turn off the PC, everything stored in memory goes away. However, it is necessary to retain the information in CMOS even when the PC is turned off so that it will be there the next time you boot.

TIP

In order to retain the data, a battery is applied to the special CMOS memory to keep it turned on, even when the PC is not. Because the battery will need to be replaced every two or three years it's a good idea to write down the answers to the setup questions so that, when the CMOS battery dies, you'll have no trouble setting up your PC again with a new battery.

Also, CMOS remembers the *system date and time*. The only way to make a permanent change in the date or time is to run setup. You can make temporary changes in date or time, but when you turn your PC off they go away. The time and date recalled by CMOS will take over when you reboot.

For most PCs, the setup program is very simple. It asks you to provide the amount of memory, types of disk drives, and type of display you have in your PC. Then it stores the answers in CMOS for use at boot time. However, there is an exception. IBM PS/2 computers use a far more comprehensive setup than most PCs. If you change your configuration for a PS/2, you will get an error message that tells you to insert a special setup disk. Since the setup program for most PCs is embedded in a certain chip in the PC, this is a somewhat different approach. The special disk is included with your PS/2 along with instructions for its use. The PS/2 configuration is very comprehensive and almost automatic.

BIOS

The next piece of the puzzle is the BIOS (Basic Input/Output System). Because BIOS is loaded into a special type of memory chip called a ROM (Read Only Memory) it is sometimes called *ROM BIOS*. ROMs are not volatile like RAM. However, since ROMs are read only, you can't save anything in them. The information in the ROM is put there at the factory using a special manufacturing process. Once the ROM is programmed, you can't change it. You have no control over the contents of the ROM chip, just as you have no control over the contents of the CPU chip. BIOS is very important to your PC, though. It is the BIOS that provides the PC with a means of communication between the CPU and such parts of your PC as the keyboard and disk drives.

There is an important distinction between the duties of the CMOS and the BIOS. While CMOS informs the PC of the *nature* of the devices attached to it, the BIOS provides a means of communicating with and managing them. Think of the CMOS as a list of devices and the BIOS as instructions for their use.

As I said, you can't do much about the BIOS. However, when you boot your PC (if it is not an IBM product that uses proprietary IBM BIOS) one of the messages you'll see on the screen is the manufacturer and version number of the BIOS chip in your computer. If you buy a "no-name" clone, you will want to check with the salesperson to make sure that the BIOS is fully compatible with IBM's. This is very important because IBM-compatible software makes use of the BIOS. If the BIOS is not fully IBM compatible, your software programs may not work correctly.

TIP

If you are experiencing serious difficulties running a variety of programs, especially those that use communications ports, you may have a BIOS incompatibility.

Although there was a time when such incompatibilities were fairly common, today's PC clones rarely experience such problems.

DOS

The area where you are most likely to experience difficulties is with DOS, the Disk Operating System. We have discussed DOS briefly before, but now we're going into a bit more detail. DOS is a set of programs that form the connection between the application program and the rest of your PC. There are three very important files and many less important utility-type programs. The three important ones are *Command.com, Ibmbios.com,* and *Ibmdos.com*. The latter two files are *hidden*. That means that you cannot see them if you list the files in the directory where they reside. Also, these two files cannot be erased without taking some special measures. In most cases you should not attempt to do anything to these two files, since changing them without going through the correct procedures can cause you no end of trouble.

When you install DOS, the installation program ensures that your *system files* (the three important files) are all of the same version. It is extremely important that you maintain the same version of DOS throughout all of the files that make up the DOS file suite. If you update from one version of DOS to another, you should also use the installation program that comes with the software to avoid version incompatibilities.

There are, as I said, several important functions, some of which may be thought of as utility features performed by DOS. These features are of two types: *internal* and *external*. Internal functions are those that are included in the *Command.com* program. Command.com is the DOS *command processor*. The command processor is the direct connection between *high-level commands* (those that you enter from your keyboard and those that are programmed into many applications programs that you run on your PC) and your PC's "internals" (the BIOS and CPU level processing). Thus it is very important that you have Command.com available to all of the programs that you run. We'll discuss techniques for accomplishing that later.

In addition to the internal functions of Command.com that allow you to run programs on your PC, there are several utilities and DOS commands. These commands are those that you can type into your computer to accomplish some simple tasks. In the next section of this chapter we'll explore some of those commands as well as the *external* commands included in DOS. External commands are those that are not part of Command.com. Instead, they are small utility programs, each with its own individual file.

What's in DOS?

When you buy a copy of DOS (or when DOS is supplied with your PC from the manufacturer) you will get several disks and a technical manual. Those disks contain the additional files and utility programs plus the three important system level programs and an installation program. There are only two manufacturers of DOS: IBM and Microsoft. Digital Research also has its own version of DOS, but it is more correctly thought of as an *extended DOS*, meaning it goes beyond standard IBM or Microsoft DOS. Not all IBM-compatible programs are guaranteed to operate correctly or completely with DRI DOS, while they would work with MS-DOS (Microsoft) or PC-DOS (IBM). The Microsoft and IBM DOS versions are very similar and are almost completely compatible with each other. However, you should never mix the two any more than you should mix versions of DOS.

For the most part you can't buy a copy of MS-DOS (the one from Microsoft). Microsoft supplies it to companies that manufacture PCs. These companies often make small changes in the implementation of the system so that they have, in effect, their own version of DOS. The fact is, however, that all of the essential functions and features are the same, regardless of the PC manufacturer's changes. These changes generally relate to the utilities and are usually additions of functionality (how the program works) instead of changes or deletions.

If you want to buy your own copy of DOS, it will generally need to be IBM's PC-DOS. You can buy that from any computer store. Table 3.2 provides a list of the most important functions of DOS and whether they are internal (part of Command.com) or external (separate programs). These are the basic commands that you will find yourself using most of the time. There are many others,

Your PC's Autonomic Nervous System

▼ *Table 3.2. Examples of Important DOS Commands*

COMMAND	DESCRIPTION	INTERNAL/EXTERNAL
Backup	Save (back up) files from one disk to another	E
Chdir or cd	Change directory	I
Chkdsk	Check disk and memory space	E
Cls	Clear the screen	I
Copy	Copy one or more files	I
Date	Display or set the date	I
Del	Delete one or more files	I
Dir	List the contents of a directory	I
Diskcomp	Compare the contents of two disks	E
Diskcopy	Copy an entire disk to another	E
Fdisk	Configure a disk in preparation for formatting	E
Format	Format a disk	E
Mkdir or md	Create a directory	I
Ren	Rename a file	I
Restore	Restore files from a backup	E
Rmdir or rd	Delete a directory	I
Time	Display or set the time of day	I
Type	List the contents of an ASCII file on screen	I
Ver	Display the DOS version number	I
Xcopy	Copy files and directories	E

depending on the version of DOS that you are using; however, these will make up the bulk of your DOS activities.

Many DOS functions change from version to version (version 4.01, for example, has more functionality than version 3.0). This is not a book about DOS and a detailed discussion of all its capabilities is beyond our scope. However, you can get detailed explanations for all of the commands and functions of your particular version of DOS by referring to the manual that came with it.

Talking to Your PC—Simple Commands

Before we get started on the details of these basic commands, you need to learn a new term: *syntax*. Syntax refers to the way that you use a command. It includes the command itself along with any *options* or *switches*. Options and switches alter the basic meaning of the command. They are also sometimes called *arguments*. Arguments follow the command and are usually separated from it by a separator character. The separator for most DOS commands is the *forward slash (/)*. This is the slash that appears on most keyboards on the same key as the question mark (?). Also part of a commands syntax are optional and mandatory arguments. These appear inside a pair of *delimiter characters* such as square brackets ([]) or curly braces ({}). Here are the rules for the DOS command syntax. The command will appear in **bold characters**. Characters and arguments within square brackets ([]) are optional. Text strings (except for switches) that you must supply are in *italics*. Switches are in regular text. For example, here is the syntax for the Dir command:

dir [*drive*][*pathname*][/p][/w]

That means that you must type the command (**dir**) followed by the drive (optional) and the pathname (also optional) of the directory you wish to list. You may also use the optional /p or /w switches, which will be described in detail with the command description. Thus, if you wanted the listing of the files on the D:> drive in the \books\chapts subdirectory the command you would type would be:

dir d:\books\chapts

followed by a carriage return (press the [Enter] key).

Backup

Purpose: Backs up one or more files from one disk to another
Syntax: **backup** [*sourcedrive:*][*path*][*filename*] [*targetdrive*] [/s] [/m][/a][/f][/d:*date*][/t:*time*][/L:[[*drive*][*path*]*filename*]]
Example: backup c:/s a:
Backs up (saves) all of the files and subdirectories on the C: drive to floppies in the A: drive.

Here are the arguments and their meanings.

Switch	Purpose
/s	Includes subdirectories in the backup
/m	Includes only files that have changed since the last backup
/a	Adds newly backed up files to the existing backup without erasing the existing backup (DOS version 3.3 or later); used with the /m switch, makes an *incremental backup* that creates a complete up-to-date backup
/f	Formats the target disk (if necessary)
/d:date	Backs up files modified on or after date
/t:time	Backs up files modified on or after time
/L:	Makes a backup log entry in filename located on drive:path; unless a filename or drive:path is specified, DOS will create Backup.log in the root directory of the source disk

You'll learn much more about the backup command and its use in the next chapter. The way I have illustrated the command shows the format for the example commands that follow. Notice that we give you the name (or names) of the command, its purpose, the syntax of the command (how you write it with any switches or options), an example of the command in actual use and, finally, a table showing the available options or switches for the command and what they mean.

Chdir or cd

Purpose: Changes from your current directory to a different one
Syntax: **chdir** or **cd** [*newpath*]
Example: cd c:\wp\docs
Changes from whatever directory you are in to the C:\WP\DOCS subdirectory.

You can use the cd command to change from any directory on your current disk to any other. You cannot use cd between disks, however. If you use the cd command and the new directory name alone, DOS will assume that you are changing to a *lower-level directory*. That means, as you will learn in the next chapter, that DOS will look for your target directory *under* the one in which you are currently located (the *current* or *active* directory). If you actually mean to change to a directory at the same level or higher than the current directory, you will need to use the *backslash* (\). This is the slash that, on most keyboards, is on the same key as the vertical line (|). If you are unsure about where the target directory is located, use a complete pathname including the disk, like this:

$$\text{\textbf{dir} } [\textit{drive:}][\textbackslash \textit{pathname}]$$

Chkdsk

Purpose: Reports the amount of memory and disk space available and checks the disk for errors
Syntax: **chkdsk** [*drive*][*pathname*][/f][/v]
Example: chkdsk c: /f
Performs check disk on the C: drive and fixes damage that it finds.

Here are the switches and their meanings.

Switch	*Purpose*
/f	Repairs errors on the disk
/v	Displays the name of each file as it scans the disk

Chkdsk is a method of testing the integrity of your hard drive. Often, when you delete a file, DOS writes another file over a portion of the old file. That leaves the rest of the old file on your disk. Of course, the remnants of the old file are useless, but they do take up space. Chkdsk finds these remnants, called *chains*, and deletes them if you wish. Without the /f switch, chkdsk simply reports errors and does not make any repairs to the disk. With the /f switch, chkdsk will repair any disk errors it finds.

Cls

Purpose: Clears the display screen
Syntax: **cls**

Cls, or "clear screen" simply erases all the information on your display and places the DOS prompt in the upper-left corner of the screen. Used in a batch file, it clears the screen and continues executing the batch file.

Copy

Purpose: Copies one or more files
Syntax: **copy** [*sourcedrive*][*sourcepath*]*sourcefile* [*destdrive*]
[*destpath*]*destfile* [/v][/a][/b]

Example: copy c:\wp\docs*.* a: /v
Copies all of the files in the C:\WP\DOCS subdirectory to a floppy disk in the A: drive and verifies that the copy can be read.

Here are the optional switches and their meanings.

Switch	Purpose
/v	Verifies that each sector on the target disk was written correctly and ensures an accurate copy
/a	Copies ASCII files
/b	Copies binary (executable) files

In most cases you won't have much use for the /a or /b switches. You can usually ensure a good copy simply by using the /v switch, which will return an error message if it cannot verify a correct copy on the target (*dest*ination) disk. It is a good idea to copy all binary files (those with .com, .exe, .sys, or .dat filename extensions) using the /v switch.

Date

Purpose: Displays or sets the system date
Syntax: **date** [*mm-dd-yy*]

The date command, issued alone, will display the system date and offer you a prompt for entering a different date in the format mm-dd-yy where mm is the number of the month (01–12), dd is the day of the month (01–31), and yy represents the last two digits of the year within the twentieth century (19yy). If you wish to change the date you can issue the command in the format shown in the syntax, which will automatically update the existing date to your new entry. However, the date command does not make a permanent date change. To do that you must use setup and write the new date in CMOS.

Del

Purpose: Deletes files
Syntax: **del** [*drive*][*path*]*filename*
Example: del c:\wp\docs*.*
Deletes all of the files in the C:\WP\DOCS subdirectory. Because you specified all files (*.*) the PC will ask you "Are You Sure? (Y/N)" before it lets you remove all of the files.

Del deletes the specified file from your disk. However, bear in mind that the file is not really erased from your disk. Rather, the directory entry for the file is altered so that you can write new files over the deleted one. If for some reason you need to completely erase the file (such as for security purposes) you'll need a utility that does so. There are several of these utilities available. DOS does not completely erase deleted files.

Dir

Purpose: Lists the files in a directory
Syntax: **dir** [*drive*][*pathname*] [/p][/w]

The dir command has two available switches, /p and /w. The /p
switch stops the directory listing at the end of each page (a page in
computerese means a screen full of data) and requests that you
press a key to continue. This prevents long directory listings from
scrolling past so fast that you can't read them. The long listing
(default) includes file creation time as well as file size for every file
in the directory (Figure 3.1). The /w switch presents the directory
listing in a wide format, omitting all information except the filename
(Figure 3.2).The wide display is useful only for browsing.

▼ *Figure 3.1. A Typical Listing of a Root Directory (Continued on
next page)*

dir c:\

Volume in drive C has no label
Directory of C:\

COMMAND COM	25276	7-24-87	12:00a
ANSI SYS	1647	7-24-87	12:00a
DESKNAV DND	299	9-22-90	5:25p
MOUSE COM	14455	8-24-87	12:00p
BKSHLF <DIR>		2-18-91	12:59p
SA EXE	4506	5-15-87	4:00p
XTREE BAT	46	5-27-90	5:14p
START BAT	4143	3-21-90	1:43p
HIMEM SYS	11304	5-01-90	3:00a
SYSMAP COM	13524	12-01-89	
XCOPY EXE	11216	7-24-87	12:00a
MARK COM	218	5-04-89	8:38p
WP51 BAT	100	7-29-90	9:13a
RAMDRIVE SYS	5719	5-01-90	3:00a
WP{WP} SET	2348	7-29-90	9:17a
WPPRS} SET	2586	7-29-90	9:21a
QEMM <DIR>		2-17-91	12:17p
WINDOWS <DIR>		2-17-91	12:17p
ED <DIR>		2-17-91	12:24p
UTILS <DIR>		2-17-91	12:25p
DOS <DIR>		2-17-91	12:25p

▼ *Figure 3.1. Continued*

NORTON <DIR>		2-17-91	12:26p
AUTOEXEC BAT	683	2-18-91	4:07p
XTGOLD <DIR>		2-17-91	12:27p
EI <DIR>		2-17-91	12:28p
FASTBACK <DIR>		2-17-91	12:29p
AMDEK SYS	12319	11-11-87	6:41a
MSCDEX EXE	19943	4-07-89	11:23a
MSLIB <DIR>		2-18-91	1:24p
CDROM BAT	52	2-18-91	1:18p
MSLROM BAT	91	2-18-91	1:32p
CONFIG SYS	583	2-18-91	4:07p

   21 File(s) 14039040 bytes free

▼ *Figure 3.2. A Typical Directory Display Using the /w Switch*

dir c: /w

  Volume in drive C has no label

  Directory of C:\

COMMAND COM	ANSI SYS	DESKNAV DND
ASK EXE	LOGIN EXE	LOGOUT EXE
MOUSE COM	MSREDIR EXE	NB COM
BKSHLF	SA EXE	SETNAME EXE
XTREE BAT	HIMEM SYS	SYSMAP COM
XCOPY EXE	WP51 BAT	RAMDRIVE SYS
WP{WP} SET	WPPRS} SET	BOOKROM BAT
QEMM	WINDOWS	ED
UTILS	DOS	NORTON
AUTOEXEC BAT	XTGOLD	EI
FASTBACK	AMDEK SYS	MSCDEX EXE
MSLIB	CDROM BAT	MSLROM BAT
CONFIG SYS	RELEASE EXE	

  26 File(s) 14039040 bytes free

Diskcomp

Purpose: Compares the contents of two disks

Syntax: **diskcomp** [*sourcedrive*] [*targetdrive*] [/1][/8]

Example: discomp a: b:

              Compares the disk in drive A: with the disk in drive B:.

discomp a: a:
Compares two disks in drive A:. You will be asked to switch between the two disks as the PC performs its compare.

Diskcomp performs a track-at-a-time comparison between two disks. This means that the two disks must be identical (both 360K 5 $\frac{1}{4}$" floppies or high-density 3 $\frac{1}{2}$" floppies, etc). You cannot perform diskcomp on hard disks. The /1 switch (that's the number one, not a lowercase L) compares only the first side of the disk regardless of disk type. The /8 switch looks only at the first 8 sectors per track. You'll learn more about sectors and other disk terms in the next chapter.

Diskcopy

Purpose: Copies the contents of one disk to another
Syntax: **diskcopy** [*sourcedrive*] [*targetdrive*][/1]
Example: diskcopy a: b:
Copies the contents of the disk in drive A: to a target disk in drive B:, sector by sector. As with the discomp command you can use only the A: drive. DOS will prompt you to periodically switch the source and target disks in the drive.

Diskcopy works exactly like diskcomp, except that it copies the disk's contents instead of comparing it. The /1 switch has the same meaning—copy only the first side of the disk. The advantage to using diskcopy as opposed to copy is that diskcopy copies the disk contents a track at a time (a track is a physical area on a disk) instead of trying to copy files. Under diskcopy, DOS doesn't care what is on the disk, it simply transfers bits until the two disks match. As in diskcomp, you must use disks that are the same type and you can't diskcopy hard disks.

Fdisk

Purpose: Prepares a hard disk for formatting
Syntax: **fdisk**

Fdisk will be explained in more detail in the next chapter. It is one of the external utilities and it provides menu guidance, so it has no switches or options.

Format

Purpose: Prepares a disk for use
Syntax: format *drive:* [/1][/4][/8][*t:tracks*][*n:sectors*][/v][/s]
Example: format a: /4
Formats the low-density 5 ¼" disk in drive A: (a high-density drive).

Use the format command to prepare any type of disk for use by DOS. You'll get more details on formatting in the next chapter. However, there are several options and switches in this command that you should understand.

Switch	Purpose
/1	Formats one side of a floppy disk only
/4	Formats a low-density (360KB) 5¼" disk in a high-density (1.2MB) drive
/8	Formats 8 sectors per track
/b	Leaves room for the system files on the disk
/s	Transfers the system files to the disk; use the /s switch to boot your PC from the disk
/t:tracks	Specifies the number of tracks to put on the formatted 3½" floppy disk; the default value is 80 (/t:80)
/s:sectors	Specifies the number of sectors per track for a 3½" disk; the value for a 720K disk is 9 (/n:9)
/v	Assigns a volume name to the disk; you will be prompted to enter a name of up to 11 characters

All of these switches are self-explanatory with the exception of the /t:tracks and /n:sectors switches. The purpose for these switches is to allow you to format a 720K disk in a 1.4MB drive (3 ½"). When you format 5 ¼" disks, you can use the /4 switch to format a low-density disk in a high-density drive. However, you cannot use those switches on 3 ½" disks to accomplish the same task. Instead, you would use the tracks and sectors switches. Thus, to format a low-density 3 ½" disk in a high-density drive you would use the following command:

Talking to Your PC—Simple Commands

format *drive:* /t:80 /n:9

Your drive designation would be either A: or B:.

Mkdir or md

Purpose: Creates a directory or subdirectory
Syntax: **md** [*drive:*] *pathname*
Example: md c:\temp
           Creates a directory called temp on the C: drive

Md simply creates a directory under whatever directory you are located in currently (the current or active directory). If you are in the root directory, md creates a *first-level* directory, also known as a *parent*. If you are in a first-level or parent directory, md creates a subdirectory under the parent also known as a *child*. You'll learn a lot more about directories in the next chapter.

Ren

Purpose: Renames a file
Syntax: **ren** [*drive:*][*pathname*][*oldfilename*] [*newfilename*]
Example: ren c:\temp\oldfile.txt newfile.txt
           Renames a file called oldfile.txt in the C:\temp subdirectory as newfile.txt. The renamed file will stay in the same directory as the old filename.

Restore

Purpose: Restores files and directories backed up using the backup command
Syntax: **restore** [*sourcedrive*] [*targetdrive*][*pathname*][/s][/p][/b:*date*][/a:*date*][/e:*time*][/L:*time*][/m][/n]
Example: restore a: c: /s
           Restores files backed up onto floppies in the A: drive to

the C: drive including all of the files in subdirectories.

Here are the switches for the restore command.

Switch	Purpose
/s	Includes subdirectories
/p	Prompts for permission to restore files that are read-only or have changed since last backup
/b:date	Restores only files last modified on or before date
/a:date	Restores only files last modified on or after date
/e:time	Restores only files last modified on or before time
/L:time	Restores only files last modified on or after time
/m	Restores only files modified since last backup
/n	Restores only files that no longer exist on the target disk

Restore must be used to restore files backed up with the DOS restore command and, prior to version 3.3, only those backed up using the same version of DOS as the version used for restore.

Rmdir or rd

Purpose: Deletes a directory or subdirectory
Syntax: rd [*drive:*]*pathname*
Example: rd c:\temp
Removes (deletes) the temp subdirectory on the C: drive. The directory must be empty before you can delete it.

Rd is the opposite of md and is used in the same manner. The only difference is that md *creates* a directory or subdirectory, and rd *deletes* it.

Time

Purpose: Displays or changes the system time of day
Syntax: time [*hours:minutes*[:*seconds*[.*hundredths*]]]

The time command works exactly like the date command. However, the hours are always expressed in 24-hour format with a value of 0–23 (0 being midnight).

Type

Purpose: Lists the contents of an ASCII file on screen
Syntax: **type** [*drive:*]filename
Example: type c:\temp\test.txt
Lists (displays) the contents of the file test.txt, which resides in the temp directory on the C: drive. Test.txt must be an ASCII file.

Type lets you display the contents of any ASCII file on your screen. To stop the scrolling of the display you can press [Ctrl][S], and [Ctrl][Q] to resume.

Ver

Purpose: Displays the version number of the installed DOS
Syntax: **ver**

Xcopy

Purpose: Copies files and directories
Syntax: **xcopy** [*sourcedrive:*][*sourcepath*]*filespec* [*targetdrive*] [*targetpath*][/a][/d:*date*][/e][/m][/p][s][/v][w]
Example: xcopy c:*.* d: /s
Copies all of the files in all of the directories and subdirectories on the C: drive to the D: drive.

Xcopy differs from copy in that it can copy directories and subdirectories, whereas copy is restricted to the files in the source directory. The directories and subdirectories referred to by xcopy must be under the directory specified as the source path. Here are the switches used by xcopy.

Switch	Purpose
/a	Copies files that have their archive bit set (This is a bit

complex and is beyond the scope of our discussion. You will rarely use it, and for more information you can refer to your DOS user's manual.)

/d:date	Copies only those files modified on or after date
/e	Copies subdirectories even if they are empty; use with the /s switch
/m	Similar to the /a switch (Beyond our scope.)
/p	Prompts you for confirmation prior to copying each file
/s	Copies directories and subdirectories
/v	Like the copy command's /v switch; verifies correct copy of each file
/w	Waits before copying files; prompts before continuing

These are the most commonly used of the DOS commands. You will use these commands both from your keyboard and within batch files. Batch files, and other similar issues, comprise the next section of this chapter.

Teaching Your PC New Skills

The next step on our road to PC mastery is the special use of the commands we have just discussed. As you learned, you can type these DOS commands and your PC will perform the function dictated by the command. When you type a command at the DOS prompt, it is called a *DOS command line*. The command line contains the command and any switches or options you add. You can also start any application program by typing the program's command line at the DOS prompt. That means if you have a word processor whose startup command is *WP*, you can run the program just by typing WP at the DOS prompt. Issuing commands in this manner is called using your PC *interactively*. But there is another way to issue commands to your PC.

Batching It

You can create a simple ASCII text file with a series of commands—one right after another, each on its own line—that will execute each of the commands one at a time until it has executed all of them. This text file has a special name. It is called a *batch file* and it always has the filename extension *.bat*. Let's suppose that your current directory is the root of your C:> drive (C:\) and that you want to launch (run) your word processor located in the C:\wordpro directory. The command to run the word processor is WP. You would perform several tasks if you were to do this interactively.

First, you would need to change to the C:\wordpro directory (*cd c:\wordpro*). Then, you must invoke the program (*wp*). Finally, when you are finished, you'd like to return to the root directory (*cd c:*). By using a batch file, you can perform all of these tasks with a single command. Here's how. We'll call our batch file Wordpro.bat. You can create this simple batch file using any ASCII text editor or by using the DOS mode of most word processors. This is the mode that produces text files without any word processing control codes. You'll know you've produced an ASCII file if you can read it on your screen using the DOS *type* command. If you see any strange looking characters, you'll know you didn't create an ASCII file.

Simply type each command exactly as you would type it at the DOS prompt. Each command sits on its own line. We'll start by clearing the screen. So your batch file would look like this.

```
cls
cd c:\wordpro
wp
cd c:\
```

That's all there is to it. Of course batch files can get somewhat more complicated, but the idea is that all you need to do is create your ASCII file in exactly the same way as you would type the commands at the DOS prompt.

Special Files You Can Build

There are two special files that you can create in virtually the same way. These two files set up your PC at boot time so that you can load menus, device drivers, and other startup programs when you first turn on your computer. These two files, Autoexec.bat and Config.sys, are simple to create, but very important. The Autoexec.bat is a simple batch file that DOS looks for right after it executes Config.sys. Let's look at the Config.sys file first.

We need to define a new term from the preceding paragraph: *device drivers*. So, before we go any further, we'd better understand what they are. Many programs and peripheral devices (such as displays, printers, keyboards, etc.) require special programs to be in place so that they can work correctly. These programs must be running in such a way that they don't interfere with other applications programs you might run. These special little programs are called *device drivers* and they are files with the file extension .sys. For that reason they are sometimes called *sys files* (pronounced "sis"). DOS takes these sys files and places them all together in one chunk of memory called the *command environment*.

The sys files are invoked from the Config.sys file. You create a Config.sys file the same way you create any batch file. You use your ASCII text editor to create a file that contains the name of each sys file in the format *device=filename.sys*. You place one device command on each line. There are also a couple of other commands that go into the Config.sys file.

When an application program is running on your PC, it may have need to use other files. For example, a database management program needs database files. A word processing program needs document files, and so on. In computerese, we say that these applications *open* the files they need, meaning that they *use* them. DOS needs to know how many of these files the application is likely to open so it can ensure that there is enough memory available. Also, applications programs place portions of themselves into special memory when they run.

These special memory locations are called *buffers*. DOS also has to know how many buffers it needs to have available for your applications. Both the number of files and the number of buffers are designated in the Config.sys file using, not surprisingly, the commands *files=* and *buffers=*. Typical values for these two parameters are files=30 to 50 (depending on the applications you are running) and buffers=15 to 20. These figures represent a range. You would, of course, include only a single number within that range.

Figure 3.3 is a typical Config.sys file. Notice the various device drivers. The ones in the \3drivers\ subdirectory are used to run a local area network. The others provide services for various other programs and peripherals. There is one additional command shown here that we haven't discussed: the *lastdrive=* command. In most cases you won't need this command. However, if you occasionally use additional drives (for example, if you connect to a local area network) you may want to add this command to designate the highest available drive on your system.

Usually, you won't need to add the sys files to your Config.sys. When you install a program or set up a peripheral that uses a sys file, the installation or setup procedure will usually do it for you. Likewise, if your application program requires more files or buffers than you have set, the application will correct your Config.sys to include them. Your best bet is to create a basic Config.sys with files= and buffers= set to average values and let your applications do the rest.

Teaching Your PC New Skills

▼ Figure 3.3. A Config.sys File

```
device=ansi.sys
files=50
buffers=15
lastdrive=z
device=\3drivers\eth503.sys /I:2
device=\3drivers\spp.sys
device=\3drivers\pro.sys 12 2 2
device=\3drivers\buf.sys
device=\3drivers\idp.sys
device=\3drivers\lgl.sys
device=c:\windows\smartdrv.sys 2048 512
device=amdek.sys /n:1 /d:amdek /p:240
```

The Autoexec.bat File

The other important program you can create is the Autoexec.bat. This is nothing more than a batch file. There are a few commands that you will always want in your Autoexec.bat. The most important of these is the DOS path. The path tells DOS where to look for various programs. In our batch file example earlier, we changed the directory from the root to c:\wordpro because that is where we had saved our word processing program. To run it DOS needed to know where it was. The easiest way was to simply move to that directory.(Never fear. We will discuss directories and subdirectories in detail in the next chapter.)

However, there is another way to tell DOS where programs are located. That is to set a *path* to them. The path command does not specifically point to a program. Instead, it points to a directory. DOS looks in all of the directories in the path whenever you load a program. If it finds the program in one of the path directories, it runs it. If it does not (and you haven't specifically told DOS where to look as in the earlier example), DOS will give you a "file not found" error. In Figure 3.4, you'll see the DOS **PATH** command as well as some others.

The figure shows a very simple Autoexec.bat file, but it demonstrates several things you might see in such a file. The first command is the path command. What it tells DOS is, whenever the user invokes a program, look for the program's files in the following directories:

C:\WINDOWS\;C:\;C:\DOS\;C:\ED\;C:\UTILS\;C:\XTGOLD\;C:\COMM

Notice that there is a semicolon (;) separating the directory pathnames. The second command is the *prompt* command. This

---

▲ *Figure 3.4. An Autoexec.bat File*

PATH C:\WINDOWS;C:\;C:\DOS\;C:\ED\;C:\UTILS\;C:\XTGOLD\;C:\COMM
prompt d_$p $g
set TEMP=C:\WINDOWS\TEMP
cls
peter

command lets you customize your DOS prompt to include such things as the date, time, or the pathname of the current directory. In this example the DOS prompt from the C:\ directory would look like this:

**Teaching Your
PC New Skills**

Fri 2-22-1991

C:\

The prompt shows the current date on one line and the current directory on the next. The $ and an additional character indicate what the prompt should look like. Table 3.3 is a list of the various elements you could include in your DOS prompt and the $ designators for them.

The set temp command sets a temporary directory for Microsoft Windows, and the command *peter* starts a batch file called Peter.bat that loads other programs. You can start a batch file or any program you wish from your Autoexec.bat. Like all batch files, Autoexec.bat will continue executing after it finishes running a program called from within it if there are more steps in the batch file. There is, however, one exception to this rule. If you want to return to the original batch file (in this case Autoexec.bat) after

▼ *Table 3.3. DOS Prompt Commands*

This Character	Gives You This Prompt
$q	The = sign
$$	The $ sign
$t	The current time
$d	The current date
$p	The current drive and pathname
$v	The DOS version number
$n	The current drivename
$g	The > character
$l	The < character
$b	The I character

running another batch file, you must use a special command named *call*. So, if we had other files or commands to execute *after* running Peter.bat, instead of simply typing *peter* we would have to type *call peter*. This only works in DOS versions 3.3 and higher; in earlier versions you cannot call a batch file and then return to the original batch.

These two files, the Config.sys and the Autoexec.bat, are sometimes referred to as *boot files*. This is actually only part of the story, however. In addition to these two files we should also include Command.com and the two hidden system files in that category. The simple purpose for Config.sys is to create the command environment. The job of the Autoexec.bat file is running your PC with the user environment you want. For example, the last command in your Autoexec.bat file (in place of our peter command) might invoke your menu program. You'll learn about user menus in Chapter 7; now, let's look into memory.

Helping Your PC Remember— How Much Memory Is Enough?

There are three types of memory for many computers. How you and your computer use this memory and how much your PC contains will have a large bearing on how efficiently your PC does its job. Broadly speaking, PCs from the 286s up can contain DOS memory and expansion memory. Expansion memory can consist of either exTended or exPanded memory, or sometimes both. Here is the whole memory story.

Think of your PC's memory as a tower. Our imaginary tower has (or can have) many floors. Each floor in our example equates to 1KB of random access memory (RAM). There is a door in the bottom of the tower. You can enter the door and use the first 640 floors (640KB) no matter who you are. Those floors are always available and it takes no special skills or tools to use them. Those first 640 floors represent the first 640KB of RAM, also called *DOS memory*. This is available in virtually all PCs and it is where all your applications programs run.

When you invoke a program by typing its startup command at the DOS prompt or in a batch file, DOS finds the program and loads it into DOS memory. All programs run from inside DOS memory. That is why we use the term *load* to describe how we start a program. We *load* a program from the disk to memory so we can *run* it. The command environment we discussed earlier also sits in DOS memory. That reduces the amount of DOS memory available for running applications.

Helping Your PC Remember— How Much Memory Is Enough?

Expanding Your Tower

Now, if you want, you can add many more floors to your tower. However, you will need special tools to open the door to them. These extra floors, above the first 640, are equivalent to *expansion memory*. If you have a 286, 386, or 486 PC, you can use this extra memory if you have installed it.

You can use expansion memory in a number of ways. For example, you can use exTended memory for *RAM drives*. A RAM drive is a block of exTended memory that DOS treats as if it were a disk drive. The advantage is that RAM drives are much faster than disk drives. The disadvantage is that their data is lost when you turn off or reboot the PC. You can use a RAM drive to temporarily hold files that contain data or documents to speed up the programs that use them.

Many programs use expansion memory to hold a portion of themselves or information that they use, thus reducing the amount of DOS memory that they require. There are two types of expansion memory; different programs use one or the other in a variety of ways. Here's the difference between them.

ExTended memory is also known as *contiguous memory* because it views all of the memory above 640KB as one *contiguous block* of available memory. RAM disks can use only exTended memory since they need a continuous block of memory available to simulate the space on a disk. Many other programs use exTended memory because it gives them large blocks of available memory in which to function.

ExPanded memory is somewhat different. Although there is, perhaps, a large block of memory, if it is configured as exPanded memory programs can use it only in blocks of 64KB at a time. These blocks move around the larger memory block under the control of a *page frame*. The page frame is sort of like a window on 64KB of the total available memory. Programs that use exPanded memory control the location of the page frame's view of the expansion memory so that it is seeing the 64KB block that the program needs at the time. Obviously, exTended memory is more practical and efficient. However, there are a number of popular programs that take advantage of exPanded memory.

You really don't need to worry much about expansion memory. When you buy your PC the only memory usually available in their standard configurations is DOS memory. If you want expansion memory, just tell your dealer. It is usually sold in blocks of 2MB and the dealer can configure it as exTended, exPanded, or both and provide any memory management tools you need to take advantage of it. From the applications you are using, your computer dealer will know how to set up your expansion memory.

Some Hidden Floors

We have missed one hidden piece of memory. In our tower, we don't actually jump right from the 640th floor into the expansion floors. There are 384 floors between the bottom 640 and the expansion. The trouble is, we have to take an elevator through them and we can't usually stop and use them. This 384KB of memory between DOS memory and expansion memory is called *high memory* and it is very hard to get at. Some of those 384 floors (384KB) are used for storage. In fact, they can be useful if we know how to unlock them.

Using special tools, you can take advantage of some of that high memory. It is true that some high memory is taken up with special drivers for your display, among other things, but a very large percentage of it is open and usable. With the special tools, called memory managers, you can put your command environment there instead of in DOS memory. That gives your programs more room to run.

If you run TSRs (Terminate and Stay Resident programs, also called *pop-ups*), you can often load them into high memory, freeing still more DOS memory. Pop-ups are little programs such as utilities, calendars, calculators, and note pads that stay in memory all of the time. To use them you simply press a predefined key combination, called a *hot key*, and they *pop up* on your screen. If you load them into DOS memory they take space away from your applications.

If you have a 386 or 486 PC the only tools you need to take advantage of that extra memory are software drivers. If you have a 286 machine, you can't open the door without a special hardware addition to your PC. The mechanics of that process are beyond the scope of this book, as are the specifics of the same process for 386s and 486s. However, your dealer can recommend the proper memory expansion tools depending on which PC you own.

How much memory do you need? Like everything else in personal computing, that depends on how you are using your computer. Certainly you need DOS memory. You will virtually always get at least that. But if you are buying a very simple machine such as the so-called "Turbo" PCs that are actually like the old IBM XTs, you may get only 512KB of RAM standard. Make sure you have at least 640KB. There are almost no worthwhile programs that can run, along with the overhead of the command environment, in only 512KB of memory.

If you buy a 286 or higher, you will always get DOS memory and high memory (1,024KB total) even though you would not have the benefit of those additional memory management tools we discussed earlier. The PC will usually be advertised as 640KB, but the extra 384KB is there nonetheless. You can add as much expansion memory as you need. Again, consult with your computer dealer to determine exactly what you need in terms of expansion memory and memory management tools.

Helping Your PC Remember— How Much Memory Is Enough?

Summary

- BIOS (Basic Input/Output System) contains instructions for managing the peripheral devices attached to the PC (keyboard, screen, ports, disk drives, etc.).
- CMOS (a special random access memory) contains definitions of the devices attached to the PC.
- DOS is the operating system. It contains instructions for running

programs and managing the processing of information entering and leaving the PC.

- You provide the configuration information on most PCs by running a special program called Setup which stores your answers in CMOS.

- In order to retain the Setup data in CMOS, a battery is applied to the special CMOS memory to keep it turned on, even when the PC is not. This battery must be replaced periodically to avoid losing the Setup data.

- DOS is a set of programs that form the connection between the application program and the rest of your PC. There are three very important files and many less important utility-type programs. The three most important ones are Command.com, Ibmbios.com, and Ibmdos.com, the last two of which are hidden.

- When you type a command at the DOS prompt, it is called a DOS command line. The command line contains the command and any switches or options you add. You can also start any application program by typing the program's command line at the DOS prompt.

- You can create a simple ASCII text file with a series of commands, one right after another, each on its own line, which will execute each of the commands one at a time until it has executed all of them. This text file has a special name. It is called a batch file and it always has the filename extension .bat.

- The Config.sys file is a boot file that sets your PC's operating environment.

- The Autoexec.bat file is a boot file that enhances the environment already set up by Config.sys by executing programs such as memory resident pop-ups and other programs from which you want to start your computing session.

- Your PC can use DOS memory, high memory, exTended memory, and exPanded memory. 386 PCs can manage all of this memory using software drivers only. 286 PCs require special add-in hardware to manage high memory.

PRACTICE WHAT YOU'VE LEARNED

1. What is the function of your PC's BIOS?

2. How does configuration information get into CMOS?

3. How does CMOS RAM retain its information after you turn off the PC?

4. What is the purpose of CMOS memory?

5. What are the two major suppliers of DOS?

6. What are the three important system files on your PC?

7. What is the purpose of the path command and where do you generally use it?

8. What is the difference between DOS memory, high memory, exTended memory, and exPanded memory?

ANSWERS

1. Contains instructions for managing the peripheral devices attached to the PC (keyboard, screen, ports, disk drives, etc.).

2. You store it there when you answer the questions in your PC's setup program.

3. It uses a small battery to make the CMOS RAM nonvolatile.

4. CMOS is used to store information regarding the configuration of your PC. It collects data about the peripherals such as memory, disk drives, ports, displays, and keyboards attached to the computer.

5. Microsoft and IBM. You can't buy Microsoft DOS because it is generally supplied only to manufacturers of PCs. You can, however, buy IBM's PC-DOS at your local computer store.

6. Command.com (the command processor), Ibmbios.com (hidden), and Ibmdos.com (hidden)

7. It tells DOS which directories on your hard disk to search for programs you execute from the DOS prompt. You generally place it in your Autoexec.bat file.

8. DOS memory is the first 640KB of RAM. This is where you run all of your applications programs. High memory is the next 384KB of RAM. Your PC stores some system drivers such as display drivers here but it is, for the most part, empty. You need special memory management tools to use it. ExTended memory is an open block of contiguous memory that takes up the rest of the memory you have installed (if you configure it as exTended memory). ExPanded memory is a different way of configuring your remaining memory (different configuration from exTended memory). It uses a page frame to access this additional memory in 64KB blocks. Only exTended memory can be used for RAM disks.

Your PC's Built-In Library of Information

Your PC is an efficient processor of information. However, the ease and success with which you use it to process that information depends, among other things, on the efficiency with which you manage its fixed storage—your computer's hard disk. You might consider the PC's hard disk to be its file cabinet of programs and data. In this chapter you will learn about:

▲ **Hard disk management**

▲ **Preparing your hard disk for use**

▲ **Directory organization and management**

▲ **Backup and recovery**

Your PC's File Cabinet

If you think of the hard drive as your PC's file cabinet, you'll have no trouble keeping it in proper order. For example, in a file cabinet you would probably keep all documents of one type together. You might have a file folder for correspondence, another for invoices, and so on. You would also probably designate certain drawers in the file cabinet as special repositories of similar information. For example, you might have a drawer designated for everything that happened in 1989, or one that contained nothing but customer files.

The point is that, in any good filing system, you will have categories and subcategories. Those divisions are always broken down based on collections of similar information. By setting up your file cabinet in this manner, you can easily retrieve any information you have filed. You don't even have to know where it is stored—you just have to know the system. Setting up your PC's hard drive is not much different from setting up the file cabinet. You create categories, called *directories*, that relate to the same categories—file drawers, for example—in your file cabinet. Then, of course, you have subcategories, called *subdirectories*, and so on.

The easiest way to visualize the organization of your hard disk, or *directory structure*, is to think of it as a *directory tree*. The directory tree is simply an illustration of the relationships of the various directories and subdirectories to each other. Figure 4.1 is an example of a directory tree.

▼ *Figure 4.1. A Directory Tree*

DIRECTORY TREE FOR VOLUME LAPTOP
C:\
          C:\DOS
          C:\BIN
          C:\HOLD
          C:\ED
                  C:\ED\TEXTFILE
          C:\CCMAIL
          C:\UTIL
          C:\PRO
          C:\WP51
                  C:\WP51\DOCS

Notice that the volume (disk name) *LAPTOP* contains a *root directory* C:\. The backslash (\) by itself indicates that you are looking at the root. The root is the highest level of file cabinet division. You might view the root as the file drawer. All of the directories, such as C:\DOS or C:\CCMAIL, might be major file folders in the drawer. And the *subdirectories,* such as C:\ED\TEXTFILE, are minor folders within the major folders.

In the case of our example, each of the directories has been set up for a specific purpose. The C:\UTIL directory, for example, is a major folder in our file cabinet that contains all of our utility programs. That means that when we install a piece of utility software on our PC, we install it in the C:\UTIL directory. Similarly, I installed my copy of WordPerfect, the word processor I use for most of my writing, in a special directory called C:\WP51. Because the word processor creates documents, I added a minor folder, or *subdirectory,* under the C:\WP51 directory, called C:\WP51\DOCS. You create these directories and subdirectories using the DOS *MD* or *MKDIR* command.

We'll discuss the specifics of organizing your hard drive a bit later in this chapter. For now, the important thing for you to understand is that there is a generally accepted method for laying out your hard disk. That method is roughly analogous to the way you would organize a file cabinet. I have seen PC users who don't use any hard disk organization. Instead they put everything in their root directory. There are two very good reasons for *never* doing that. First, you are only allowed a certain number of directory entries in a single directory. How many depends on which version of DOS you are using.

The second reason is that you will find it very difficult to manage your program and data files if they are all in one huge directory. Many applications have quite a few files that go along with them (WordPerfect has several dozen for example) and the filenames are not always indicative of the program they belong to. Thus, if you want to delete a program for some reason, you are very likely to leave several files taking up space you might need for something else. If you organize your applications and their accompanying files in their own directories and subdirectories, you'll have no trouble identifying the files you want to delete.

Your PC's File Cabinet

Preparing the Cabinet to Receive Its Library of Files

Before you can set up your new file cabinet, you may have to prepare it. Potentially, there are several steps in this process. However, before we get too tangled up in details, here is a bit of information about hard disks in general. When you purchase a new PC, depending on where you buy it, your hard disk may or may not be ready to use. If it is, the information that follows won't be a lot of use to you unless you have a major problem that requires you to *rebuild* your hard drive.

That doesn't mean that you have to get out the screwdriver and soldering iron. The term *rebuilding* in reference to hard drives actually refers to the disk, not the drive. It means that you will need to perform the tasks we are about to discuss and then *restore* your backed up files. You won't have to rebuild your drive unless something happens that destroys all, or a significant portion of, the files and data in your file cabinet.

On Your Mark—Low-Level Format

Most PCs purchased from computer stores come with the hard disk ready for use and the DOS files already installed. If your computer store doesn't provide that service, *at no additional cost*, go to another computer store. If, however, for one reason or another, you find that you have to prep the hard drive, here are three important rules to follow.

TIP

1. Read the drive manufacturer's instructions for preparing the hard drive.

2. Read them again.

3. Read them one last time before starting.

Not all disks are the same. There are many different procedures for preparing hard drives for use. Often the manufacturer will include special programs on a separate floppy disk that you must use. *Use them!* Here are the whats and whys of hard disk prep.

Preparing the Cabinet to Receive Its Library of Files

Hard disks must be low-level formatted before you can begin to use them. This is a special formatting technique that prepares the hard drive for DOS formatting. Low-level formatting checks every sector of the disk to make sure that it is good. If it finds a bad sector it marks it and creates a special bad sector table. This table and the mark prevent DOS from trying to place data on the bad sector.

Low-level formatting is a very lengthy process (a 40MB drive can take over an hour) and should never be attempted without the specific instructions and tools from the drive manufacturer. Almost all modern drives come from the factory low-level formatted and there are very few reasons to do it yourself. If the manufacturer recommends it, however, you can be certain they will supply a special program and complete instructions, including *when* it might be necessary. Most PC users will never, in their entire lifetimes, have to low-level format a hard disk.

After the hard disk receives its low-level format, it must be set up to work as a DOS hard drive. That means that it must be divided up into *partitions* or *volumes*. Partitions are divisions on a hard drive that carry the root designators C:\, D:\, E:\, etc., that you discovered earlier. Depending on the version of DOS you are going to use, you will either be restricted to partitions of no more than 32MB, or there will be no limitations on partition size. At least one partition on your drive must be designated as a DOS partition. Usually, that is the C:\ partition. That partition should contain the special files that boot your PC. But we're getting a bit ahead of ourselves.

Most hard drives are at least 20MB, and many are much larger. You can take larger drives and break them up into several partitions. For example, if you had a 40MB drive, you could create a *primary DOS partition* of 32MB and a secondary partition of around 10MB. The primary partition would be your C:\ drive and the smaller one would be the D:\ drive. Although we don't actually have two physical drives, DOS views the two partitions exactly as if we did.

Get Set—Define the File Cabinet

In order to create these partitions, you use the DOS program *FDISK*. FDISK is a special program that comes with all versions of DOS. It allows you to partition the physical drive, determine the types of partitions and their sizes, and create the *FAT* and *directory structure*. There's a new term: FAT. The FAT (File Allocation Table) contains information that DOS uses to help it locate files on the hard drive. The physical locations of the files are located in the FAT while the names, sizes, and other data about the files are in the directory. These two areas of the hard disk must be prepared before DOS can use them.

Once you have completed using FDISK (it is a very simple program to use, providing all of the special prompts you will require) you are ready for the final step, DOS formatting. FDISK varies somewhat among versions of DOS, so check the DOS manual that comes with your PC for specific instructions. Again, you won't need to do this unless you buy a PC with an unpreped hard drive or you decide at some time in the future to change the size or number of your partitions. If you do make changes in the future, remember that running FDISK will wipe out all the data on your drive. You need to have a way of restoring data, usually from a backup, after you finish your work.

TIP

Never perform any alteration of your hard disk without two complete backup copies of your programs and data.

Go—Format the Hard Drive

The final step in preparing your hard drive is the DOS format. You simply use the FORMAT command from a copy of DOS on a floppy in your A:> drive. Always use the /S switch on the FORMAT command when you format the C:> drive, since you will need to transfer the *system files* in order to make the drive bootable. If you are formatting other drives (such as the D:> or E:> drives) you won't want to make them bootable, so you won't use the /S switch.

The DOS format sets up the DOS partitions to actually receive files. Like FDISK, FORMAT will wipe out all of the data on your disk. So don't forget to make two backups. Why two backups? It is possible that you will have a damaged backup, for any of a number of reasons. For example, you may have used a damaged floppy disk during backup. When you are about to completely wipe out everything on your disk, you'll want to be absolutely certain that you have a good backup copy in order to restore the data after you finish your format.

Once you have completed the DOS format, you are ready to begin setting up your directory structure and loading programs and data onto your hard disk. There are several rules of thumb regarding hard disk organization, and that is what the next section is all about.

Preparing the Cabinet to Receive Its Library of Files

Organizing the Library into Logical Areas

While all hard disk layouts are not the same, there are some generalizations that we can make. Obviously, each individual PC user has different requirements, will be using different applications, and will have more or less sophistication depending on his or her individual needs. The approach taken here is a generic one that you can fit to just about any situation. We'll assume the C:> drive for the purposes of this discussion because that's where you'll keep most of the basic files and programs you'll be running. If you have a D:> drive, or other higher level drives, you will usually use them for additional programs or data.

For starters, it's not a good idea to put a lot of programs in your root directory. All that you should put in the root (C:\) are those files that are necessary for booting your PC. Those files include *Command.com* and device drivers (*sys files*), *Config.sys*, and *Autoexec.bat*. Additionally, there may be certain batch files that you use in bootup. However, it will be an unusual root that has more than about a dozen files.

Begin at the Beginning—The Key Directories

The first directory you should create (using MD or MKDIR) is the DOS directory (C:\DOS). The DOS directory contains all of the other files and programs that come with your version of MS-DOS or PC-DOS. There are quite a few of these and you won't need all of them. Read through your DOS manual and learn what each of these files do. If they don't apply to you, get rid of them. Remember, you have a lot of space on your shiny new hard drive now, but it won't be long before you'll be asking why you didn't get a bigger one in the first place. You can extend that time by putting only the files you really want on your drive.

The next directory you should make is the BAT directory (C:\bat). This is where you'll keep any batch files you create (except, of course, Autoexec.bat). These batch files will sort of grow up over time as you learn more about your PC and DOS. They can be tremendously useful in running complex functions and programs. Additionally, you can use batch files to create menus. However, if you are using a commercial menu program, there is a strong probability that it will create its own directory.

The next two directories are optional since they won't apply to all users. This is a matter of personal preference; however, most users will eventually have them. The first is the UTILS (C:\UTILS) directory. UTILS is for all of the little utility programs that you'll collect over the years. Many are public domain or shareware programs (you'll learn about PD and shareware in Chapter 8). Typically these programs are for performing useful little functions such as locating files or browsing text files.

The second directory is HOLD (C:\HOLD). HOLD is what I call a *holding tank*. You use HOLD as a temporary storage place for just about anything you might be doing on your PC. For example, if you are using a word processor, you may want a location to temporarily store documents in process. When you have finished with the document, you may want to move it from the holding tank to a permanent home in a subdirectory under your word processor's directory. You'll find as you use your PC more and more that you have a million and one uses for a holding tank. Some users name their holding tanks TEMP. You can name your tank anything you want, but it is a good idea to have one.

There are very few other generic directories that you'll need to create. Just remember the rules:

1. Only boot and sys files go in the C:\ root.
2. Keep separate directories for DOS and batch files.
3. Build a directory for utilities and one for use as a temporary "holding tank."
4. Create separate directories for each category of software or data. Attach data as subdirectories under the directories containing the programs they address (i.e., documents under word processors, databases under database management programs, etc.).

Other Directories

When you install a new program it will usually create the necessary directories and subdirectories for you automatically. Generally, the installation program will ask you if you want to use the default (the directory name and path that the installation program assigns) or create your own. In 99 times out of 100 you'll be safe accepting the installation program's suggestions. However, if you already have a directory with the same name, you'll want to suggest a change to the program. If you get an error message during an installation process that says *"unable to create directory,"* that means that the directory already exists. Before you automatically allow the installation to proceed, you should ensure that you're not about to overwrite existing files.

During installation, many programs will ask if you want them to modify your Config.sys and Autoexec.bat files. In most cases it's a pretty good idea to allow the modifications. Usually the modifications have to do with the PATH statement and the addition of device drivers to the Config.sys file. The next section discusses the use of the DOS directory structure by applications programs.

Putting Files in the Cabinet

Once the installation program for your application has created the necessary directories and subdirectories for the application, you have two ongoing tasks. First, there may be data files associated with the application. You will need to keep the data subdirectories as free of superfluous files as possible. You can do that by deleting any unwanted data files periodically and by deleting backup files if the application creates them. It is, of course, a good idea to keep backup files as long as you are working on a particular data file. But once you are finished there is little reason to keep a duplicate copy, especially if you perform backups regularly.

Keeping Your Hard Drive Running Efficiently

The second task you have is *defragmenting* the hard disk from time to time. When DOS places a file on your hard disk, in order to make use of as much disk space as possible it might break up the file (fragment it) and place pieces of it in small available spaces on your hard disk. When your hard disk is new and you don't have a lot of files on it, there are no small spaces, so DOS doesn't try to fill gaps. But every time you delete a file, you leave a gap. DOS would like to see that gap filled, so the next time you install an application or create a data file DOS will try to fill the open space.

The problem with that, unfortunately, is that fragmented files or programs don't perform as well as unfragmented programs do. Over time, your computer may begin to feel as if it is performing somewhat sluggishly. Often, when a disk becomes badly fragmented, the holes aren't big enough to be of any use to DOS. So, unfortunately, they just sit empty. That means that, given enough unusable holes, you'll have a fair amount of unusable disk space. The good news is that there are utility programs, called defragmenters (or *defraggers*), that can reorganize the physical placement of files on your hard disk to fill the holes while avoiding fragmenting files. In other words, defragging your hard disk returns it to the condition that it was in before you started deleting and adding files. The benefit is twofold. First, you'll get your old performance back. Second, you'll make more efficient use of disk space.

There is a small caveat regarding defraggers, however. Even though they are, for the most part, pretty safe and reliable, they work by physically moving files around on the hard disk. That means that they go through a series of copies and deletes. Of course, any time you do that, you take the chance of damaging data. Be sure that you have a good backup of your entire hard disk before you attempt to defrag it.

Putting Files in the Cabinet

Keeping the File Cabinet Organized

The first task we discussed, "cleaning up" your hard drive periodically, can be accomplished easily with the help of a class of utility called a *disk manager*. Disk managers allow you to see all of the files and directories on your disk in the *directory tree* format we saw at the start of this chapter. Once you can see all of your files laid out neatly in their proper directories and subdirectories, you will quickly recognize which ones you must keep and which ones you can safely get rid of.

The problem with attempting to clean up unwanted files on a hard disk, especially a large one, is that you can never get the "big picture." Without an overall view of the disk it is easy to miss files of certain types that, if you knew they were there, you would delete. Also, some applications create temporary files and don't have the courtesy to delete them when they are no longer needed. Some of these files can be quite large, taking up a lot of precious disk space.

Disk managers also have a number of facilities that can be of great help in organizing your hard disk. Besides allowing you to view the disk, its directories and files, disk managers allow you to delete files and directories, create directories, copy files, and move files from one directory to another. They are tools for quickly viewing and manipulating the files and directories.

If you have more than one volume (or disk, or partition, if you prefer) here is a trick for keeping the fragmentation on your C:> drive to a minimum. Since it is the addition and deletion of data that tends to fragment a hard disk, consider putting data that is in a constant state of change in special directories on the D:> drive. That way you will fragment the D:> drive more than the C:> drive. When you add new applications to the C:> drive, they will have fewer holes to fill and will tend to install in *contiguous* (adjacent) sectors. This type of installation (contiguous rather than fragmented) tends to preserve the overall performance of your hard drive.

Summarizing, then, if you follow the hints above for creating directories, allow applications to create their own directories, defragment your hard disk from time to time, and use a disk manager to help you move, copy, and delete files, you'll be able to maintain a tight, well-organized hard disk. Such hard disks perform better and give you the overall feeling that your PC is running lean and mean.

What Do You Do If the Library Burns Down?

This may be one of the most important sections of this book. When you have spent months, or even years collecting applications and data on your PC the last thing you want is for a hard disk crash or other system malfunction to destroy everything on your disk. Worse, and more likely, you don't want a user error such as the infamous *DELETE* *.* (delete everything in this directory) to wipe out weeks of work accidentally. In this section we'll discuss backup and recovery techniques.

AXIOM

There are only two kinds of computer users. Those who back up and those who wish they had.

You can take my word for it. You will, some day, fit into one of those two categories. Losing your hard drive is a little like burning down the library. If you aren't backed up, you'll lose everything.

Backing Up

There are two kinds of backup techniques. You can use the DOS backup command, or you can use a third-party backup program such as Fastback. There are advantages to the third-party approach. First, third-party backup programs are usually significantly faster than DOS. In fact, that's their claim to fame. Second, third-party backup programs are not sensitive to the version of DOS being backed up or restored.

Occasionally, you'll try to restore a DOS backup only to get an error that says something to the effect of "wrong DOS version." What the message is trying to tell you is that you backed up under one version of DOS and you're trying to restore under a different one. And, unfortunately, it won't let you. For those two reasons, especially the speed, I prefer third-party backup programs. An added benefit is that, in addition to being faster, third-party programs often use fewer floppy disks. Now, what does backing up mean?

When you copy a file from one disk onto another, as you learned earlier, you are, actually, transferring an image of the file. That is why, in order to ensure a perfect copy, you use the DISKCOPY command. The problem with DISKCOPY, though, is that it transfers an entire disk, sector by sector, to another disk. Obviously you won't be able to use diskcopy to transfer the contents of a 40MB disk to a 360KB floppy. Fortunately, there is another way.

Backup programs use a special copying format that transfers files a bit at a time. So that there will be no confusion when you go to restore backed up data, these programs add special information about the files and the order in which you backed them up in a special section of the file called a *header*. The header information allows you to fill each backup disk completely full. So, if you were in the middle of backing up a file when the target disk (the one you are backing up *onto*) filled up, you just put the next disk in the floppy drive and continue. When you restore, the files are replaced on the hard drive a bit at a time and the header information ensures that you are placing the backup disks in the right order.

Grandfathering: Another Way to Back Up Your Data

Backing up can take a while on large hard drives so many people don't like to do it. How often you back up is dependant on how often you put new data on your hard disk. If you don't add new programs or data every day, there's no reason to back up every day. But if you use your PC for business, and you are updating data daily, you should back up daily. To shorten the process, you can use a technique called an *incremental backup* for most days. If you back up daily, you should use a technique called *grandfathering,* which will be explained shortly.

If you grandfather, the last backup of each week must be a full backup instead of incremental. Incremental backups back up only that information which has changed or is new since the last backup. Full backups back up the entire hard disk. Obviously, incremental backups are faster. Here is how grandfathering, the only correct way to do daily backups, works. Even if you don't do daily backups, you should implement some variation on grandfathering.

First, the reason for grandfathering is that it allows you to keep a sort of history of your hard disk. If you should encounter a virus, for example, you would only restore the virus by restoring from the backup of the day before. You would need to go back several days, weeks, or even months to find a clean backup.

To grandfather, you start by making a complete backup of the hard disk. You first clean off all files that you don't want in the backup and make sure that the disk is free of virus contamination. This backup is called a *baseline.* You take that backup and keep it in a safe place. Then you start doing daily backups. You will need a set of backup disks for each day of the week on which you intend to perform a backup. Each day except the last day of the week can be an incremental backup. The last day must be a full backup because that is the only day you are going to keep. Put the last day's backups away. Start over again with incremental backups the following week.

At the end of the month, you'll have four (usually) sets of full backups. Those will be the ones from the last days of each week in that month. Keep the last one as the monthly backup and put it in a safe place. Start over again at the beginning of the next month. At the end of a year, you'll have a set of twelve monthly backups for the preceding year. Now, continue as before, except that you keep only the preceding twelve months.

At the end of the first month in the new year, you'll no longer need the first month in the preceding year. You will always have the most recent twelve months, the current month's weeklies, and the current week's dailies, plus the original baseline. There is almost no catastrophe that can befall your hard disk from which you won't be able to recover using this technique.

If you ever have to restore data to your hard disk from backups, there are a few rules. First, you must restore using the program that you used to back up. That means that if you used the DOS backup, you must use the DOS restore, usually for the same DOS version. If you used Fastback or some other third-party backup program, you must use its restore program. You can't mix programs. Also, you'll need the restore program, and sometimes with third-party programs, a setup program. It is a good idea to have a special disk that you keep with your backup that contains everything you'll need to restore your lost files.

Remember that in the event of a complete hard disk loss you'll have also lost the restore program. So be sure you create a disaster kit. Backup and restore can be used in other ways, too. For example, suppose that the only thing you use your PC for is your business database. You can write a batch file that backs up only the database everyday when you finish using it. That way if you ever lose your data, you can restore only that file. You can also often restore a single file that you may have inadvertently damaged. You'll then lose only the data entered since your last backup. That's a whole lot better than losing the entire file. It does take a while to locate a single file in a large backup, but it's better than the alternative.

What Do You Do If the Library Burns Down?

Summary

- By setting up your hard drive like a file cabinet with categories and subcategories broken down based on collections of similar information, you can easily retrieve any information you have filed.
- Create categories, called *directories*, that relate to the same categories and subcategories, called *subdirectories*, and so on.
- Never put all of your files into a single root directory.
- There are three basic steps to preparing a hard drive for use. First, if necessary, low-level format the disk. Most manufacturers already do that for you. Second, perform a DOS FDISK to set up partitions. Finally, format the disk so that it can receive data.

- Never perform any alteration of your hard disk without two complete backup copies of your programs and data.

- All that you should put in the root (C:\) are those files that are necessary for booting your PC. Those files include *Command.com* and device drivers (*sys files*), *Config.sys*, and *Autoexec.bat*.

- When you install a new program it will usually create the necessary directories and subdirectories for you automatically.

- Defraggers are utility programs that reorganize the data on your hard disk so that it is as contiguous as possible, thus improving hard disk performance considerably.

- Use a disk manager to help you move, copy, and delete files. It helps you see the "big picture" of all of the files on your hard disk.

- Some day, you will need to restore the data on your hard disk from a backup. Therefore, it is only logical that you need to perform backups regularly.

- There are two kinds of backup techniques. You can use the DOS backup command, or you can use a third-party backup program such as Fastback.

- If you use your PC for business and you are updating data daily, you should back up daily. To shorten the process, you can use a technique called an *incremental backup*. If you back up daily, you should use a technique called *grandfathering*.

PRACTICE WHAT YOU'VE LEARNED

1. What is a directory tree?

2. Why should you never place all of your files in a single directory?

3. What does the term "rebuilding a hard drive" mean?

4. What are the steps in preparing a hard drive for use (if it hasn't already been prepared when you receive it)?

5. What should you put in your PC's root directory?

6. What is a "defragger"?

7. What is the single most important task you should perform on your hard disk?

8. What is a "grandfather backup"?

ANSWERS

1. A directory tree is an illustration of the relationships of the various directories and subdirectories on a disk to each other.

2. First, you are allowed only a certain number of directory entries in a single directory. Second, you will find it very difficult to manage your program and data files if they are all in one huge directory.

3. It means formatting the drive and then restoring the backups of all files that were on the disk.

4. First, low-level format (only if the manufacturer of the drive recommends it). Second, use FDISK to produce DOS partitions (or volumes). Finally, format the disk using the DOS Format command with the /s (transfer the system files) option.

5. All that you should put in the root (C:\) are those files that are necessary for booting your PC. Those files include Command.com, device drivers (sys files), Config.sys, and Autoexec.bat.

6. A defragger (defragmenter) is a software program for reorganizing your hard disk so that there are no fragmented files, all files occupy contiguous sectors, and your hard disk runs more smoothly and quickly.

7. Backing up

8. Grandfathering is a technique whereby you back up daily keeping the weekly backups for a month, and the monthly backups for a year. All grandfather backup plans should start with a single "baseline" backup that is kept permanently in a safe place.

Printing

Connecting printers to your PC can be one of the most frustrating of computer activities. Printers come in a bewildering variety of types, styles, shapes, and sizes. The methods of connecting them can be equally bewildering. In this chapter I'll introduce you to the basic types of printers, give you a bit of detail on the finer points of choosing and connecting a printer, and end up by introducing you to the mysteries of printer control codes. In this chapter you will learn about:

▲ **Dot matrix and daisy wheel printers**
▲ **Laser printers**
▲ **PostScript printing**
▲ **Printer control codes**

A Printer by Any Other Name

There is such a wide variety of types of printers that it is probably a good idea to try to categorize them in some way. Unfortunately, printers, unlike many other types of peripheral devices, are not quite so easy to describe. One would think that simply saying that the device prints on a page would be enough. But that is not the case. There are line printers, page printers, ink jet printers, laser printers, dot matrix printers, daisy wheel printers, and plotters—the printers that aren't printers—just to name a few.

Prices range from around $100 to tens of thousands of dollars. There are printers that are several printers in one. There are discussions of printer "engines" and the relative merits of 9- and 24-pin printers in the trade magazines. So many buzzwords—so little time to figure them all out. If you go to your favorite computer store and ask for a "printer," it's anyone's guess what you'll walk out with. Well, relax. You're about to become a printer maven. By the time you're through with this chapter, your confusion will be over and you'll walk confidently up to that computer salesperson and walk out with exactly what you want. We'll start by defining a few basic printer concepts.

Basics

You can begin your quest for a printer by deciding exactly what you want to do with it. If you are printing very few sophisticated documents, no graphics, and price is an important issue, you might benefit from the class of printer called the *dot matrix printer*. These simple, low-cost printers can cover a wide range of basic needs. But, as you will soon see, they have some limitations. Also, there are some dot matrix printers that are a bit more expensive and can do a few more tricks than the bare bones models.

Another type of printer, appropriate for typing text only, is the daisy wheel or *letter quality* printer. These are less common these days than they used to be, due largely to the improvements in *near letter quality* dot matrix printers. The daisy wheel printers are appropriate for use as text only printers for letters and reports in venues such as law offices. There are, however, some drawbacks to the daisy wheel, as you will soon see.

The third type of printer in common use is the *laser printer*. Laser printers are capable of printing anything your computer can produce that's printable. They are used for graphics and text. They are sophisticated and, generally, at the top of the printer price range. Finally, there is the laser's little sister, the ink jet printer. Ink jets are almost as high quality as laser printers and cost somewhat less.

If you need to produce sophisticated technical drawings, you might include plotters in your discussion of printers. Plotters are devices that work very much like printers with the exception that they generally use one or more small pens to draw and write on the page. They can take several sizes of paper and are used, generally, in engineering, technical, and drafting applications. We won't spend time with plotters here since they are a rather specialized breed.

Theory

Before we continue, it would be useful to discuss a little bit of printer theory. How, exactly, does a printer work? Without getting too deeply involved in the engineering, printers work by converting electrical signals from your PC into physical motion of either a print head, laser beam, or jet of ink. In order to ensure that, no matter what printer and PC you connect together, the printer can print what the PC tells it to, printers used standardized signals called *character sets*. These character sets are always produced the same way by the PC and the applications running on it so that the printer will have no difficulty understanding what is expected of it.

There are many different character sets. Usually, there are two or three standard sets that virtually all printers and PCs are set up to understand, "right out of the box." Then, if you want additional character sets, you may need to have some special software that "teaches" your printer the new characters. There are several ways to do this, depending on the printer. Often these character sets are called *fonts*. The basic character sets available on virtually all printers are the ASCII characters (128 printable characters including letters, numbers, and punctuation) and the IBM extended characters (same as the ASCII set plus several graphics characters for drawing lines, boxes, and special symbols). Additional fonts are available for the more sophisticated printers, such as laser printers and ink jets.

All printers, regardless of type, basically fall into two categories: mechanical and electronic. The mechanical printers (dot matrix, high-speed line printers, and daisy wheel printers) are considered *line printers*. That means that they print a line at a time. With the exception of high-speed line printers (large, expensive, industrial-strength printers that print using a high-speed band of characters that covers the entire width of the page on which it is printing), these mechanical printers tend to be slower and noisier than the electronic printers.

Electronic printers, such as the lasers and ink jets, are considered to be *page printers,* meaning that they print a page at a time. As a group they are quieter, faster, more versatile, and more expensive than the line printers. There is one application, however, where you will have to use a mechanical printer in preference to an electronic printer. If you are going to print wide reports, such as inventories or financial spreadsheets, you may need to use 14"-wide computer paper. Only the mechanical printers come in a wide-carriage style to accommodate that paper.

While we're on the subject of paper, that is another distinction between printer types. Mechanical printers can often take two styles of paper. If the printer has a *tractor* (the spiny wheels on either side of the print roller), it can use *continuous feed* computer paper. That's the paper with the little holes along each side of the sheet. This paper comes in long strips with the individual sheets perforated so you can tear them off the long continuous sheet. This is good paper for continuous feed applications such as long reports or form letters. You just set the paper feed and start printing.

Some mechanical printers also have the ability to take single sheets of paper, one at a time or in quantity, using a *cut sheet feeder.* The cut sheet feeder lets you use a stack of single sheets. Cut sheet feeders can be expensive and often are mechanical monsters that don't work smoothly. Unless you spend a fair amount for a mechanical printer, the single sheet capabilities are very limited. Almost all of these printers are more at home with the continuous feed mechanism.

Virtually all electronic printers use single sheets. They have paper trays that can handle a variety of paper sizes, except for really large sheets. Some even have the ability to manage envelopes. In general, the paper handling capacity of these printers is similar to the abilities of the smaller copier machines. You'll understand why a little later on. Now, on to the specifics of the simplest of printers, the mechanical breed.

Simple Pleasures—Printing the Easy Way

In general, the simplest type of printer is the dot matrix. Dot matrix printers work by forming characters using a combination of dots. The dots are produced by a *print head* that contains tiny pins (often 28/100ths of a millimeter in diameter). Depending on the character to be produced, a pattern of these pins strikes the paper through a ribbon, similar to a typewriter ribbon, to produce the character on the page.

There are 7-, 9-, 18- and 24-pin dot matrix printers, the number of pins relating to the print head. The more pins in the print head, the closer together the dots can be placed (because there can be more dots in the character) and the smoother the character appears. The 24-pin dot matrix printers are often called *near letter quality* (NLQ) printers because they produce characters that come very close to the quality produced by daisy wheel (or *letter quality*) printers (Figure 5.1).

Although there are both *serial* and *parallel* dot matrix printers, most are parallel. And that, the type of connection, brings us to our next important subject. Printers can be either serial or parallel connection. Most simple printers are parallel. That means that the entire character is transferred to the printer at one time. These printers connect to the *printer ports* on your PC and use LPT1 through LPT4 as their connection. When you print to a parallel printer, you must tell your application to which port you have the printer connected.

▼ *Figure 5.1. A High-end Dot Matrix Printer*

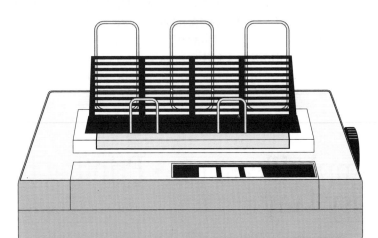

Any Port in a Storm

Most PCs contain only a single printer port (LPT1) even though
DOS can support more. If you want to add more parallel printers
to your PC you'll need to buy an add-in board with more printer
ports on it. Parallel printers use a connection cable that has a special
connector called a *centronics* connector on the printer end and a 25-
pin connector similar to a serial connector (but opposite in gender)
on the PC side.

   Serial printers, on the other hand, use a regular serial cable
(sometimes called a modem cable) and connect to one of the
communications ports (COMM1–COMM4) on your PC. The PC
transfers characters to the serial printer a bit at a time. Obviously,
character transfer speed is slower on serial printers than it is on
parallel printers. There is another benefit to parallel printers over
serial printers. The parallel printers are infinitely easier to configure (set up). You'll usually be up and printing on a parallel printer
within moments of opening the box. I've taken days to properly set
up a serial printer.

Seeing Dots

In terms of print speed, dot matrix printers provide reasonable speed, though nowhere near the speed you get with a page printer. Also, some of the less expensive printers use a technique of printing each line twice, the second time with a slight offset, to get the effect of near letter quality without the expense of a 24-pin print head. This technique can work fairly well, considering the cost, but slows the printer down considerably. You'll usually get about a page per minute or a little more out of a dot matrix printer. Electronic printers can produce four to eight pages per minute.

Another shortcoming of dot matrix printers is that they have little or no ability to produce either graphics or sophisticated fonts. These printers are good, general-purpose workhorses, low in price and sophistication while being easy to use and set up. Along with the dot matrix printer in the mechanical classification is the daisy wheel or letter quality printer. These printers are not as popular as they used to be for a variety of reasons. First, the improvements in dot matrix technology have all but eliminated the daisy wheel's market niche. Second, daisy wheels are noisy, slow, and expensive as compared with dot matrix NLQ printers.

However, sometimes you'll see one of these printers available and, if the price is good enough, you might be tempted if all you print is text. Daisy wheels are very similar in construction and capability to typewriters. If you want a different typestyle or font, you need to change the daisy wheel. The daisy wheel print head is so called because the individual characters are on rays that radiate out from the center of the wheel like the petals of a daisy. Remember that daisy wheels can do no graphics at all. For the price, you'll usually be better off with a low-end laser printer if you need high-quality text.

The benefits to these simple printers are low cost and ease of use. The drawbacks are slow speed, noise, and limited capabilities. In my office, I use a laser printer for virtually all daily work and a dot matrix printer for mailing labels for mass mailings. For home computer use, you may do very well with a good NLQ dot matrix printer. If you need more horsepower, however, you may need the laser printer or ink jet, our next topics of discussion.

The Ultimate in Sophistication— The Laser Printer

Throughout this chapter we've been nibbling around the edges of laser printers and ink jets. Now, we'll get into some detail. First, a bit of explanation for how these devices work. The laser printer is very much like a typical small copier. In fact, the main part of the printer, called the *engine*, is generally the same as found in such popular copiers as Canon. The main difference is that, instead of copying the image of an original drawing or typescript onto another sheet, the laser printer transfers images from your PC. Beyond that difference, there are, for the most part, only similarities.

Laser printers, because of their sophistication, have far more capability and, unfortunately, far more complexity than dot matrix printers. For example, most laser printers can connect either to the serial or parallel port. They are, most often, connected to the serial port, which increases hookup complexity. The laser printer, like a copier, requires periodic changes of toner and drum. The dot matrix printer just needs a new ribbon from time to time. A typical laser printer can produce around 3,000 pages from a single dose of toner (Figure 5.2).

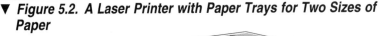

▼ *Figure 5.2. A Laser Printer with Paper Trays for Two Sizes of Paper*

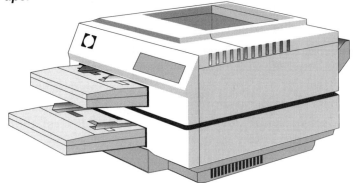

Standards

There are two laser printer standards. These standards refer to the way in which the printer produces its output, the printed page. The first standard is the HP (based upon the Hewlett-Packard LaserJet). This is a font-based standard. That means that different fonts (character sets) must be installed on the printer in order to use them. This installation process is accomplished by installing *font cartridges* in the laser printer itself, or by using *soft fonts*, which you download into the laser printer from your PC. In any event, the number of fonts that you can install at one time depends on the amount of memory installed in your laser printer. In order to get any flexibility at all from your laser printer, you'll need at least 1MB of memory in it.

The other type of laser printer is the PostScript laser printer. We'll look into PostScript shortly; however, the main difference between PostScript and HP-type laser printers is that PostScript doesn't require preloading of fonts with cartridges or soft fonts.

Although the HP LaserJet, the original popular laser printer, cost around $3,000 when it was introduced in 1985, today's LaserJets and LaserJet clones cost considerably less. They are also much smaller, taking the marketing lead of the "personal copier." There is almost nothing in the way of printing that you can't do with laser printers. They provide a good medium resolution of 300dpi (dots per inch); publication quality masters for printing are often around 1,000dpi, and this resolution is now available on high-quality laser printers. There are even color laser printers, although they are expensive and difficult to use.

If you are doing any type of graphics or desktop publishing requiring pictures or different typestyles, you probably want a laser printer. Almost all programs using printers provide the capability of printing on a laser printer. Unless you purchase a PostScript printer, in most cases you'll set up your application to print to one of the HP LaserJet series printers, regardless of the manufacturer of your laser printer. The operator's manual that comes with your printer will tell you which one.

What Else Do You Need?

You'll also need a collection of fonts for your printer. When you buy the printer, you'll get a limited number of common fonts. However, you will soon find that you'll want much more flexibility. Generally, the best buy for your money is the soft font collections available from many sources. Be sure that the soft fonts you purchase are compatible with your laser printer. If you have a PostScript printer, you won't want soft fonts.

Laser printers are fun. Using some reasonably inexpensive drawing or desktop publishing software, you can produce everything from cartoons to newsletters and brochures. If you plan on doing that kind of work with your laser printer, you'll want to look into collections of *clip art*. Clip art is bits and pieces of cartoons, logos, drawings, and ornamentation that you can use in your documents.

The term clip art comes from the days when newspapers and other publishing concerns would buy collections of these drawings, clip them out, and paste them into their own page layouts. By so doing they avoided hiring artists to draw the many small illustrations they used in their publications. By using computer clip art and a laser printer with your desktop publishing software you can do the same thing. Clip art collections range in size from a few dozen images to hundreds (even thousands on very large professional collections) and in cost from free to over $1,000. The complexity ranges from simple line art to sophisticated art and photography.

Typical laser printer speeds range from about four pages per minute for text only to over eight. These speeds are for text using a single simple font only. When you see a specification for print speed, that is what you are seeing. Remember that one of the reasons you are purchasing a laser printer is to print graphics. Depending on the printer, there are a couple of ways that graphics are handled. First, if you have enough memory in the printer, the entire graphic gets stored and then, after the first print, multiple copies come fairly fast. However, if you usually don't print lots of copies of a single page, that may be of limited use.

If you don't have enough memory, the graphic, which is usually much larger than text-only pages, cannot be completely loaded into the printer. A portion is loaded and printed, and then the rest is loaded and printed. What all of this boils down to is, when you go to buy a laser printer, test it thoroughly before you buy. Ask the salesperson to print out 15 to 20 pages of pure text in a simple font. Time the test and decide if you can live with the results. Then do the same test with a more complex font. Finally, ask the salesperson to print some complex graphics for you. You'll find that the graphics pages print much more slowly, even as much as a few minutes per page, than the text pages. This is typical of all laser printers.

At today's lower prices, laser printers can be a very good choice as a general-purpose printer. In many cases, you'll find that the cost of a laser printer will be more than justified by its versatility and the additional speed for many printing tasks. For virtually all general-purpose printing, such as letters and reports, the laser printer provides an extremely professional product at a reasonable cost.

The only real difficulty you may experience is setting up the printer. In that regard, I recommend that you follow the manufacturer's instructions to the letter. Today's laser printers have lots of options, which can be confusing. The best bet is to set up your printer as simply as possible to get it working. Print a few pages and experiment with fonts. Then, when you've begun to become familiar with the printer, start trying out some of the "bells and whistles" available on most lasers.

As we discussed earlier, there is an alternative to the laser printer called the ink jet. Ink jet printers have many of the same capabilities as laser jets. They cost a bit less and generally do not have the stamina to be used in high-volume printing applications. They can do many graphics applications almost as beautifully as lasers; however, they sometimes lack the fineness of line and gray scale differentiation of the more expensive laser jets. One benefit of ink jets is their ability to manage color printing less expensively than color lasers. Ink jet technology is maturing, and in the near future we should see ink jet printers with full laser printer quality at prices significantly lower than lasers.

The Ultimate in Sophistication— The Laser Printer

Paper and Toner

There is one last word on laser printers. I told you earlier that these printers require toner cartridges in much the same way as typical copiers do. These cartridges can be a bit pricey, depending on the type of printer you have. There are services that rebuild and refill used toner cartridges for much less that the cost of a new cartridge. Often these companies can refill a toner cartridge ten or more times, resulting in significant savings over buying new ones. However, there is a caveat.

Some companies use the "drill and fill" technique. This means pretty much what it says. They drill a hole in the toner cartridge, fill it with toner, fill the hole, and send it back to you. You will not get either very good or predictable results from this approach to toner cartridge refurbishment. In order for the job to be done right, the refurbisher must disassemble the cartridge, clean it completely, repair or replace worn parts, and then refill it. If you are sending your toner cartridges to a refiller, be sure they are doing the whole job.

TIP

Never send your laser printer toner cartridge to a refill service that does only a "drill and fill." Cartridges must be disassembled and cleaned before refilling for consistent results.

Along with toner, the other expendable associated with laser printers is paper. Any paper that is acceptable to a plain paper copier is acceptable to a laser printer. Heavy paper, such as letterhead, can sometimes cause the printer to jam. If you are going to print on letterhead, be sure to follow the laser printer manufacturer's advice with regard to paper weights.

Also on the subject of paper, you'll get fewer pages per toner cartridge if you are printing a lot of dense graphics or are printing a lot on porous paper (such as some of the textured letterhead papers). You can use regular photocopier or laser printer bond paper (also called xerographic paper) and get the best balance of utility and toner cartridge efficiency. High gloss papers will require you to clean your printer's drum or corona wire more frequently.

Some printers also require that you replace the drum periodically. Some use toner cartridges that include the drum. The drum and the corona wire are the major elements that allow an image to be transferred to a sheet of paper. They must be kept clean and the drum must be kept out of bright sunlight. If you are beginning to see smudges or gaps on the printed page, you may need to clean your printer's corona wire or drum. Follow the printer manufacturer's instructions very carefully for doing this since these two elements are extremely delicate.

PS: What Is It?

The last section described the HP approach to laser printers and the way this class of printer uses fonts. Each font in the HP-type laser printer is set up as a collection of characters in a particular type style. You load those character sets into the laser printer and the printer, under control of your PC and the application running on it, prints the characters. Graphics, on the other hand, are created as *bit maps*. Bit maps are sets of instructions to the laser printer that define the nature of every dot on the printed page. Remember that a laser printer simply prints many thousands of dots on the page with varying degrees of light or dark. The degree of light or dark is called the *gray scale*. If you look at a laser printed page with a magnifying glass you can see the dots. Most standard laser printers print 300dpi (dots per inch).

The PostScript laser printer works a bit differently. Instead of defining graphics and characters as individual objects to be downloaded to the memory of the printer for printing, PostScript printers use the PostScript *page definition language* to define all of the characters and graphics on the page at once. There are no fonts in the sense of the HP printers. Instead, PostScript defines each character in a large program prior to printing. The program is sent to the printer, which is intelligent. Then the printer interprets the PostScript program and produces the dots that result in the printed page.

PostScript was created by Adobe Corporation. The main difference between PostScript and HP-style printers is that PostScript printers, such as the Apple Laser Writer, have a small computer inside them that actually interprets the PostScript instructions to produce a page. PostScript laser printers produce much better line definition, gray scale interpretation, and smoothness of curves than other types of laser printers. They are, as you might guess, somewhat more expensive than the "other guys." They are, however, also somewhat easier to use since they require no external font cartridges or soft fonts.

There are, of course, some limitations on the number and style of fonts available. The standard PostScript printer has either 35 or 45 fonts, depending on which level of the PostScript standard the printer supports. Font capability comes included with your PostScript printer when you buy it. Also, much of the memory limitation, which can trouble HP-type printers, is not a problem with PostScript. Since PostScript doesn't store fonts (it creates them on the fly as it needs them) it doesn't need massive storage to hold font sets. The other side of that, however, is that there must be sufficient memory to hold the page definition program generated when your application prints a PostScript page.

There is another problem with PostScript. Not all applications support PostScript printers. If your application does not support PostScript, you will not be able to print except under two conditions. First, there are some utilities, many of them free, that convert standard ASCII text into PostScript files. The second way to print is available if your PostScript printer has a non-PostScript mode. For example, the Apple Laser Writers include a mode of operation that emulates a Diablo dot matrix printer. While you won't be able to print graphics or fonts with either of these "work-arounds," you will be able to print simple text. There is yet another solution emerging, however.

There are already a few companies producing laser printers that conform to either the HP standard or the Adobe PostScript standard. Additionally, there are several companies that have produced PostScript cartridges that make your HP-type printer PostScript compatible. The end result of both of these approaches is that you can have your cake and eat it, too. You can print PostScript when you have applications that support it, and use the simpler HP standard if your application won't handle PostScript.

In most cases where an add-on produces the PostScript (such as the cartridges), you'll find that the additional quality, which helps justify PostScript's higher cost, is not quite up to that of a "real" PostScript printer. But most of the dual-purpose printers produce excellent quality in either mode of operation.

There is one additional accessory that you might want to look into if you are using your laser printer for professional graphics work. We saw earlier that typical laser printers have a resolution of 300dpi, and that professional quality laser printers could have a resolution of up to 1,000dpi. Of course, the 1,000dpi machines are very expensive, but there is an alternative.

Several companies produce add-in boards for many popular laser printers that increase resolution to 400 x 600dpi, or even 1,000dpi. These accelerators do not increase the cost of the printer to that of the high-powered machines. They do, however, produce excellent results. The same companies that produce these add-in cards also produce other add-ins that accelerate print speed significantly.

Keeping Your Printer Under Control

Printers need help to know what they should print. Earlier in this chapter we looked at how printers, especially mechanical ones, convert the electrical impulses in your PC to characters on a sheet of paper. But there is a bit more to the story. In order for printers to know what character set they are supposed to print, or add special characteristics to a typeface, such as adding boldface, they must have a special character or set of characters. These characters are called *control characters*. Control characters don't show up on the printed page. They simply tell your printer what to do.

In most word processing programs, you never see the control codes. They are embedded in special files called *printer drivers*. Because there are many different kinds of printers, built by many different manufacturers, there is no universal set of control codes that works for every printer. However, that's not really as confusing as it sounds. Most printers use at least some of the same codes. Most of the differences lie in the special printing features unique to a particular model of printer. But because there are differences, we need individual printer drivers for our applications that use printers.

Virtually all printers except PostScript printers need these control codes. PostScript printers don't because they use the PostScript page definition language to set them up. If your application supports PostScript printing, the functions handled by control codes are managed for you. But if you use just about any other printer, you'll find that all but the simplest applications require printer drivers.

Some applications allow you to embed special control codes within printing commands. This can be a little complicated. Until you become completely familiar with your printer, the applications, and the required codes, your best bet is to keep your printing as simple as possible. When you are ready, if your application allows it, you'll find that control codes are generally just combinations of characters preceded by a special *control character*. The control character is little more than a special character that would not be likely to occur in a normal line of text. An example might be a double percent sign (%%), or a combination of the control key with some other key. This control character signals the printer that the next character or characters are not to be printed; rather, they are instructions to the printer.

Driving Your Printer

You'll have very little to do with control codes and they vary significantly from printer to printer, even though the functions they perform may be remarkably similar. The important thing to remember about control codes is that they are the reason for printer driver files. You must match the correct printer driver to the printer you plan to use.

There usually are generic printer driver files in many simple programs. They tend to cover a broad range of printers instead of being unique to an individual printer. For example, you might find that your program has a generic printer driver, one for HP laser printers, and a few for the more exotic printers. In that case, you'll learn that many of the functions of which your printer is capable are not available. This is because the drivers have concentrated on those control codes that cover the most generally used and commonly included features of a wide variety of popular printers.

A good trick to try if you can't find a printer driver for your particular printer is to try to use the generic driver. It will often work. Another thing to do is check your application's user manual for lists of printers that hold certain control codes in common. See if your printer uses a driver from another, included printer. Finally, you can check the operator's manual for your printer. Often the manufacturer will list other printers similar enough to have compatible printer drivers.

If all else fails, call the developer of your application and ask what driver to use for your printer. Often developers don't have drivers for every printer when they introduce their product, but they do have a continuing program of new driver development. They may have developed a driver for your printer since you got your software. Usually, developers will provide the driver at no additional cost.

Control codes don't, generally, require your attention. However, they are implicit in printer drivers and if your printer won't work properly with a particular application, they are the first thing you should suspect. Check the printer driver to be sure that you installed the correct one when you installed your application. And, in the case of printer trouble, here's a hint.

TIP

Don't fuss with a recalcitrant printer. If your printer generally works fine until you install a new application, and you have done everything the application's operator manual tells you to do without success, call the developer of your software and get help. You can grow old and gray fighting a printer problem and the developer probably has an immediate answer.

Summary

- Begin your quest for a printer by deciding exactly what you want to do with it. Use determines what type of printer you should buy. Price helps to determine which one you will end up with.

- There are three basic types of printers: dot matrix, daisy wheel, and lasers. In addition, as subsets of the basic types, there are ink jets (similar in function to lasers) and high-speed page printers. For most users dot matrix, laser, or ink jet printers cover the ballpark.

- Printers work by converting electrical signals from your PC into physical motion of either a print head, laser beam, or jet of ink.

- Printers used standardized signals called *character sets* always produced the same way by the PC and the applications running on it so that the printer will have no difficulty understanding what is expected of it.

- Mechanical printers can use either cut sheets of paper or, if they have tractors, continuous sheets. Electronic printers, such as lasers, almost always use cut sheets only.

- There are 7-, 9-, 18- and 24-pin dot matrix printers. The more pins in the print head, the closer together the dots can be placed and the smoother the character appears.

- Parallel printers connect to the *printer ports* on your PC and use LPT1 through LPT4 as their connection.

- Serial printers connect to the *COMM ports*, COMM1 through COMM4.

- Parallel printers are faster and easier to set up than serial printers.

- For all types of printing, graphics and text, you'll need a laser or ink jet printer. Either one produces just about anything your PC tells it to. They are, however, somewhat more complex and expensive than dot matrix printers.

- There are two general standards for lasers: HP and PostScript. HP (the standard used by Hewlett-Packard LaserJets) is a bit-mapped standard that requires additional fonts for different character sets. PostScript is a page definition language that composes documents a page at a time and creates its own fonts as it goes.

- When you see a manufacturer's print speed specification on a laser printer, it refers to the number of pages per minute for simple text only.

- Laser printers require toner cartridges, just like photocopiers.

PRACTICE WHAT YOU'VE LEARNED

1. Name three basic types of printer.

2. What is the difference between tractor feed and sheet feed?

3. What is a dot matrix print head?

4. What size print heads are available for dot matrix printers?

5. Describe the cable used to connect a parallel printer to your PC.

6. What are the benefits and drawbacks to dot matrix printers?

7. What are the two general types of laser printers?

8. Name an inexpensive alternative to the laser printer.

9. What precaution should you take if you are refilling laser printer toner cartridges?

10. What is PostScript? How does it differ from HP-style printing?

ANSWERS

1. Dot Matrix, Letter Quality, and Laser printers

2. Tractor feed uses tractor wheels to feed continuous sheet paper through the printer. Sheet feed cannot handle continuous feed paper. It must use single or cut sheets.

3. The print head for a dot matrix printer is a block containing up to 24 tiny pins that strike the paper through a ribbon, much like a typewriter ribbon, to create a character on the page.

4. There are print heads with 7, 9, 18 or 24 pins available for dot matrix printers.

5. It will have a centronics connector on the printer end and a 25-pin connector, similar to an RS232 connector but of opposite gender, on the PC end.

6. The benefits to dot matrix printers are low cost and ease of use. The drawbacks are slow speed, noise, and limited capabilities.

7. The two types are HP (and workalikes) and PostScript.

8. The ink jet printer

9. Be sure that the refiller completely rebuilds the cartridge. Avoid "drill and fill" operations that simply replace the toner.

10. PostScript is a page definition language. It creates all fonts and graphics as a program which is interpreted by the printer using its on-board computer. HP-type printers require that you send complete fonts to the printer for storage and use. PostScript printers generally give better definition and character resolution.

Can We Talk?: Using Your PC to Telecommunicate

Now that you have your new PC up and running complete with printer, it's time to explore some of the uses to which you can put it. One of the most useful capabilities of PCs is their ability to communicate with other computers. However, computer-to-computer communications often requires a bit of legerdemain. And that is what this chapter is all about. In this chapter you will learn about:

▲ **How PCs communicate**

▲ **Modems and how to use them**

▲ **Communications software**

▲ **Modem command strings**

▲ **Connecting to computer bulletin boards**

Hey, PC—The Phone's for You!

Earlier in this book, I introduced you to the ports on your PC. In the last chapter you learned about the printer ports (LPT1–LPT4). In this chapter our emphasis is on the serial ports (COMM1–COMM4). These are the ports that are used to connect your PC to the outside world by way of modems. Modems are devices that convert the electrical signals in your PC into audio tones that can travel over telephone lines. They also convert the tones back to signals that your PC can understand. We'll discuss that process in detail in the next section.

How Do PCs Communicate?

Computers can communicate using modems and telephone lines as easily as if they were sitting side by side connected to each other directly. That is, if you have the modems and the computers set up properly. That can become a bit difficult at times. How does the process work? First, you need some special software in the computers called communications, or *terminal* software. Terminal software interprets your input to your PC and converts it to signals that can be sent to a COMM port. It then guides the signals to the proper COMM port for transmission.

The COMM or serial port has either 25 or 9 pins in its connector. For most communications all that are required are the 9 pins. The 9-pin connector is a subset of the 25-pin connector. It simply ignores the pins that are not usually used. This connector is sometimes called an *interface* or *communications interface*. The interface conforms to a standard called *RS-232C*; for that reason it is also occasionally referred to as an RS-232 interface. The RS-232C standard dictates the nature of the electrical signals appearing on each of the 9 or 25 pins in the connector.

The modem (Figure 6.1) connects to the COMM port by means of a 9- or 25-wire cable. When the signals get to the modem, they are converted to a package of tones of special frequencies. If you listen to these tones, they sound like so much static or noise. But each tone carries special information that the modem on the other end of a

▼ *Figure 6.1. A Modem*

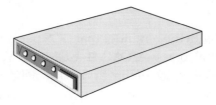

telephone line can interpret and convert back to the individual signals for the 9 or 25 pins in the COMM port on the distant computer. The tones are sent out of the sending modem on regular telephone lines. In fact, you usually use your terminal program to dial a telephone number for the distant computer in exactly the same way that you would use your telephone to dial your mother-in-law.

When the modem on the other end hears a ring (just like a telephone hearing a ring signal) it answers the phone as if it were a telephone set. The answering modem (called the *distant end*) notifies the terminal program on the distant computer that a call is coming in to it. The terminal program then begins to receive data from the sending PC. All computers using modems and terminal programs operate just about the same way. This method of communications has a fancy name to describe it: *asynchronous communications*. Most PC users just call it "modeming."

And Now, the Details

There are a few issues to consider when you connect a modem to a COMM port. For example, you may or may not have a COMM port in your PC. You may decide to use an *internal modem* (more about that when we discuss modems). You may, believe it or not, have more than one modem or COMM port on your PC. For that reason, it's best if we take a small side trip in our discussion of modeming to understand what goes on in and around the COMM ports. If you are going to have trouble connecting to the outside world, this is one of the places, so you need to be prepared to handle it.

COMM Ports Revisited—What Are IRQs and I/Os?

Let's start out with the reminder that DOS permits your PC to have up to four serial ports—COMM1–COMM4. Your terminal program must know which of these ports it will be using to talk to the modem. You determine that when you set up the terminal software. However, DOS also needs to know the differences between the COMM ports so it can communicate with the terminal program (remember that DOS is the connection between the PC's internals and the application program).

Furthermore, if you happen to be using more than one of the COMM ports (for example, COMM1 for a modem and COMM2 for a printer) the PC needs a way to allow each port to do its job in turn without conflicting with the other. There are two methods the PC uses to accomplish these two tasks. Let's take the "which port am I using?" task first.

Every device in your PC that communicates between the PC's operating system and the outside world uses the PC's Input/Output (I/O) system. That includes the keyboard, display, printers, modems, or anything else that turns the PC's internal signals into something viewed or used outside. Just like the houses along a street, these devices need addresses so the PC will know where they are. These addresses are called *I/O addresses*. Each device or port has a unique I/O address. That way, when an application needs to send a signal to the COMM1 port, it tells the PC (through DOS) "I need to talk to the COMM1 port." DOS then says, "the COMM1 port is located at I/O address. . .(depending upon the address)." The application then can route its signal to the right port.

In reality, most programs that need to access an I/O address already know what the address is and send their request to access the address directly through DOS. However, we can't afford to have several signals attempting to access the same or different addresses at the same time. To allow this would cause such confusion that the PC could not process information and would simply go on strike. In order to prevent I/O anarchy, PCs have a system of *interrupt requests*, also called *IRQs*. Every I/O device (device with an I/O address) also has a unique IRQ. No two devices can have the same IRQ or attempts to access either device will lead to very unpredictable results.

When an application needs to access a particular address, it issues an interrupt request unique to that address. The CPU then says, "OK, go ahead. . .it's your turn." If there are two addresses responding to the same IRQ, the PC will become confused.

These two concepts, I/O addresses and IRQs, are very important because you must make sure that you do not have two devices attempting to share the same address or IRQ. Since many devices allow you to change their IRQ or I/O address, you must watch this carefully. As you will soon see when we discuss internal modems, this can cause you some real headaches if you are not careful.

What Is a Modem?

We've pretty well had an introduction to modems and what they do. However, there is much more to the issue of modems than might at first be obvious. Basically, there are two types of asynchronous communications modems. There are internal modems, actually add-in cards for your PC with a modem on it, and external modems, boxes that plug into the COMM port on your PC. The modem we discussed above was an external modem. It connected to the COMM port of the PC using a 9- or 25-pin cable. Then, the telephone line plugs into the modem.

The internal modems don't need the 9- or 25-pin connector since they actually plug onto the mother board inside your PC. They have a connector on them so that you can plug the phone line directly into them. Now we come to the problem with internal modems. There is a real potential for address and/or IRQ conflicts. If your PC has a COMM1 port, what will your internal modem use? If it is also set for COMM1 (you set the COMM port in an internal modem with small switches on the printed circuit board) you will have these conflicts.

TIP

The symptom of IRQ or address conflicts is random operation, inability to access the modem consistently, your PC "locking up" or "freezing" (a situation where you can't get any response to keystrokes and you have to reboot the PC), or other unpredictable, inconsistent, and unexplained operation.

There are two solutions to this problem with internal modems. Both solutions assume that you already have a COMM1 port that came installed in your PC. If you did not receive a COMM1 port (a situation that happens occasionally with very low-cost clones— you have to buy the COMM port as a separate add-in board) you won't have any problems. Simply set up the internal modem for COMM1 and it will work just fine.

The first solution is to disable the PC's COMM1 port. You do this, depending on your PC, by changing the switch settings on the mother board, or, if the PC has an add-in COMM board, on the add-in board. Read the PC's instruction manual very carefully to see how to do this, or ask your dealer to do it for you. Once you disable the COMM1 port, you can set the internal modem to COMM1 and it will work correctly. However, you will no longer have an additional COMM port. If you need the other port for a printer or other serial device, you'll probably want to try the second method.

This method is somewhat less successful. However, just in case you need it, here it is. Leave the PC's COMM1 port as it is and set the internal modem to COMM2. However, when you set up your terminal software, you'll need to remember that the modem is on COMM2. There is a test that you can perform to ensure that your modem and terminal program are on the same wavelength. Set up your terminal program to communicate with the modem and then type AT. If the program responds with OK, the terminal program is communicating with the modem correctly. If it does not, you need to check to make sure that both the modem and the terminal program are set for the same COMM port. There could, however, be other problems, which we'll look at now.

Speeds

Besides making certain that the terminal program and the modem are on the same port, there are two other issues that you must address. One, parity, we'll take up in the next section. The other, modem speed, is appropriate for discussion now. Modems operate at many different speeds. Modem speeds are measured in *bits per second*, or *bps*, the number of bits that pass through the COMM port in a second. The typical modem speeds expressed in bits per second, sometimes called *data rates*, available on most terminal programs are: 300, 1200, 2400, 4800, 9600, and 19200.

The problem is that not all modems support all of these speeds. Most modems are either 1200 bps, 2400 bps, or 9600 bps modems. The 1200 bps modems support 300 bps as well, even though there is almost no need for this slow speed. The 2400 bps units will also support 1200 and 300 bps. And the 9600 bps modems, also called high-speed modems, support all of the data rates including, sometimes, 19200 bps.

All but the high-speed modems are very straightforward. They operate very simply and have very few quirks. However, the high-speed modems can become quite complex. They have special modes of operation and are very inconsistent from manufacturer to manufacturer. That means that the high-speed modem of one manufacturer will not communicate at full efficiency, using all of its advanced features, with that of another manufacturer. While it is true that they will communicate, different manufacturers add different special features not usually compatible with the special features of other manufacturers. This doesn't mean that you can't use high-speed modems reasonably universally. It only means that you may have difficulty configuring them for best results.

Keeping It All Together

In making sure that your modem and your terminal program work together, the COMM port is one thing that has to be the same on the modem and the terminal program. The other is modem speed. If you have a 2400 bps modem and your terminal program is set for 9600 bps, the two will never communicate. You must have the terminal program set for the same or lower speed as the modem. Unless locked at a particular speed, modems can "fall back" to a lower speed if you attempt to use the lower speed from your terminal program. However, they cannot step up to a higher speed.

There is one more thing you should know about modems. Back in the early years of generally available "popularly priced" modems, Hayes Microcomputer Products produced a series of modems that used a command language based on commands that began with the characters AT. Over time, this command language, the commands you use to set up the features of the modem, has become a *de facto* standard. Thus, virtually all terminal programs expect the AT command set. What that means to you as a modem buyer is that you should always stick to modems that are Hayes compatible. We'll discuss these commands a bit later in this chapter in the section on modem command strings.

TIP

When shopping for a modem, a good, general-purpose modem would be a 2400 bps external Hayes-compatible modem. This is the best compromise for utility, ease of use, universality, and price.

This Program's Terminal

Now, we'll go into a little more detail regarding the terminal program that you will use to communicate with your modem and, ultimately, with the computer at the distant end. First, let's review the purpose for comm or terminal programs. The PC needs a way of communicating through the COMM port to the modem. It also needs a way to take advantage of the modem's features and to simplify computer-to-computer communications. Term programs provide those facilities.

If you happen to be using Microsoft Windows 3.0, you received a terminal program with your software. Although Windows' term program is very simple to use, like a lot of "free" programs included with other programs, this one is limited in its capabilities. The program was written for Microsoft by Future Soft Engineering, the same company that produces an excellent, but very complex, term program called DynaComm.

You could perform some very elementary communications without using a term program. However, you would find the process tedious and confusing, not to mention restrictive. Terminal programs provide several services to you that help make communicating simple. Some of these services are shown in Table 6.1.

The term program supplies these services by providing you with menu choices for achieving the objectives and, through its internal programming, translating your request into the language that DOS and the modem understand. For example, if you wanted to change the data rate of your modem, you could do it by "talking" directly to the modem with AT commands issued through your term software. Then, you could use a menu choice to match your term program's speed to the modem.

You could dial the phone number of a distant computer directly from the term program, or you could let the term program do it automatically by preloading the phone number into a "phone book" (included in most terminal software) and then selecting it when you want to dial. You could go through all of the steps required to connect to a distant computer manually, or you could write a simple "script" that lets your term program do it for you. Basically, good terminal programs automate as much of the connection process as possible so that you can make a connection simply by selecting a menu choice.

This Program's Terminal

▼ *Table 6.1. Terminal Program Services*

- Controlling the modem setup

- Establishing an end-to-end connection between two computers

- Automating the computer-to-computer connection process

- Transferring files between two computers

Setting Up Term Programs

In order to work with your modem, your term program will need some preliminary setup. The extent and complexity of this setup varies with the program, so be sure to read the operator's manual that comes with your software. There are basically two steps to setting up your terminal software to communicate with a distant computer. The first step sets up the term program to work with your modem. The second sets up the combination of the terminal software and the modem to communicate with the distant system. You usually perform the first step only when you set up the software for the first time or when you buy a new modem. The second step must be performed for each distant or remote system to which you want to connect. Once performed, though, the second step does not need to be repeated unless the remote system changes.

We discussed the basics of matching the term software to the modem in the last section. Generally, all you need is to be certain that the speeds and COMM ports match. In the case of the more complex high-speed modems there may be other adjustments you'll need to make, but those are described in the modem's operators manual.

When setting up to communicate with a remote computer, however, there are two additional parameters you'll need to set. These are the number of data bits per character (including the number of stop bits) and the *parity*. Every character has a certain number of *data bits* that contain the information that makes up the character. You learned earlier that most characters in a PC had eight bits. You also learned that serial communications meant sending out characters one bit at a time. Modems use serial communications.

Think about how those serial bits must look to the computer at the other end of your communication. As far as the computer knows, it is simply seeing a stream of bits. There is nothing to tell it where the last bit of one character and the first bit of the next character are. All it sees is bit after bit after bit. There must be a way of determining where one character ends and the next begins. It turns out that asynchronous communications systems have a way of doing exactly that. They insert extra bits that are always of a certain type or pattern between characters. These special bits are called *stop bits*. They signal the end of a character and tell the distant computer that the next bit it sees is the start of a new character. Stop bits are usually longer in duration than the data bits.

Most PC systems use eight data bits. In that case, they would also usually use one stop bit. Occasionally some systems use only seven data bits. Those systems generally use two stop bits. However, the 8,1 combination is by far the most common and you can count on it as a starting point for setting up your end-to-end communications. Now on to the other issue: *parity*.

All communications systems need a way to determine whether they are communicating correctly. One of those methods is to use a *parity check*. A parity check is a primitive method of adding one or more bits to each character leaving the sending system. The receiving system checks the bit when the character arrives to see if it is the same as when it left. If it is, the receiving system assumes that it has received the data correctly. Obviously there aren't too many ways to use one or two bits to determine with any reliability the accuracy of a data transmission. So parity is often set to *none*, meaning that the system isn't going to bother to check. This is usually OK since there are more sophisticated ways of checking file transfers, which you will learn in a moment. However, there are two other possible parity settings besides none. They are *odd* and *even*.

Generally speaking, you will see the odd and even parity settings with seven-bit data. The most common setup between PCs connected by modem is eight data bits, one stop bit, and no parity bit. That is abbreviated N,8,1 (No parity, 8 data bits, 1 stop bit). For almost every serial connection (interestingly, this applies to serial printers as well as modems) you will use the N,8,1 setting. Now, let's review briefly where we are in our modem/term setup.

The first thing we need to do is make sure that the general setup between our modem and our term program is correct. That means the data rates and COMM ports must be the same. This won't change unless you change modems. The next task is to see that you have set your term program to match that of the distant computer with which you want to communicate. That means setting speed (usually the same as your modem, but occasionally lower—you won't need to change the modem since it will "fall back" to the lower speed mandated by the term program), number of data bits and stop bits, and the parity bit (usually N,8,1). That's all there is to it.

File Transfers

There is one other task your term program can perform for you. From time to time you might want to transfer a file *to* the distant computer (called an *upload*) or *from* the distant computer (called a *download*). There are some issues to confront when you want to do this. The most important issue is getting the file to its destination without it being damaged by noise or other interference. To perform file transfers, terminal programs use any of several generally accepted *file transfer protocols*.

File transfer protocols are methods of transferring files by packaging them up in pieces and transferring the pieces. Each piece is checked at the destination using a *cyclic redundancy check*, or *CRC*, which is simply a mathematical calculation of all of the bits in the package. If the results of the distant end's calculation match the calculation at the sending end, the package (called a *packet*) is considered correct. If it is different, the distant end asks the sending end to send the packet again.

There are several generally accepted file transfer protocols. When you use one of these protocols (usually included as part of your term program) you must be sure that both the sending and receiving end are using exactly the same protocol. Some of the common ones are: XMODEM, YMODEM, YMODEM BATCH, ZMODEM, and KERMIT.

Xmodem is very simple and provides some protection against file corruption during transfer. It uses small packets of only 128 bits so transfers can take a while to complete. YMODEM is better, using larger packets (1,024 bits) and a more sophisticated CRC. YMODEM BATCH is the same as YMODEM except that it lets you transfer several files, one after another, automatically. ZMODEM is considered among the best and most sophisticated of the file transfer protocols, and KERMIT is slow but very good for transferring files over noisy telephone lines due to its superior error checking and correction.

When you want to transfer a file, most term programs use the generic procedure shown in Table 6.2.

▼ *Table 6.2. Transferring a File Over a Phone Line*

1. Tell the distant end that you want to transfer a file.

2. Select the file to transfer and notify the distant end.

3. Select the distant end protocol.

4. Notify your term program of the file being transferred.

5. Select the same protocol for your end as you did for the distant end.

6. Commence the transfer.

This Program's Terminal

The term programs on both ends will prompt you for these steps and you can follow the prompts easily. Once the transfer has started, the two computers will establish their own private communications, a process called *handshaking*, which ensures that both computers are communicating correctly and using the same transfer protocol. Then the sending end will start transferring packets to the receiving end. If a period of time goes by when no packet is received at the receiving end, it will terminate the transfer and give you a *timeout error*. That means that it waited and received nothing so it assumed that something was wrong enough to terminate the transfer.

The other error you can receive is a *bad block error*. This means that the CRCs didn't match at the sending and receiving end. Don't worry. The program will resend the bad packet until it gets it right or determines that it can't. If the receiving side determines that it can't receive due to too many bad packets (or blocks—the two terms have the same meaning) it will terminate the transfer and give you an appropriate message.

Stringing Along with Your Modem

The AT command set, mentioned earlier, which Hayes Microcomputer Products introduced in the early days of commercial modems is a set of commands that you use to configure your modem. All Hayes-compatible modems have two operating modes: the data mode and the command mode. In the data mode, these modems simply transfer data. In the command mode, however, you can change their configuration in a variety of ways.

There are several basic AT commands that are common to virtually all Hayes-compatible modems. These commands are always preceded by the two characters AT. The AT commands are anywhere from one to several characters, often a combination of letters and numbers. The commands may often be strung together after the initial AT, which means "attention." The AT then gets the modem's attention or, as some users put it, "wakes up" the modem. Then the commands may be added in what is called a *command* or *setup string*.

For example, the command for dialing a phone number is D. If you add a T, the modem knows that you want to dial over a touch tone phone system. Then, of course, you need a phone number to dial. So, if you string these commands together: ATDT555–1234, the modem knows that it is supposed to use tones to dial 555–1234. As soon as it dials the number (completes the command string) the modem waits for a response. The response, hopefully, is the modem on the distant end answering.

There is a very wide variety of modem setup commands. The extent of these codes depends on the manufacturer of the modem. However, there are several that are common to just about all Hayes-compatible modems, regardless of manufacturer. For your reference, Table 6.3 lists a few of the most common AT codes and their meanings. I suggest that you look to your modem's operator manual for more details.

You can use these codes from your terminal program whenever you are in direct communication with your modem. What that specifically means depends a bit on your terminal program. Generally, terminal programs have a mode where you use them from a set of menus or a phone book and another mode where you are connected directly to the modem. In that mode, anything you type on your screen goes straight to the modem and anything coming out of the modem goes to the screen.

When you have your modem set up to echo the characters you type, you may actually see two of each character. This is because the

▼ *Table 6.3. Typical "AT" Modem Commands*

COMMAND	DESCRIPTION
AT	Attention (precedes other commands)
A/	Repeat the previous command
A	Answer the phone
B1	Select standard Bell 212A 1200 baud speed
D	Dial the phone number that follows the command
E	Don't echo commands
E1	Echo commands
H	Hang up the phone
L - L3	Set speaker volume (L is lowest, L3 is loudest)
M	Turn the speaker off
P	Pulse dial type phone
S0 - S??	These are special *registers* (memory areas inside the modem) that have different numbers and meanings depending on what manufacturer's modem you have. Usually, S0-S27 are reasonably consistent from manufacturer to manufacturer. The "S registers" are rather complicated and their specific definitions are beyond the scope of this book. For more detail, refer to your modem's operator manual. There can be several hundred S registers in complex modems.
T	Tone dial type phone
Z	Reset the modem's registers
&W	Write the current configuration to the modem's memory

modem always returns the character you type if the connection is correct. If you add local echo, you'll see your typing on the screen whether the modem is properly connected or not. If it *is* properly connected, you'll see the echo *and* the modem's returned character. It's a good idea not to have local echo on so that you can quickly tell if the modem is communicating with your PC and term program.

You can also connect directly to the distant end in this mode simply by typing the access setup string such as the ATDT555–1234 above. As soon as the distant end answers, you'll be in direct communication with the modem, and therefore, the PC on the distant end. The only difference between letting the term program dial and doing it yourself is that if you do it yourself, you have to actually type the string. If you dial automatically (sometimes called *autodialing*) or as part of a script, the dialing string is sent by the term program automatically.

Term programs, modems, and AT command sets vary from manufacturer to manufacturer. You won't really know the capabilities of your particular products until you read the accompanying user manuals. But they all behave pretty much alike and have, at their core, many similarities. Now, we'll put all of this theory to some good use and have a bit of fun with computer bulletin board systems.

BBSing—The Most Fun You Can Have with a Phone and a PC

Computer bulletin board systems (BBSs) are, in some respects, the CB radios of the computer world. BBS programs are relatively inexpensive and anyone with a computer, modem, and an extra telephone line can set one up. BBSs are often designed to provide special services or subjects of conversation for those who connect to them. For example, there are bulletin boards that specialize in online games, messages, or conferences, files of all kinds for downloading by BBS members, and a variety of other specialties.

Many bulletin boards have special interest groups, known as SIGs, to discuss anything from technology to UFOs. There are also a great many "adult" bulletin boards with mature humor and graphics for downloading. In short, you can find a BBS for just about any subject or taste right in your own home town. In order to locate the bulletin boards in your area, you can usually ask your local computer store. If you are buying a modem, ask the salesperson for a list of local "boards." Some areas have lists that are posted on the boards and   computer stores will often copy them and make them available to their customers.

When you find a board that looks interesting, all you need to do is phone it with your modem. The BBS lists usually tell you how to set the modem, but if they don't, start out with 1200 or 2400 bps, N,8,1. You'll get most of them on the first try. Don't be surprised if the phone is busy. Many of these boards, especially the "kiddie boards" (BBSs that specialize in online games), are in use almost constantly. Keep trying, and eventually you'll get through. When you do, you'll probably find that there are some limits as to what you can do on the board until the sysop (system operator, in other words, the person running the BBS) increases your privilege level. You'll probably have to answer a short questionnaire or send a note to the sysop requesting full privileges. Most boards are free, but a few charge a nominal fee.

The usual attraction for BBSers is that availability of free software. This software, called freeware or a variation called shareware, is present in abundance on bulletin boards. It costs nothing to download. The shareware will cost a nominal fee if you decide to keep and use it. We'll look at shareware in detail in Chapter 8.

Another attraction is BBS networks. These networks, with colorful names like Fido and Relay, are connections of hundreds of boards all over the world. Through a series of board to board relays you can send messages and carry on conversations with people worldwide who have similar interests to yours. The only problem is that it can take a while for the relays to get messages to their destinations. Using these networks, though, you can chat in much the same way as you would on a CB or Ham radio, excepting the delays, of course. Again, there is usually no cost.

If you are a BBS novice, sign onto one of the boards that looks like it might have the kinds of discussions or software that you would find interesting and "lurk" (sit in on discussions by reading messages without sending any) awhile to get the feel of the board. Then, if you have questions, ask. Most BBSers are very friendly and always willing to help new users learn the ropes.

Different Strokes

Aside from the fun of bulletin boards, there are a couple of variations that are quite useful. One variation is electronic mail (E-mail). Systems such as MCI Mail provide a method of sending electronic messages, faxes, and telegrams throughout the world right from your PC. For the small business with employees who travel a lot, services like MCI Mail and laptop PCs with modems provide an inexpensive way for out-of-town staff such as salespeople to keep in touch with the office. These services do have a cost associated, but it is usually fairly reasonable, and in some cases, downright cheap. MCI Mail, for example, is accessible from anywhere in the United States via an 800 number.

Another variation on the BBS is the conferencing system such as BIX (The Byte Information Exchange, a service of Byte Magazine) and CompuServe. These systems are large national or international services that are a combination of the BBS and E-mail systems. They generally cost a bit to use, but they are a wealth of information and data. These systems, often associated with trade magazines, professional organizations, or other special interest groups, have everything from experts on a range of subjects eager to discuss their specialties and answer questions, to online databases of information on a variety of subjects. In fact, the subject of online databases could take up an entire book by itself.

What's an ANSI?

There is one additional subject that we should touch upon if you are going to "modem" to bulletin board systems. Most terminal programs have the capability of emulating (acting like) special types of computer terminals. That's one of the reasons they are called "terminal" programs. Two of the most common terminal emulators are VT100 and ANSI. The VT100 is a Digital Equipment Corporation screen that is used with certain minicomputers. It is black and white (no color display capability) and uses a very simple character set. You won't have much need for this unless you happen to be connecting to Digital's minicomputers over some sort of corporate network.

The ANSI emulation, however, is the one you'll want to use with just about all BBSs. It allows you to see the color that the BBS generates for some interesting graphics and menu screens. Many boards are very colorful. To use the ANSI emulation, just set your term program for it (the operator's manual will tell you how) and be sure that you have a file called ANSI.SYS in your root directory and a line in your Config.sys file that says "device=ansi.sys" (without the quote marks, of course). If you don't have your PC set up in this manner, you'll see a lot of strange characters and other "garbage" when you log onto a BBS. That garbage is a sure indication that you are on an ANSI BBS and you don't have your PC and term program set for ANSI emulation.

Summary

- Modems are devices that convert the electrical signals in your PC into audio tones that can travel over telephone lines.
- Modems need some special software in the PC called communications, or *terminal*, software that interprets the input to your PC and converts it to signals that can be sent over a phone line. It then guides the signals to the proper COMM port for transmission.
- Internal modems are actually add-in cards that go inside your PC.
- External modems connect to the COMM port using either a 9- or 25-wire cable and special connectors.
- Internal modems require care in setting up because they can conflict with other boards and ports in the PC.
- Modems operate at different speeds measured in *bits per second*, or *bps*, which means the number of bits that pass through the COMM port in a second. Typical modem speeds, or *data rates*, are: 300, 1200, 2400, 4800, 9600, and 19200.
- A good general-purpose modem is a 2400 bps external Hayes-compatible modem.
- Term programs control the modem setup, establish an end-to-end connection between two computers, automate the computer-to-computer connection process, and transfer files between two computers.
- Term programs require preliminary setup to work with modems. The extent and complexity of this setup varies with the program.
- Terminal programs use any of several generally accepted *file transfer protocols* to transfer files by packing them up in pieces and transferring the pieces.

- Some common file transfer protocols are: XMODEM, YMODEM, YMODEM BATCH, ZMODEM, and KERMIT.

- There are several basic commands that are common to virtually all Hayes-compatible modems. These commands are always preceded by the two characters AT. Hence the term "AT commands."

- Term programs, modems, and AT command sets vary from manufacturer to manufacturer, so you won't know the capabilities of your system until you read the accompanying user manuals.

- Aside from the fun of bulletin boards, there are a couple of variations, such as electronic mail, which are quite useful in that they allow you to send electronic messages, faxes, and telegrams throughout the world right from your PC.

PRACTICE WHAT YOU'VE LEARNED

1. What is a modem?

2. What does the modem use to communicate?

3. What two functions of your PC's operating system must you be especially careful about when you are adding internal modems or other add-in cards?

4. What is the safest way to install an internal modem in your PC?

5. What two things must you do if your modem and terminal program are to work correctly together?

6. What are some of the functions of the terminal program?

7. Why do we need stop bits?

8. What is a CRC?

9. What are AT commands?

10. Why do you need ANSI?

ANSWERS

1. A modem is a device that converts the electrical signals in your PC into audio tones that can travel over telephone lines.

2. Terminal software, the PC, a serial (or COMM) port, and telephone lines

3. The I/O address and the interrupt request (IRQ)

4. Disable COMM port 1 in your PC and set up the internal modem for COMM 1

5. They must both be set to the same COMM port and the same data rate.

6. Controlling the modem setup, establishing an end-to-end connection between two computers, automating the computer-to-computer connection process, transferring files between two computers

7. To distinguish between the end of a transmitted character and the beginning of the next character

8. Cyclic Redundancy Check. This is a method of ensuring that files transferred between two PCs make the journey between the sending PC and the receiving PC intact.

9. AT commands are used to set up or configure the modem for a communications task.

10. ANSI is used to allow your PC to respond to color graphics created using the ANSI standard (as is common on bulletin board systems). To take advantage of ANSI color, you must load the Ansi.sys file using your Config.sys file at boot time.

7

My PC's All GUI !: Using Graphic Interfaces

GUI, pronounced "gooey," is one of those wonderfully graphic computer acronyms. It means Graphical User Interface. This chapter is about user interfaces, graphical and otherwise. In that classification we include menu systems of all types, especially those that are graphical in nature. In this chapter you will learn about:

▲ **Menu systems in general**

▲ **Menu shells**

▲ **Desktop-type menus such as GEM**

▲ **The best known GUI: Microsoft Windows**

What's on the Menu?

Menu systems cover a rather wide range of different types. There are very simple menus, consisting of a list of choices for which you select a number or a letter. There are menus with a colored bar, also called a *light bar*, that you move among selections. There are pull-down and pop-up menus. These menus are sometimes part of other menus called *desktops*. And, there are full graphical interfaces that use *icons* (small pictures) to represent menu choices instead of words. All of these menus are also applicable to specific types of programs. The purpose of a menu is to make your use of the PC easier, faster, and more intuitive. Believe it or not, regardless of what generation the salesperson touts your new software as, there are uses for each one of these menus.

AXIOM

If a menu doesn't make your computing easier, by default it is making it more difficult. Menus are worthless until proven useful. The state of the art isn't worth beans if it doesn't help the state of your computing.

No matter how "old" the style of a menu appears, there may be a valid application for it. For example, I once worked for a gentleman who was obsessed with having the programs his company sold look "90s." To him that meant fancy graphical interfaces. The fact was that, for some of those programs, the combination of the application's intent and the people who would be using it dictated a very simple, "old-style" menu. It didn't look zingy and, as he put it, "90s," but users had no trouble figuring out how to use it. Old or not, it was a wonderful menu.

Remember, not all PC users are computer mavens. Some just want to get their work done and actually view PCs as an intrusion rather than a benefit. With all of that in mind, I wholeheartedly recommend a menuing system of some kind. But don't let yourself be carried away by some artificial criterion for state of the art glitz. Match the menu to your needs.

Making Your Selection

There are a lot of issues that go into selecting a menu. In fact, there are a couple of levels of menus. The first is the interface to your PC. *Interface* is just a trendy way of saying "how you and your computer communicate." You can communicate at the DOS prompt level. Programmers and many power users love that. It seems to give them added control.

I'm about as much of a power user as you're likely to find, and my personal system is fully menued using Microsoft Windows. Having said that, when I work on a development project for a client I give them the menus and I work from the DOS prompt. Why? When I work on my own system, the applications that I use are straightforward, like word processing and database management. I want to get at and into the application as fast and easily as I can. I have dozens of such applications and I can't remember them all. Some method of organization is a must. Menus, actually GUIs, work very well for me in that venue.

However, when I am producing a system for a client, I need to get in and out of special development environments fast. A menu actually holds me up. Also, I want to see how things work without the interference of a menu. I am, in essence, creating an environment for my users. I have to be outside of it to create it. Here's the point. Menus, of whatever type or style—including no menu at all—must meet the specific needs and skill level of both the user and the application(s).

These are two extremes, but they serve to illustrate that the user interface, DOS prompt, or GUI, has its place. That place is dictated by the use and the user. The first level of menus, the main interface to your PC, will go a long way toward improving your efficiency with your PC. The second level, inside the application, is really not within your control. But you should avoid like sin any application that is so hard to use by virtue of a misplaced menuing system that you can't get any real power out of it. Enough said—what types of menus are available to you?

Types of Menus

The first, and most primitive (don't let that term bother you, it just means that the system is quite simple) menu is the kind that lists your choices and lets you choose a number or letter to make a selection. That type has a couple of benefits. First, it takes up almost no memory. Second, it is so easy to create, you can do it yourself with simple batch files. Just create a batch file that prints out several menu choices labeled 1,2,3, and so on. Then make a batch file for each choice—1.bat, 2.bat, 3.bat, etc.—with each batch file performing the task described on the menu. For example, if choice number 1 was "Run WordPerfect," your 1.bat batch file would load WordPerfect and execute it. By typing 1 (executing 1.bat) you would load your word processor. It's easy, it's primitive, and it works very well.

The second generation is the "moving bar" menu (Figure 7.1). This requires special programming you probably can't do yourself. But there are a great many "menu programs" that do it for you. You

---

▼ *Figure 7.1. A Moving Bar Menu*

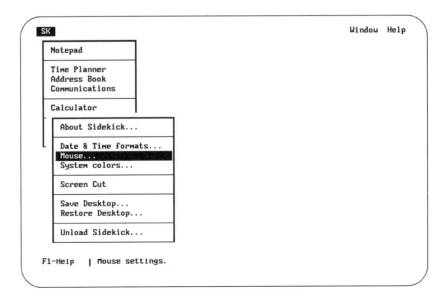

simply fill in some blanks in the program with commands that resemble simple DOS batch file commands, and the menu program creates a menu. The menu looks like a list of choices, just like its primitive predecessor, but instead of selecting a number or letter, you use the cursor arrows to move a light bar up and down the menu. When you reach your selection you hit [Enter] and the menu does the rest. These are also low memory users and fairly simple to construct and use.

The third type of menu is the Lotus menu (Figure 7.2). This is a menu bar across the top of your screen like the popular Lotus 1-2-3 spreadsheet. Each choice invokes another set of horizontal menus until you have made the final choice and invoked a program. These can be hard to use and are a precursor to the next type. That type is the *pull-down* menu. It starts out looking like the Lotus menu, but instead of invoking tier after tier of horizontal menus, each selection drops a set of additional choices below it. These choices are in the form of moving bar menus. The bar across the top is, appropriately, called the top or menu bar. The moving bar

What's on the Menu?

▼ *Figure 7.2. The Lotus Menu*

```
A1: '                                                          MENU
Worksheet  Range  Copy  Move  File  Print  Graph  Data  System  Quit
Global,  Insert,  Delete,  Column,  Erase,  Titles,  Window,  Status,  Page
          A         B        C        D       E        F        G       H
1
2
3
4
5
6
7
8
9
10
11
12
13
14
15
16
17
18
19
20
18-Apr-91  04:22 PM                              NUM
```

menus that appear under a top menu choice are called *drop-down* or *pull-down menus*. This type of menu is typical of the *desktop system* such as the GEM menus.

Finally, the most sophisticated of menu systems is the GUI (Figure 7.3). GUIs require a real graphics environment. You can't use them otherwise. The visual difference between a GUI and other systems is that a GUI does not use menus. Instead, it uses *icons*. Icons are little pictures that represent a menu choice. When you select an icon, you either invoke a program, or you invoke another icon. GUIs have another big distinction. They are always used with mice. The speed and ease with which you can use a GUI are based, in part, on the speed with which you can move your mouse to the icon and click on it. Obviously, GUIs are meant for machines with more power, graphics, and memory.

Menus can be very useful. Which type you select depends on a lot of factors. I have pointed out the differences between the various types of menus in general terms. Now, let's explore some of these in more detail, including their uses, system requirements, and some representative products.

▼ *Figure 7.3. Windows 3.0—A GUI Screen*

Should You Shell Out for a Menu?

One of the methods some applications use to allow you to return to the DOS prompt temporarily is called "shelling." When you shell out of a program, a small piece of the program remains in your PC's memory, sort of as a place marker. That small piece remembers what you were doing in the program at the time you shelled to DOS so that you can return to exactly the same point you left. Then, the program leaves you at the DOS prompt to do whatever you needed to do before returning to the program. You don't have quite as much memory as you would otherwise have since a little piece of your application is taking up space.

Menu shells work in a similar manner. They leave a little bit of themselves in memory and let you shell out to a program—sort of the opposite of shelling *from* a program. Then, when you are through running your application, you return to your menu. These menus, in view of today's memory hungry applications, may not be as practical as they might first appear. However, they have their place and, in some cases, work just fine.

One of the better menu shells is part of DOS 4.01. Since it is actually part of DOS it is reasonably well constructed, fairly simple to use, and not particularly memory hungry. Its appearance is quite modern. It uses a moving bar for making your selection and it permits *hierarchical menus*. That means that you can have menus that, instead of invoking programs, invoke other menus. These lower-level menus are sometimes called *submenus*.

Submenus are the best way to set up your PC's menuing system. For example, you might have a main menu that offers *Word Processing, Databases, Utilities,* and *Spreadsheets*. The Word Processor choice might invoke a submenu that offers *WordPerfect, Spelling Checker,* and *Text Editor*. The Database selection might offer *dBASE IV, Telephone List, Mailing List,* and so on. Each generic category appearing on the main menu leads to a submenu of specific choices. You'll find this technique applicable to virtually all user interfaces.

How They Work

Menu shells leave a little piece of themselves in memory. Sometimes they leave that piece in exTended or exPanded memory (if you have it) so that they don't take up space in your DOS memory. In general, however, menu shells are intrusive enough into DOS memory as to impede your normal computing. Any shell that leaves more than a few hundred bytes is very likely to get in your way.

Another aspect of menu shells that may make them less than attractive to the novice user is that they usually must be programmed. Virtually all popular shells are, actually, a sort of DOS batch file–like programming language that lets you create your own menuing system. Most folks who simply want to use their PCs have no interest in becoming programmers at any level, easy or not. Writing batch files is elementary, even trivial.

TIP

Most menu shells that claim to be "just like DOS batch files" really are somewhat more complex. If you want to build your own menus, hold out for a system that asks little more of you than filling in a few blanks with the programs or submenus you want to use. There are several menu shells available that make no more than those limited demands.

Down the Right Path

While we're on the subject of menu shells and other, similar, types of menu systems, a few words about the DOS path is in order. Menu shells need to be set up so that your PC can find them when the program they called finishes running. There are two ways to ensure that your menus will have many happy returns. One way, if you are using home-brew batch files, is to always make the last command in the batch file the one that calls the menu back. For example, suppose that you had a menu batch that did no more than print some menu choices on the screen. When you selected one of the numbered choices at the DOS prompt, you actually called another batch file named that number.

Let's say that your menu file is called *Menu.bat*. It has six choices, numbered 1 to 6, the first one being WordPerfect. You have six other batch files, 1.bat, 2.bat, 3.bat, and so on. 1.bat changes to the WordPerfect directory and starts WordPerfect when you type 1 at the DOS prompt. All of these files are in a directory called C:\MENUS. So the last commands in your 1.bat (and all of the other five numbered batch files) should be:

Should You Shell Out for a Menu?

```
CD C:\MENUS
MENU
```

The change of directory back to the directory where you placed all of your menu batch files ensures that DOS can find the Menu.bat file. Then, you invoke that file with the command *MENU*, which returns the menu choices to your screen. Another method, which usually works fine, is to make sure that the directory containing your menus is in the DOS PATH statement in your Autoexec.bat file. The reason it only *usually* works is because there are certain combinations of subdirectories that can confuse DOS. But if you keep your directories and your menus simple, you'll have no trouble. One rule that you already know applies here. Keep all of your menu files together in their own directory.

Commercial menu shells, should you decide that they are for you, will usually install in their own directory with the appropriate changes made to the DOS PATH statement as part of their installation. In that case you will have no need to worry about these matters. A final word on shells. They often have one additional benefit. Many come with accessories such as calculators, notepads, and calendars, that improve their usefulness. Also, many have built-in special menus for performing DOS functions such as file copying, naming, and deleting. The best of these require almost no programming at all and consist of fill-in-the-blanks type setup. For the money, these shells can be very beneficial.

A Gem of a Desktop

One of the menu styles that has found favor in recent years is the *desktop* or graphical work surface. Graphical work surfaces were first introduced by Apple Computer, and the Macintosh has long been a model for ease of use. Many Macintosh users joke that they can do almost anything that doesn't specifically require text (such as word processing) without ever touching the keyboard. The difference between the Mac work surface and the menu systems we have discussed thus far is that the Macintosh uses *icons* instead of words and prompts to describe files.

Each directory is represented by a small picture of a file folder. The individual files inside the folder (directory) are represented by small pictures indicative of the file's purpose. For example, Foxbase, a well-known database management program available on the Macintosh, uses a picture of a fox as its icon. If you click your mouse on the icon, the program loads and starts. You never type a thing. If you click on the folder, it has the same effect as switching to the directory (using the DOS CD command) on a PC. Early Macintosh users became so loyal to their graphical work surfaces that software companies in the PC world began to take notice.

A company named Digital Research decided to take advantage of this technique (mice on a graphical work surface instead of typing commands at a prompt) and developed a similar menuing system called *GEM*. GEM uses the same file folder metaphor for directories that you see on the Macintosh. It also allows some limited use of other icons for applications programs. There are good things and bad things about the GEM desktop menu system. Many of these things apply to graphical work surfaces in general.

First, in order to use a graphical desktop like GEM, you need a PC and display that can do graphics. That usually means either an EGA or VGA monitor. You also usually need a fair amount of memory since graphical work surfaces take a lot of memory and must act like a shell, leaving part of themselves in memory when you execute a program. Third, you can't really use a graphical program without a mouse. That means that you will have to have a graphics environment (graphics display, lots of memory, and a mouse) before you can take advantage of GEM or any other graphical user interface.

Another drawback, for some, is that GEM is not very colorful, even though it uses a color display. All of the work surface is, basically, black, white, gray, and blue. It uses the color display to get good definition and to allow the use of color programs. GEM is also not terrifically fast at executing programs. On the plus side, GEM can be purchased with a nice collection of "desktop accessories," such as a calculator, a calendar, and a notepad. The accessories add value to GEM since you can begin to develop a coordinated work surface containing your applications, tools, and accessories.

GEM was the first of the PC GUIs, and for that it deserves a lot of credit. Even today, current versions of GEM are acceptable work surfaces, even though Windows is far more popular. GEM, like Windows, also has lent its "look and feel" to applications programs written using it as the *graphical engine*. The graphical engine is the part of a program that gives it the ability to work in a graphics environment. Today, in the PC world for the most part, if you are graphical, you are either GEM or Windows. Each engine is at the heart of a very different type of graphical system. For all of that, you can run GEM programs on top of Windows (you can run Windows and then also run a GEM-based application). Unfortunately, you can't have it the other way around.

GEM seems to be losing ground to Microsoft Windows at a rapid pace. But there are still many excellent programs that have been developed using the GEM interface. And, while it doesn't have the glitz and features of Windows, GEM is a capable, easy-to-use GUI if your applications aren't too demanding. For real GUI power, however, you will probably want to turn to Microsoft Windows. Windows is more than just a GUI, it is a complete computing environment. GEM, too, is an environment, albeit not as complete as Windows.

So, What's It All Mean?

This brings us to another topic for discussion. What is the difference between a work surface, menu, GUI, and environment? To a greater or lesser extent, all of those qualify as an environment. Anything that presents a user interface is, after all, a computing environment. When we speak of *environments* we usually mean something that goes beyond the work surface. Our simple menus, for example, don't do much of anything except call a few applications programs. GEM, like Windows, has the ability to do somewhat more than call a few programs.

They both have the ability (Windows much more than GEM) to control, or at least manage, memory usage. They have the ability to work with interrupts and addresses, especially when controlling printer and COMM ports. Again, Windows does these two things much better than GEM. Finally, the icons are more *tightly coupled* to the applications than menu choices on our simple menus. That means that it is much easier to run your programs from the GUI and return to the GUI work surface than it is to manage your applications from a simple menu.

You also have more control over how your programs, graphical or not, will run. In short, a complete computing environment such as GEM or Windows takes control over the "uncooperative" aspects of your PC and its programs so you don't have to. In the next section, we'll explore the most popular and powerful of PC GUIs, Microsoft Windows.

Do You Do Windows?

The Microsoft Windows GUI is today's premier graphical user interface. Actually, Windows is much more than an interface. It is a complete work environment. PC environments must provide much more than just a GUI. They must provide a complete system of user interface and PC control. They provide the control aspects by acting as a *surface* on the PC's operating system. That means that the environment, in this case, Windows, provides functionality that the operating system, by itself, does not. Then, it must connect with the operating system in such a manner that neither the operator nor the application program realizes that there are really two entities at work: the environment and the operating system— in this case Windows and DOS. There are a great many good books on Windows, most of which go into excruciating detail. Here, we've opted for a bit simpler, less strenuous discussion.

In the case of Windows and DOS, Windows covers up, for many users, some of the warts on DOS. For example, most versions of DOS are not multitasking. That means that, by itself, it cannot do two things at once. However, with the addition of Windows, some degree of multitasking capability emerges. You can actually run several programs at the same time if the processor allows it (you need the 80386, 80386SX, or 80486). DOS memory management also leaves something to be desired. With Windows (and Windows-specific applications) all of the memory in your 80386 or 80486 becomes available to you. These are examples of the use of the environment to add oomph to the PC's operating system.

Do You Do Windows?

In the Mode

Windows can operate in three different modes. The *real* mode, which you invoke by typing *win /r* to start the program, is the most compatible of the three. You use the real mode when you want to use Windows on an older or somewhat unsophisticated PC, such as the IBM XT. It also allows you to run many programs that were designed for early versions of Windows. The *standard* mode, invoked by typing *win /s* to start up, is the normal mode for Windows. The standard mode allows some access to exTended memory and, unlike the real mode, allows switching between Windows applications. Finally, if you are using a 386 or 486, you can use Windows' *386 enhanced* mode. This mode, the most powerful Windows mode, can take advantage of all memory management and multitasking features of both Windows and your PC. You start Windows in the 386 enhanced mode by typing *win /3*.

In addition, Windows provides a complete graphical interface. All menu selection is by icon, using a mouse. Running Windows without a mouse is possible, but very awkward. Windows also is most effective on a color display. In fact, the most useful configuration for Windows is by no means trivial. You should have a 386, 386SX, or 486 PC with 3MB or 4MB of memory and at least a 40MB hard drive. This is a fairly serious PC. The implication is that Windows is for fairly serious PC users.

Getting It Going

Another aspect of Windows that would lead you to believe (somewhat erroneously) that serious users only need apply, is that the types of applications that can take maximum advantage of the Windows environment are mostly business applications. That means that there are limited programs for the casual user. That will probably change over time as the prices for high-power PCs continue to come down. In any event, Windows has a great deal to recommend it for the serious PC user, so I'll offer some insights into this, some say revolutionary, product.

First, installing Windows is fairly simple. All you need do is stick the first disk in your A:> drive and type SETUP. From that point, all you need to do is follow the prompts and fill in the blanks. You should be quite familiar with the hardware your system uses, since Windows will ask you such things as what type of monitor and mouse you have. The questions are quite straightforward, but if you feel uncomfortable discussing your PC's configuration, by all means let your dealer install Windows for you.

Once you have installed Windows, you'll find that your screen is divided into *groups*. These groups are, visually, boxes that contain icons representing applications. During the installation, Windows will have searched your hard drive for programs that it recognizes. When it finds one, whether it be a Windows or non-Windows application, it will make note of it and provide an icon in the proper group.

One GUI Fits All

That brings us to a short digression. There are both Windows and non-Windows programs. The applications that are considered Windows applications are those that have been written specifically for use in the Windows environment. In fact, Windows applications will not work outside of Windows. You must have Windows to run them. The non-Windows applications are those that were written before Windows was popular and can run outside of the Windows environment. These are the common PC applications you run every day on your standard PC without anything except DOS, and perhaps a simple menu.

There are several programs that come with Windows 3.0. Most of these programs are pretty simple to use but lack much of the sophistication of larger, standalone programs that do the same thing as the "free" Windows programs. For example, there is, as we saw earlier, a terminal program. In addition there is a Rolodex-style database, a simple word processor with a fair number of useful features, a notepad, and a recorder. The recorder is a program that lets you record keystrokes (or mouse clicks) and assign them to a single key. This technique is called *keystroke macros* and lets you perform a complex process by selecting a single key. Another included program is the file manager, which lets you manipulate files (copy, delete, rename, etc.) and view the files and directories on your PC in the form of a directory tree.

Windows applications take advantage of all of the available capabilities of Windows in terms of memory management, multitasking, and so on. Non-Windows applications cannot use these capabilities. In fact, Windows must make some special concessions to run these "primitive" programs. Those concessions are in the form of *Program Information Files* (PIFs). PIFs are special files that tell Windows all about the non-Windows programs they describe. When you install Windows, you also install a *PIF editor* that lets you create PIFs for your non-Windows applications simply and quickly. Then Windows refers directly to the PIF instead of the application.

The Windows System Files

There are two other important Windows files, but there is no need of going into extensive detail, because the Windows manual and a couple of Windows information files do a pretty good job of describing them in depth. These files are the *Win.ini* and *System.ini* files. Between them they contain all of the information that you need (or, if you prefer, that *Windows* needs) for configuration. Much of what is in these two files is created during the installation process. However, there are two ways to change them, should your needs change or should you want to fine tune your Windows installation.

The first way to alter these files is through what amounts to running the setup program again. In reality, you do this from within Windows itself using the Windows Control Panel. The other way is simply by editing the files using an ASCII text editor.

The two files contain somewhat different types of information. Bear in mind that the information contained in Win.ini and System.ini is essentially configuration information. It controls the extremely complex job of configuring Windows to your specific use.

The Win.ini file contains largely environmental information (Figure 7.4). This information includes such things as the kind of keyboard or mouse your PC uses. It includes the fonts that your PC will use for both screen display and printing from standard applications (special fonts for specific applications are included here also, under the headings for those applications). Also, the Win.ini file is updated every time that you install a new Windows application. These applications may have special file or memory handling requirements, customized fonts for printing, or a variety of other specialized parameters. During the installation of the application (which you must do from within Windows) the Win.ini file gets an automatic update. Unfortunately, non-Windows applications have no way of updating this file, and thus cannot take advantage of the special features of Windows.

▼ *Figure 7.4. A Typical Win.ini File Screen*

```
[windows]
load=
run=
Beep=yes
Spooler=no
NullPort=None
device=PostScript Printer,PSCRIPT,LPT1:
BorderWidth=3
KeyboardSpeed=31
CursorBlinkRate=448
DoubleClickSpeed=657
Programs=com exe bat pif
Documents=
DeviceNotSelectedTimeout=15
TransmissionRetryTimeout=45
swapdisk=
NetWarn=1
MouseThreshold1=4
MouseThreshold2=0
MouseSpeed=1

[Desktop]
Pattern=(None)
Wallpaper=(None)
```

TileWallpaper=1
GridGranularity=0
IconSpacing=80

[Extensions]
cal=calendar.exe ^.cal
crd=cardfile.exe ^.crd
trm=terminal.exe ^.trm
txt=c:\windows\notepad.exe ^.txt
ini=notepad.exe ^.ini
pcx=pbrush.exe ^.pcx
bmp=pbrush.exe ^.bmp
wri=write.exe ^.wri
rec=recorder.exe ^.rec

[intl]
sCountry=United States
iCountry=1
iDate=0
iTime=0
iTLZero=0
iCurrency=0
iCurrDigits=2
iNegCurr=0
iLzero=1
iDigits=2
iMeasure=1
s1159=AM
s2359=PM
sCurrency=$
sThousand=,
sDecimal=.
sDate=/
sTime=:
sList=,
sShortDate=M/d/yy
sLongDate=dddd', 'MMMM' 'dd', 'yyyy

[ports]
; A line with [filename].PRN followed by an equal sign causes
; [filename] to appear in the Control Panel's Printer Configuration dialog
; box. A printer connected to [filename] directs its output into this file.
LPT1:=
LPT2:=
LPT3:=
COM1:=9600,n,8,1
COM2:=9600,n,8,1
COM3:=9600,n,8,1
COM4:=9600,n,8,1
EPT:=
FILE:=
LPT1.OS2=
LPT2.OS2=

[Windows Help]
Xl=173
Yu=50
Xr=481
Yd=374
Maximized=1

[fonts]

```
Modern (All res)=MODERN.FON
Script (All res)=SCRIPT.FON
Roman (All res)=ROMAN.FON
Symbol 8,10,12,14,18,24 (VGA res)=SYMBOLE.FON
Tms Rmn 8,10,12,14,18,24 (VGA res)=TMSRE.FON
Courier 10,12,15 (VGA res)=COURE.FON
Helv 8,10,12,14,18,24 (VGA res)=HELVE.FON
CG Times (WN) 6,7,8,10,12,14,18,20,24 (VGASCR)=VGASCR0.FON
Univers M[ (WN) 6,7,8,10,12,14,18,20,24 (VGASCR)=VGASCR1.FON
Univers Md (WN) 6,7,8,10,12,14,18,20,24 (VGASCR)=VGASCR1.FON
[PrinterPorts]
PostScript Printer=PSCRIPT,LPT1:,15,45
Generic / Text Only=TTY,None,15,45

[devices]
PostScript Printer=PSCRIPT,LPT1:
Generic / Text Only=TTY,None

[Solitaire]
Back=10
Options=73

[colors]
Background=0 0 0
AppWorkspace=64 128 128
Window=255 255 255
WindowText=0 0 0
Menu=0 128 128
MenuText=0 0 0
ActiveTitle=128 64 64
InactiveTitle=64 128 128
TitleText=255 255 255
ActiveBorder=128 128 128
InactiveBorder=255 255 255
WindowFrame=0 0 0
Scrollbar=224 224 224

[ToolBook]
startupUnits=inches
startupHeight=5760
startupWidth=8640
startupSysColors=true
startupSysBooks=
startupBook=tourbook.tbk

[Clock]
iFormat=1

[Terminal]
Port=COM1

[Paintbrush]
width=864
height=864
clear=B/W

[PostScript,LPT1]
feed1=1
feed15=1
device=2
orient=1

[spooler]
```

```
priority=high
netupdate=yes
netspool=yes
inactivealert=always

[SciCalc]
layout=1

[PostScript,LPT1.OS2]
feed1=1
feed15=1

[PostScript,LPT2]
feed1=1
feed15=1

[MSWrite]
Backup=1
Font1=Courier,48,0
Font2=AvantGarde,32,0
Font3=Bookman,16,0
Font4=Helv,32,0
Font5=Helvetica-Narrow,32,0
```

Do You Do Windows?

The System.ini file contains far more complex and detailed information (Figure 7.5). Most of this information relates to the way that Windows interacts with your PC and its operating system. Both of these files have a simple text file format that looks very much like a batch file. Each line is a separate parameter consisting of a keyword, an equal (=) sign, and a switch. The switch can be a value, or it can be a logical expression such as true, false, on, or off. Unless you either understand these files very well, or have specific step-by-step instructions, I strongly urge against attempting to modify them since errors can bring about unpredictable results.

▼ **Figure 7.5. A Typical System.ini File Screen**

```
[boot]
mouse.drv=mouse.drv
286grabber=vgacolor.gr2
386grabber=vga.gr3
fixedfon.fon=vgafix.fon
oemfonts.fon=vgaoem.fon
fonts.fon=vgasys.fon
display.drv=vga.drv
shell=C:\WINDOWS\progman.exe
network.drv=msnet.drv
language.dll=
comm.drv=comm.drv
sound.drv=sound.drv
keyboard.drv=keyboard.drv
```

```
system.drv=system.drv
[keyboard]
subtype=
type=4
oemansi.bin=
keyboard.dll=
[boot.description]
mouse.drv=Microsoft, or IBM PS/2
display.drv=VGA
network.drv=3Com 3+Share
language.dll=English (American)
keyboard.typ=Enhanced 101 or 102 key US and Non US keyboards
system.drv=MS-DOS or PC-DOS System
[386Enh]
SystemROMBreakPoint=FALSE
mouse=*vmd
EGA80WOA.FON=EGA80WOA.FON
EGA40WOA.FON=EGA40WOA.FON
CGA80WOA.FON=CGA80WOA.FON
CGA40WOA.FON=CGA40WOA.FON
display=*vddvga
ebios=*ebios
keyboard=*vkd
network=*vnetbios, *dosnet
IgnoreInstalledEMM=off
device=*vpicd
device=*vtd
device=*reboot
device=*vdmad
device=*vsd
device=*v86mmgr
device=*pageswap
device=*dosmgr
device=*vmpoll
device=*wshell
device=*vhd
device=*vfd
device=*vpd
device=*parity
device=*biosxlat
device=*vcd
device=*vmcpd
device=*combuff
device=*cdpscsi
local=CON
FileSysChange=off
TimerCriticalSection=10000
UniqueDOSPSP=TRUE
PSPIncrement=5
MinTimeslice=20
WinTimeslice=100,50
WinExclusive=0
Com1AutoAssign=2
LPT1AutoAssign=10
MaxPagingFileSize=3048
prvmFILES=60

[standard]

[NonWindowsApp]
SwapDisk=I:\windows\temp.swp
```

Once you have completed your installation, you can move icons from one group to another simply by *dragging* the icon to the new group box. You can create new groups or add new files to your groups by selecting *New* from the *Files* menu on the program manager. The *Program Manager* is a shell, of much the same type that we discussed earlier. When you load Windows, the first window that appears is the Program Manager. All of your other groups are windows inside the program manager. If you want to change an existing application's icon, path, or other properties, you select *Properties* from the File menu in the Program Manager.

Windows provides a limited supply of rather dull and generic icons. Most Windows applications have their own icons, but if you want to dress up your non-Windows applications (which obviously wouldn't have icons since they were never intended to use them) you'll need to locate one of the many available icon collections. These collections, some commercial, some shareware or freeware, are available from a variety of sources. Ask your computer store about icon collections or check on your local BBS if you got excited enough over the last chapter to sign onto one or more of them.

Do You Do Windows?

Simplifying

Occasionally, you'll find that you like everything Windows does for you, except that, like me, you've added so many programs that you find the Windows groups to be excessively crowded. There are a couple of approaches to this. One is to arrange your groups differently, and put groups inside groups. This technique is called *nesting* and is about the same as the hierarchical menus we discussed earlier. A scheme that seems to work well is to arrange groups by application instead of by type of program. For example, if you are a writer, you might put all of your writing tools in one group (arranged by type of program) or you might open up a group for books in progress (clicking on a book name brings up the current chapter in progress), another group for your newsletter, and so on.

The second approach, organizing the books into one group, newsletter in another, requires more maintenance since you will be launching (starting) applications programs (such as your word processor) from a document instead of starting the application and then finding the document. Obviously, you'll have to update the *properties* of the icon when you finish one chapter and start another one. This approach would probably not be particularly practical if you work on a large variety of short projects. The point is that you can organize your groups in a variety of ways to suit your needs.

If, on the other hand, you still find your work surface too crowded, there are several third-party Windows shells that take the place of the Program Manager. These third-party shells all take different approaches to the organization of the work surface. They do nothing, however, to alter the underlying interface between Windows and your PC. Unfortunately, some of the features of these third-party shells can be a bit ill-behaved with Windows, so you'll want to explore your options very carefully before you buy a third-party shell.

There are three major benefits to using Windows. First, it offers a customizable work surface that doesn't require a rocket scientist to set it up and make it your own. Second, Windows manages PC resources such as memory very well for Windows applications, and not too badly for non-Windows ones. Windows also greatly simplifies printing by automating the printing resources of your PC after initial installation. Finally, Windows exploits the capability for advanced PCs (386, 486, etc.) to multitask.

One drawback to Windows is that it is only an environment over DOS. It is not a complete operating system in itself. That means that if the basic capability to do some task doesn't exist within DOS, the best Windows can do is simulate it. You can't create something in DOS using Windows that was never there in the first place. Also, Windows is not yet well-behaved with some third-party enhancements such as memory managers or shells. Future versions of Windows should overcome some of this and improve its cohabitation with other programs.

Summary

- The purpose of a menu is to make your use of the PC easier, faster, and more intuitive.

- The types of menus generally available range from simple ones where you make a choice by typing a letter or number to more sophisticated moving bar menus, graphical desktops, and full graphical user interfaces.

- The Lotus menu is a menu bar across the top of your screen like the popular Lotus 1-2-3 spreadsheet. Each choice invokes another set of horizontal menus until you have made the final choice and invoked a program or function.

- The most sophisticated of menu systems is the GUI, which requires a real graphics environment. The visual difference between a GUI and other menu systems is that a GUI does not use menus. Instead, it uses *icons*.

- Menu shells leave a little bit of themselves in memory and let you shell out to a program. Then, when you are through running your application, you return to your menu.

- Hierarchical menus means that you can have menus that, instead of invoking programs, invoke other menus. These lower-level menus are sometimes called *submenus*.

- Menus need to be set up so that your PC can find them when the program they called finishes running.

- GEM, a type of GUI, uses the same file folder metaphor for directories that you see on the Macintosh and allows some limited use of other icons for applications programs.

- An environment is more than a simple work surface such as a GUI. It includes how the applications are coupled to the menus, how the environment handles such things as COMM ports and Printing, and other aspects of the user/computer interface that go beyond menus.

- Windows adds some degree of multitasking capability allowing you to run several programs at the same time if the processor allows it. Windows and Windows-specific applications also can use all of the memory in your 80386 or 80486.

- Windows can operate in three modes: Real, Standard, and 386 enhanced. The 386 enhanced mode allows full exploitation of the 386, 386SX, and 486 CPUs.

- The win.ini and system.ini files are used to configure Windows to your particular system and requirements.

- The Windows Program Manager is a menu shell used by Windows to organize program icons on the work surface. When you load Windows, the first window that appears is the Program Manager.

PRACTICE WHAT YOU'VE LEARNED

1. What is the purpose of a menu system?

2. What is the main visual difference between a GUI and other menu types?

3. What is the difference between a menu system and an environment?

4. Name two popular GUIs that are also environments.

5. What are three operating modes for Microsoft Windows?

6. What are the two important configuration files in Windows and what is each used for?

7. How are menus handled in Windows?

8. If you find your Windows work surface too crowded, what is your other alternative besides changing your groups?

ANSWERS

1. The purpose of a menu is to make your use of the PC easier, faster, and more intuitive.

2. GUIs don't use menus; instead, they use icons to identify what you would normally consider to be menu choices.

3. A menuing system simply invokes various programs. It is not particularly tightly coupled to the computer's operating

system. A complete environment, on the other hand, is closely interwoven with the operating system to help you control such aspects of your computing as memory management and, if available on your PC, multitasking.

4. Microsoft Windows and Digital Research GEM

5. The real mode, standard mode, and 386 enhanced mode

6. The Win.ini file contains configuration information such as fonts, keyboard type, display type, and the specific information required by Windows applications. Printer drivers for applications are designated here, too. The System.ini file contains system-level configuration information.

7. Applications are indicated by icons that you can organize into groups of applications that are, in some manner meaningful to you, grouped based on some common theme.

8. Use a third-party shell to replace the Windows program manager shell. You may find that a different graphical approach provided by one of these shells is more acceptable to you.

8

Psssst...
Wanna Buy Some
Cheap Programs?

While it's true that you can spend a lot of money on sophisticated applications software, you can also spend as little as nothing. This chapter discusses some sources of low-cost or free software programs. We will explore the mysteries of software pricing. The chapter also contains a brief section on computer piracy. In this chapter you will learn about:

> ▲ **Low-cost commercial programs**
>
> ▲ **How developers and dealers price their software**
>
> ▲ **The concept of shareware**
>
> ▲ **What public domain software is**
>
> ▲ **Why software piracy is a bad idea**

The Bargain Basement

Not all software needs to cost an arm and a leg. Software prices vary greatly depending on several factors. First, it is not true that, unlike hardware, software prices are coming down. The top end "best sellers" will always cost a lot of money. Companies like Lotus Development, WordPerfect, Ashton-Tate, and Microsoft spend fortunes to develop and promote their products. The introduction of Microsoft Windows 3.0 cost several million dollars. Followup advertising has been equally expensive. Large software companies simply must sell their products for top dollar.

On the other hand, just like the store brands of products at your local supermarket or drugstore, there are low-cost versions of the high-priced products. Unlike those store brands, however, the low-end software products often lack some of the functionality of more expensive programs. That doesn't mean that they don't work as well, many work better. These programs are produced by small companies that don't pay huge overheads in staff and advertising costs. They simply must work correctly or they won't sell.

One factor virtually all low-cost programs have in common is that they depend on word-of-mouth and good press to gain followers. Many years ago, before the laptop computer revolution, a tiny company in Bothell, Washington, decided that there would soon be a huge market for laptop software. So Traveling Software was born to find and distribute software designed especially for laptops. Their first product was LapLink, a program for transferring information and files from a desktop PC to a laptop. It was a low-cost program and it revolutionized the use of laptop computers because it provided a practical way to take your work with you. The program was sold through Traveling's catalog. In those days, they did almost no advertising. Still, the program sold vigorously and won several awards.

The point is, unless you really need software from one of the big guns, you may not need to spend top dollar. It's true that you also may not get all of the bells and whistles, but if you don't need them, why pay for them? Here's how to decide if you need to smash your piggy bank. First, decide what generic function you want to perform. Do you need a database? A word processor? A spreadsheet?

Then, decide which expensive best-seller you would buy if you had unlimited funds. Once you know what you would buy if money was no object, decide why you would make that choice.

The Bargain Basement

AXIOM

Nobody ever lost their job for buying (*insert product name here*) is just about the worst reason for buying a product. Safety means nothing when buying software. What matters is functionality, bug-free operation, and good support. If you can get all of that with a no-name product, buy it.

It may develop that you need to spend a bundle for an industrial-strength desktop publisher simply because you can't get the functionality you need any other way. But don't assume that from the start. There are low-end DTP programs just as there are low-end word processors, spreadsheets, or database programs. The next question, of course, is how low is low. There seem to be a few "price points" that are popular in the software trade. Oddly, the price points haven't changed much over the past several years and probably won't change much over the next few.

Pricing Games

Software pricing is a different game from pricing hardware. When you set a price for hardware you figure the cost of materials plus the cost of manufacturing. Then you add development costs amortized over some predetermined number of units sold, throw in something for promotion, some overhead, and finally, your profit. It all makes a fairly neat pricing formula. Not so with software. Most companies pick a popular price for similar software and that's what the package costs.

Popular prices are $79.95, $99, $129, $149, $199, $239, $495, $695, $795, and so on. Software marketers have the idea that prices below a certain point, usually around $129, represent "impulse buys." That means that, if the price is low enough, you'll whip out your credit card and buy, even if you never take the software out of the box. All they have to do is make the program attractive enough to catch your attention. The fact is that many of those low-cost programs are worse than useless. But some represent real bargains.

Once you have decided upon what you want in your program, start shopping. Remember, if you buy a program through the mail, you can't return it if it's not what you want. So you have to be sure. On the other hand, if you buy in a computer store, especially one of the better known chains, you can usually try the software out in the store. Your best bet is to seek one of the bargain software chains like SoftWarehouse or Egghead Discount Software. Go to the store and tell the salesperson what you want. You need whatever parts of the functionality of a best seller, only you want to spend less than half the money for a *workalike*. Here is where you may get a surprise.

There may not be a close enough workalike for your purposes. However, you can often save as much as a third off the high-priced program at these discount chains. Other sources of low-cost commercial software are Radio Shack and Sears. You'll also be surprised at how many large office supply stores and book stores carry computer software. But the problem with those sources is that they don't buy large enough quantities to get the best prices. The typical computer store (nonchain) gets a mere 35 percent to 45 percent discount off of suggested retail price. That means that they can't give you a very big discount and still make any money. The big chains, however, buy at prices that are closer to distributor pricing. That means that they get as much as 60 percent off retail. They can afford to give fairly serious discounts to serious buyers.

An excellent time to buy software is when you are buying hardware. If you are reading this prior to buying your PC, here's a tip for you.

TIP

If you are buying hardware, decide on what software you will need and buy it at the same time. Larger dealers will often give away some software to make a hardware sale.

Also, many hardware manufacturers include some software with their hardware. Finally, there is a class of software that is usually a pretty good bargain. This software is called *integrated software*. Integrated software is a single program that contains a word processor, spreadsheet, database, communications program, and some other accessories and utilities. One of the best known integrated packages is SmartWare from Informix. Another is Enable. These programs are less expensive than the combined prices of the individual applications they include. Also, the integrated applications have the advantage of working well together.

Try It, You'll Like It. If You Don't, Don't Pay for It

In 1982 the PC marketplace changed radically. That was the year that Jim Button and Andrew Fluegelman invented shareware. The idea was if users could try a product, they would buy it if they liked and needed it. If not, they would simply not use it. Commercial software developers know that only a percentage of the software they sell will actually see long-term use. They count on the fact that lots of people will buy their software to try it because that's the only way they can use it legally. Quite a few software dollars get spent so that users can put the package on the shelf and never touch it again. That's a pretty expensive experiment.

Button and Fluegelman had other ideas, though. They decided that if they let everyone freely copy their software and try it—at no cost—the people who want to continue to use it would pay for it. They also had almost no overhead or advertising costs, so their software was priced at around a tenth of the price of comparable commercial products. Did the scheme work, or did these two entrepreneurs go quietly broke while hoards of wild-eyed PC users robbed them blind by not paying for their software?

Actually, back in 1982, Jim Button was still working for IBM. The concept of shareware was so successful that he left IBM and started ButtonWare, considered one of the most successful shareware companies in existence. The result of the experiment from your perspective is that you can now find hundreds of programs available on exactly the same terms. Try the program. If it does your job, send your money to the author. Often you will get a professionally prepared manual, and sometimes another copy of the program with additional functionality. Where do you find shareware?

Where to Buy 'Em

There is a surprisingly large number of sources for high-quality shareware. One of the most accessible is the wealth of local bulletin boards. Most boards have large collections of shareware. In fact, one of the driving forces behind the shareware revolution has been the proliferation of these BBSs. Another source, occasionally, is your local computer store. Usually, the stores that carry shareware are the smaller, local shops. But there are some stores that specialize in shareware. One such store is Wizardware in Bethlehem, PA. Wizardware also has a mail order catalog. Typically, you'll pay a very small fee to cover the cost of disk duplication to the store. Then, if you decide to keep the program, you'll send the shareware price directly to the developer.

A third source for shareware is mail order. Many of the popular computer magazines carry ads for shareware disks. Again, you'll pay a very small fee to cover disk duplication. Then, the price of the shareware is due only if you decide to keep the program. Many of the mail order sources as well as local stores that carry shareware participate in local computer fairs. Virtually every city of any size has periodic computer fairs or "swap shops." These PC flea markets are wonderful sources for used PCs and shareware. As they say on television, watch your local newspaper for time and location.

Safety

How do you know your shareware is safe? We'll discuss viri in depth in the next chapter, but there are some precautions you can take. First, if you buy shareware from a store or mail order house, be sure you know something about the source. Most of these vendors either retain the developer's disk labels or use their own. Avoid unlabeled disks or disks with handwritten labels. If the disk is professionally labeled with the source's name on it, it's probably safe. Although it would be nice to get a shrinkwrapped box, only the larger shareware developers like ButtonWare go to that expense. Most simply provide a disk with the program name on it and the manual included as a text file. If you register the software (pay the shareware fee) you may get more.

Try It, You'll Like It. If You Don't, Don't Pay for It

If you download your shareware from a BBS, you are at somewhat more risk, as you'll see in the next chapter. In any case, you'll need a special utility called an *unzipper* if you want to use shareware. We will discuss unzippers in the last chapter. However, here's a brief description. In order to save disk space and get all of the shareware program's files on as few disks as possible, most shareware authors use a file compression utility called Pkzip. You will need the opposite program, Pkunzip, to uncompress the files.

Both Pkzip and Pkunzip are available on most BBS systems. They are a special type of shareware called *freeware* or *public domain* software. We'll discuss that in a moment. However, if you are using Pkzip and Pkunzip only for your own personal need, you don't have to pay a thing for them. If you want to use them as part of a software product or in a business, you'll need to purchase a special license.

Why Buy Shareware?

Is shareware "good stuff"? Actually, most popular shareware is at least comparable in quality and support to commercial software. Much of it is better. There are two reasons for this. One reason is that shareware authors depend on word-of-mouth to sell their software. They don't invest money in advertising. If their programs are poorly written and badly supported, they won't see any registration fees and they'll go broke. Also, they usually support their programs themselves. That means they don't have big support staffs. So they can't afford to have buggy software. The registration fees are so low that they must depend on the software to work correctly and be easy to use. Shareware authors can't afford big support investments, so they make sure that their programs will require as little support as possible.

The second reason is that shareware authors have joined together in the Association of Shareware Professionals to ensure that their programs meet acceptable quality standards. The ASP logo on a shareware product tells you that, in principle, anyway, the author believes in producing good products at fair prices. Interestingly, the distinction between shareware and commercial software has blurred with some of the larger shareware companies like ButtonWare.

ButtonWare's extremely popular shareware database program, PC File, is available on most BBSs. If you register it, you'll pay a very low price for a full-featured version with a real manual and lots of functionality. There is even a network version. In addition, you can buy a spreadsheet and a word processor from ButtonWare for as little as 25 percent of the price of typical commercial products. Attesting to the popularity of shareware, PC File has sold almost a million copies, making it, by anybody's measurements, a best seller.

Absolutely Free!

There is a class of software that you can have at no cost. Freeware, or public domain software, is software that the author has decided to make available to the world at large without any monetary compensation. That doesn't mean that you can change the software, though. Usually, the author retains the copyright. That means that he or she still owns the program. It's just available for you to use at no cost.

That brings up an interesting aspect to computer software. In virtually all cases, no matter what you paid for an application, you don't own it. You simply own a license to *use* it. Usually, you can use only a single copy at a time. In these cases the author or the company that holds the copyright actually owns the software. So, considering freeware, the author still owns the program, but you are granted a license to use it at no cost. That also might mean you can distribute the program as well. But in just about all cases you can't *sell* it. You can only give it away.

What's Available?

What kinds of programs are in the public domain? We have discussed one such program: Pkzip written by Phil Katz. However, the Katz program may not be sold or included with another program without paying for a license to do so. That is another aspect of freeware. Often you can have a copy for your own use, but if you want to do any more with it you have to pay. Another type of freeware you might see comes from public universities. These are programs that are the result of university research. The universities place the program in the public domain as a stimulus to programmers working on similar programs. Often the programming code for the program is also available so that other developers can incorporate the public domain programs into their own applications.

Freeware is not limited to scholarly pursuits by any means. On bulletin boards across the country you'll find public domain software in plentiful supply. Much of this harvest is of excellent quality. You'll find many font sets for word processors and desktop publishing programs, lots of clip art, and other graphics. There are also a great many utilities and the occasional large application. Often the larger applications are watered-down versions of a commercial or shareware program. If you like the freeware version, you might want to purchase the real product.

How do you know you have freeware? Usually there will be a notice in a text file (sometimes called a *readme file*) that the program is in the public domain. If you find such a notice, it will usually be accompanied by a copyright notice and any restrictions the author has placed on the use or redistribution of his or her program.

Don't expect extensive documentation (user manuals) with most freeware. Often, the program is an outgrowth of some other programming the author is doing. Or, it might be a utility the author created that he or she felt would be useful to other users. In these cases, about all you can expect is a set of instructions for using the software. If the software is a set of fonts or other graphics, instructions for using it, including the programs with which it is compatible, will usually be in the readme file.

This Is an Act of Piracy, Captain Bligh!

With all of this talk about low-cost and free software, you might be tempted to view all programs as readily available for whoever wants to use them under similar arrangements. Not so at all. Commercial software is protected by fairly strict licensing laws. More and more, in companies of all sizes, PC users are accepting the fact that there are rules that govern how you can use and distribute commercial software. The bottom line is that it is illegal to share copies of commercial software. This sharing of software is called *software piracy*. Here are some of the ways that commercial software is licensed and can be used legally.

First, it is almost always legal to make a single backup copy of a program. This is a good idea and, for the most part, is encouraged by software developers. The reason for making the copy is that you should protect yourself against damaging the distribution disks of your program. By making a copy and installing your software from the copy, you protect the original from damage. Most software licenses contain permission to make this copy.

Licensing

Let's digress a little into the realm of software licensing. Most software vendors place their distribution disks inside a sealed envelope with the software license printed on the outside. By opening the envelope and removing the disks you assent to the terms of the license. Almost all software licenses are similar. For single-user software they point out that you don't own the program, you are only granted a license to use it. They also give (or don't give in rare cases) permission to make that one backup copy. And they almost always say that you can't share, resell, or reverse engineer the software (reverse engineering means disassembling the software to reveal its code). Multiuser licenses (for use on local area networks) tell you how many users may share the program on a network.

There are a few gray areas of software licensing. For example, some software is licensed by the *user*. That means that if you buy the software, you are the only person allowed to use it. You cannot loan it to your friends, even if you are not using it at the time. Some programs are licensed by the workstation. That means that you may install it on a single PC and anyone who wants may use it. Usually, that also means that you can uninstall it from that PC and move it to another. The rule of thumb is that you can only install the program on a single PC at a time. If you have a program installed on several PCs, even though only one is in use at a time, are you abiding by the license? That depends.

For example, if you use a desktop PC and a laptop computer, can you put the same program on each machine? Obviously you won't use them both at the same time. Most licenses would prohibit such an action. However, most software developers are realistic enough to understand that users simply want to be able to use their software no matter whether they are in the office or on a plane. They usually won't enforce the license and make you buy two copies.

Suppose we take that example a step further. In addition to the desktop PC and the laptop, you decide that you also want a copy on your home PC so that you can take work home. In this case, the developer would probably draw the line and tell you to buy a second copy. There is something logical and reasonable about the desktop/laptop scenario that doesn't quite fit with adding the program to extra desktop PCs. For example, suppose you have several offices that you spend time in occasionally. Should you be permitted to use a single copy of a program and share it among all the PCs, even though you only use one at a time? Most developers would tell you no. . .enough is enough.

There is another gray area which, strictly speaking, violates most licenses. However, under the right conditions, most developers actually encourage this violation. Most large companies have an organization called an information center. Information centers provide a variety of resources to PC users within the company. One of their most useful functions is providing a lending library of software. On the surface that sounds very illegal. However, most software vendors encourage it. Why? Simply because it encourages sales of their products to the company. If users get to try a

This Is an Act of Piracy, Captain Bligh!

product, and they like it, they will buy it. This is a variation on the shareware concept.

What does it take to make an info center lending library work? First, there must be few enough copies of individual programs that the library is not seen to be distributing in competition with other sources of supply. Second, the loan period must be short enough (usually a week or less) to demonstrate that the borrower only wants to evaluate the product. Finally, there must be a written agreement between the company and the borrower that he or she will remove the software from the evaluation PC when the software is returned to the library. The idea is that the software is only on a single machine at a time.

If you have questions about your rights under a software license, don't open the envelope. Call the developer and ask. Once you open the envelope, you own the software and you must abide by the license. You can usually return unopened software to your computer store. Also, if you do need to resolve a license issue with a developer, get it in writing. Never count on somebody's word over the phone.

Software piracy is illegal and it is unethical. We won't argue the ethics here, but the usual rationale for protecting the rights of the author is that it is costly to develop and distribute software. The revenues from the sale of the program support those who develop and distribute it. By stealing the program you are depriving those people of justly earned income. But that is really not the issue. The issue is that piracy is against the law and you can be prosecuted for it. The Software Publishers Association (SPA) has waged a very successful awareness campaign against software piracy. The result is that the courts are handing out stiffer and stiffer penalties for software copyright and license violations. In the words of the SPA, "don't copy that floppy." Enough said!

Summary

- There are many sources of very low-cost commercial software. You don't need to buy the most expensive unless you really need all of the functionality (which most users don't).

- Shareware is an excellent way to try a program before you buy it.
- Shareware pricing is the lowest in the industry for high-quality programs.
- There are many good programs in the public domain that will cost you nothing.
- Shareware and freeware are available on most local bulletin boards, from the smaller local computer stores that specialize in it, at PC "swap meets" and computer fairs, and through mail order.
- Software piracy (sharing programs) is illegal and you can be prosecuted for it.
- There are many variations on software licenses. Read the license carefully and don't open the envelope containing the program's disks if you don't completely agree with the license's terms.
- You are usually allowed a single backup copy of a software program.

PRACTICE WHAT YOU'VE LEARNED

1. How is software usually priced?

2. What is an impulse buy?

3. What are the important factors when selecting a software program?

4. When is one of the best times to buy software if you want the best prices?

5. What are the benefits of shareware?

6. What is software piracy?

7. What are some of the ways that a program might be licensed?

8. What steps should you take if you don't agree with the license terms on a program you have just purchased at your local computer store?

ANSWERS

1. It is based on typical pricing for similar products. This is sort of a variation on "what the market will bear."

2. The concept that if a product is priced low enough shoppers will buy it whether they need it or not

3. Functionality, bug-free operation, and good support

4. When you are buying hardware

5. High quality, low cost, chance to try before you buy

6. Illegal copying and distribution of licensed, copyright programs, neither shareware nor in the public domain—sharing of commercial programs

7. By the user, by the workstation, or for multiple users on a network

8. Don't open the disk envelope, call the developer with your question, get the developer's answer in writing. If you can't agree, return the software with the disk envelope still sealed and buy a different product.

9

I Think There's a Virus Going Around

Every PC user has, I'm sure, heard about viri. The fact is that, on PCs anyway, there is a lot more talk about them than there is actual threat from them. Viri do occasionally cause computer users difficulty; however, it is possible to avoid virus contamination with a fair amount of certainty. In this chapter you will learn about:

▲ The differences between viri and buggy or corrupted programs

▲ What a virus, worm, and trojan horse are

▲ How to avoid viri

▲ How to test for virus contamination

Can Your PC Get Sick?

PCs are just as subject to illness as people are. However, just as it is rare for people to be made sick on purpose, it is quite unusual for computers to be purposely infected. Most computer "illnesses" are the result of carelessness, bugs in a program, or hardware failure. However, your PC can experience virus infections, so it is useful to know what a virus is and how to avoid it.

More Buzzwords

There are a few buzzwords that computer users toss around when they talk about viri. So, it would probably be a good idea to get some definitions out of the way before we proceed. We'll start with *virus*. A virus is a program fragment that attaches itself to a legitimate program. The virus has a *payload*, which means that it is intended to do some sort of damage. The virus cannot act on its own. Its *logic bomb* goes off only when you execute the program to which the virus is attached. Most viri are designed to do their damage at some date in the future. Meanwhile, every time you execute the infected program, it, in turn, infects other programs, increasing the probability that you will execute an infected program at the time that the virus is set to do its damage. That sounds a bit convoluted, so here's an example.

How They Work

Let's suppose that you have exposed your PC to a virus. The virus enters your PC as a passenger on an infected program. Computer viri are similar to biological viri in that they attach themselves to the victim. They can't function alone—they must become part of an executable program. Because of that characteristic, they make the executable program somewhat larger than it is supposed to be.

Once the infected program is in your PC, the virus can't do anything until you execute (run) the program. At that point, unless it is time for the virus to do its damage, the virus will only *propagate*. That means that it will attach itself to another executable program.

By the time the virus's payload is set to do its damage, it may have infected most of the executable programs on your hard disk. That means that there is a higher probability that you'll pick an infected program to run at the time the logic bomb is set to go off.

The damage can be anything (depending on how malicious the virus's creator was) from a silly message on your screen to total destruction of all of the data on your disk. The program that brought the virus into your PC is called a *vector* or a *trojan horse*. Viri generally are set to "go off" on some specific date such as Friday the 13th, April Fools' Day, or some other "meaningful" date.

Worms

A worm is quite different from a virus. Worms are programs that can stand alone. They do not need an executable program to function since they are, themselves, executable. Worms generally are able to *replicate* (reproduce) themselves. They execute on their own—they don't need to have you run them. The usual intent of a worm is to steal system resources until the system can no longer function. For example, they replicate until they completely fill your hard disk, leaving no more room for storage. And they execute to the extent that nothing else on the PC is able to run.

In a multitasking system, worms will start running in the background and use computer resources until other programs can no longer run. On a network, worms will run over the network until network performance degrades unacceptably. Worms on networks usually have the ability to seek out network resources and use them up, thus infecting the workstations of users on the network.

Typical Viri

There are a great number of viri flying around the PC world. One company, McAfee Associates in Santa Clara, California, has researched and cataloged most active viri and produced software for detecting and removing them. Later in this chapter I'll tell you how to contact them, but now it might be interesting to see the breadth of viri in the computer community. Figure 9.1 is a list, courtesy of McAfee and Associates, of some of the more common PC viri, the kind of damage they do, and how to get rid of them. Bear in mind that this list is constantly increasing in size. Minor variations (called *mutations* or *strains*) in a virus change its signature (a method of detecting a virus using a CRC—cyclic redundancy check) materially while retaining its ability to do damage.

▼ *Figure 9.1. Typical Viri, Courtesty of McAfee and Associates*

VIRUS CHARACTERISTICS LIST V71
Copyright 1989, 1990 McAfee Associates

The following list outlines the major characteristics of the known IBM PC and compatible virus strains identified by SCAN. The number of known variants of each virus is also listed. This number is listed in parenthesis beside the name of the strain. The total number of known viruses appears at the end of the list. The Clean-Up virus I.D. code is included in brackets.

```
================================================================
Infects Fixed Disk Partition Table————————————————+
Infects Fixed Disk Boot Sector————————————————+ |
Infects Floppy Diskette Boot ————————————————+ | |
Infects Overlay Files————————————————————+ | | |
Infects EXE Files————————————————————————+ | | | |
Infects COM files——————————————————————+ | | | | |
Infects COMMAND.COM—————————————————+ | | | | | |
Virus Remains Resident————————————————+ | | | | | | |
Virus Uses Self-Encryption——————————————+ | | | | | | | |
Virus Uses STEALTH Techniques———————————+ | | | | | | | | |
 | | | | | | | | | | Increase in
 | | | | | | | | | | Infected
 | | | | | | | | | | Program's
 | | | | | | | | | | Size
 | | | | | | | | | |
 | | | | | | | | | |
```

Virus	Disinfector	V V V V V V V V V V	V	Damage
Dot Killer Virus [Dot]	Clean-Up	. . x x x	944	O,P
Father Christmas [FC]	Clean-Up	. . . x x	1881	O,P
3445 [3445]	Clean-Up	x x x . x x	3445	O,P,D,L
Mirror [Mirror]	Clean-Up	. . x . . x	928	O,P
Polish-2 [P-2]	Clean-Up	. . x x x	512	O,P,D
Polish 217 [P-217]	Clean-Up	. . . x x	217	O,P,D
Happy Day [Happy]	Clean-Up	. . . x x	453	O,P
Monxla [Monxla]	Clean-Up	. . . x x	939	O,P
USSR [USSR]	Clean-Up	. x . . . x	575	O,P
Polimer [Polimer]	Clean-Up	. . . x x	512	O,P,D
DataLock [Data]	Clean-Up	. . x . . x	920	O,P
Carioca [Carioca]	Clean-Up	. . x . x	951	O,P
529 [529]	Clean-Up	. . x x x	529	O,P,D
Spyer [Spyer]	Clean-Up	. . x . x x x . . .	1181	O,P
Taiwan4 [T4]	Clean-Up	. . x x x x x . . .	2576	O,P,D
Keypress [Key]	Clean-Up	. . x x x x	1232	O,P,D
Casper [Casper]	Clean-Up	. x . x x	1200	L,O,P,D
1605 [1605]	Clean-Up	. . x x x x	1605	L,O,P,D
Violator [Vio]	Clean-Up	. . . x x	1055	O,P,D

Name	Method		Size	Codes
Blood-2 [B-2]	Clean-Up	. . . . x	427	O,P,D
Wisconsin [Wisc]	Clean-Up	. x . x x	825	O,P,D
Christmas-J [C-J]	Clean-Up	. . x x x x	600	O,P
Austria [Austria]	Clean-Up	. . . x x x	Overwrites	
Leprosy-B [Lepb]	Clean-Up	. . . x x x	Overwrites	
Whale [Whale]	Clean-Up	x x x x x x x . . .	9216	L,O,P,D
Invader [Invader]	Clean-Up	. x x . x x x x x .	4096	B,L,O,P,D
Scott's Valley [Sval]	Clean-Up	. x x . x x x . . .	2133	L,O,P,D
Black Monday [BMON]	Clean-Up	. . x x x x x . . .	1055	L,O,P,D
Nomenclature [Nom]	Clean-Up	. . x x x x x . . .	1024	O,P,D
Anthrax - Boot [Atx]	M-Disk	. . x x	N/A	O,P,D
Anthrax - File [Atx]	Clean-Up	. . x x x x	1206	O,P,D
651 [651]	Clean-Up	. . x . x	651	O,P,D
Paris [Paris]	Clean-Up	. . . x x x x . . .	4909	O,P,D,L
Leprosy [Lep]	Clean-Up	. . x x x x x . . .	Overwrites	
Mardi Bros. [Mardi]	M-DISK	. . x . . . . x x .	N/A	B,O
1253 - Boot [1253]	M-DISK	. . x . . . . x x x	N/A	O,P,D,L
1253 - COM [1253]	Clean-Up	. . x x x	1253	O,P,D,L
AirCop [AirCop]	M-DISK	. . x . . . x . . .	N/A	B,O
400 (5) [400]	Clean-Up	. . x . x	Vary	O,P,D
P1 (3) [P1r]	Clean-Up	. x x . x	Vary	O,P,D,L
Ontario [Ont]	Clean-Up	. x x x x x	Vary	O,P,D
1226 (3) [1226]	Clean-Up	. x x x x x x . . .	1226	O,P,D
V2100 [2100]	Clean-Up	. . x . x x	2100	O,P,D,L
Plastique (3) [P1q]	Clean-Up	. . x x x x x . . .	3012	O,P,D
Wolfman [Wolf]	Clean-Up	. . x x x x	2064	O,P
Doom2 [Dm2]	Clean-Up	. . x . x x	2504	O,P,D,L
Flip [Flip]	Clean-Up	. x x x x x x . . .	2343	O,P,D,L
Fellowship [Fellow]	Clean-Up	. . x . . x	1022	O,P,D,L
Flash [Flash]	Clean-Up	. . x x x x	688	O,P,D,L
1008 [1008]	Clean-Up	. x x x x	1008	O,P,D,L
Stoned-II [Stoned]	Clean-Up	. . x . . . . x . x	N/A	O,B,L
Taiwan3 [T3]	Clean-Up	. . x x x x x . . .	2905	O,P,D,L
Armagedon [Arma]	Clean-Up	. . x x x	1079	O,P
1381 [1381]	Clean-Up	. . . . . x x . . .	1381	O,P
Tiny (7) [Tiny]	Clean-Up	. . . x x	163	O,P
Subliminal [Sub]	Clean-Up	. . x x x	1496	O,P
Sorry [Sorry]	Clean-Up	. . x x x	731	O,P
RedX [Redx]	Clean-Up	. . . x x	796	O,P
1024 [1024]	Clean-Up	. . x x x	1024	O,P
Joshi [Joshi]	Clean-Up	x . x . . . . x x x	N/A	B,O,D
Microbes [Micro]	M-DISK	. . x . . . x x . .	N/A	B,O,D
Print Screen [Prtscr]	M-DISK	. . x . . . x x .	N/A	B,O,D
Form [Form]	M-DISK	. . x . . . x x .	N/A	B,O,D
July 13th [J13]	Clean-Up	. x . . . x	1201	O,P,D,L
5120 (2) [5120]	Clean-Up	. . . x x x x . . .	5120	O,P,D,L
Victor [Victor]	Clean-Up	. . x x x x x . . .	2458	P,D,L
JoJo [JoJo]	Clean-Up	. . x . x	1701	O,P
W-13 (2) [W13]	Clean-Up	. . . . x	532	O,P
Slow [Slow]	Clean-Up	. x x . x x x . . .	1721	O,P,L
Frere Jacques [Frere]	Clean-Up	. . x . x x x . . .	1811	O,P
Liberty [Liberty]	Clean-Up	. . x x x x x . . .	2862	O,P
Fish-6 [Fish]	Clean-Up	x x x x x x x . . .	3584	O,P,L
Shake [Shake]	Clean-Up	. . x . x	476	O,P
Murphy [Murphy]	Clean-Up	. . x x x x x . . .	1277	O,P

Can Your PC Get Sick?

Name	Tool	Pattern	Size	Flags
V800 [V800]	Clean-Up	x x x . x	none	O,P,L
Kennedy [Kennedy]	Clean-Up	. . x . x	308	O,P
8 Tunes/1971 [1971]	Clean-Up	. . x . x x x . . .	1971	O,P
Yankee - 2 [Doodle2]	Clean-Up	. . . . x x	1961	O,P
June 16th [June16]	Clean-Up	. . . x x	1726	F,O,P,L
XA1 [XA1]	Clean-Up	. x . . x	1539	F,O,P,L
1392 [1392]	Clean-Up	. . x x x x	1392	O,P,L
1210 [1210]	Clean-Up	. . x . x	1210	O,P,L
1720 [1720]	Clean-Up	. . x . x x x . . .	1720	F,O,P,L
Saturday 14th [Sat14]	Clean-Up	. . x . x x x . . .	685	F,O,P,L
Korea (2) [Korea]	M-DISK	. . . . x x .	N/A	B,O
Vcomm (3) [Vcomm]	Clean-Up	. . . . . x	1074	O,P,L
ItaVir [Ita]	Clean-Up	. . . . . x	3880	O,P,L,B
Solano (2) [Solano]	Clean-Up	. . x . x	2000	O,P,L
V2000 (3) [2000]	Clean-Up	. . x x x x x . . .	2000	O,P,L
1559 [1559]	Clean-Up	. . x x x x	1554	O,P,L
512 (4) [512]	Clean-Up	x . x x x x	none	O,P,L
EDV (2) [EDV]	Clean-Up	x . x . . . . x x x	N/A	B,O
Joker [Joke]	Clean-Up	. . x x x		O,P
Icelandic-3 [Ice-3]	Clean-Up	. . x . . x	853	O,P
Virus-101 [101]	Clean-Up	. x x x x x x x . .	2560	P
1260 [1260]	Clean-Up	. x . . x	1260	P
Perfume (2) [Fume]	Clean-Up	. . . . x	765	P
Taiwan (2) [Taiwan]	Clean-Up	. . . . x	708	P
Chaos [Chaos]	MDISK	. . x . . . . x x .	N/A	B,O,D,F
Virus-90 [90]	Clean-Up	. . x . x	857	P
Oropax (3) [Oro]	Clean-Up	. . x . x	2773	P,O
4096 (2) [4096]	Clean-Up	x . x x x x x . . .	4096	D,O,P,L
Devil's Dance [Dance]	Clean-Up	. . x . x	941	D,O,P,L
Amstrad (5) [Amst]	Clean-Up	. . . . x	847	P
Payday [Payday]	Clean-Up	. . x . x x x . . .	1808	P
Datacrime II-B [Crime-2]	Clean-Up	. x . x x x	1917	P,F
Sylvia/Holland [Holland]	Clean-Up	. . . . x	1332	P
Do-Nothing [Nothing]	Clean-Up	. . x . x	608	P
Sunday (2) [Sunday]	Clean-Up	. . x . x x x . . .	1636	O,P
Lisbon (2) [Lisb]	Clean-Up	. . . . x	648	P
Typo/Fumble [Typo]	Clean-Up	. . x . x	867	O,P
Dbase [Dbase]	Clean-Up	. . x . x	1864	D,O,P
Ghost Boot [Ghost]	M-DISK	. . x . . . . x x .	N/A	B,O
Ghost COM [Ghost]	Clean-Up	. . . . x	2351	B,P
New Jerusalem [Jeru]	Clean-Up	. . x . x x x . . .	1808	O,P
Alabama (2) [Alabama]	Clean-Up	. . x . . x	1560	O,P,L
Yank Doodle (3) [Doodle]	Clean-Up	. . x . x x	2885	O,P
2930 [2930]	Clean-Up	. . x . x x	2930	P
Ashar [Brain]	Clean-Up	. . x . . . . x . .	N/A	B
AIDS (3) [Aids]	Clean-Up	. . . . x	Overwrites	
Disk Killer (2) [Killer]	Clean-Up	. . x . . . . x x .	N/A	B,O,P,D,F
1536/Zero Bug [Zero]	Clean-Up	. . x . x	1536	O,P
MIX1 [Ice]	Clean-Up	. . x . . x	1618	O,P
Dark Avenger (2) [Dav]	Clean-Up	. . x x x x x . . .	1800	O,P,L
3551/Syslock [Syslock]	Clean-Up	. x . . x x	3551	P,D
VACSINA (2) [Vacs]	Clean-Up	. . x . x x x . . .	1206	O,P
Ohio [Ohio]	M-DISK	. . x . . . . x . .	N/A	B
Typo Boot [Typo]	M-DISK	. . x . . . . x x .	N/A	O,B
Swap Boot [Swap]	M-DISK	. . x . . . . x . .	N/A	B

Name	Disinfector	Characteristics	Size Increase	Damage Fields
Datacrime II [Crime-2]	Clean-Up	. x . . x x	1514	P,F
Icelandic II [Ice-2]	Clean-Up	. . x . . x	661	O,P
Pentagon [Pentagon]	M-DISK	. . . . x . .	N/A	B
Traceback (2) [3066]	Clean-Up	. . x . x x	3066	P
Datacrime-B [Crime-B]	Clean-Up	. x . . x	1168	P,F
Icelandic (2) [Ice]	Clean-Up	. . x . . x	642	O,P
Saratoga [Ice]	Clean-Up	. . x . . x	632	O,P
405 [405]	Clean-Up	. . . . x	Overwrites	
1704 Format [170x]	Clean-Up	. x x . x	1704	O,P,F
Fu Manchu (2) [Fu]	Clean-Up	. . x . x x x . . .	2086	O,P
Datacrime (2) [Crime]	Clean-Up	. x . . x	1280	P,F
1701/Cascade [170x]	Clean-Up	. x x . x	1701	O,P
CASCADE-B (9) [170x]	Clean-Up	. x x . x	1704	O,P
Stoned (2) [Stoned]	Clean-Up	. . x . . . . x . x	N/A	O,B,L
1704/CASCADE [170x]	Clean-Up	. x x . x	1704	O,P
Ping Pong-B (2) [Ping]	Clean-Up	. . x . . . . x x .	N/A	O,B
Den Zuk (3) [Zuk]	M-DISK	. . x . . . . x . .	N/A	O,B
Ping Pong (3) [Ping]	Clean-Up	. . x . . . . x . .	N/A	O,B
Vienna-B [Vienna]	Clean-Up	. . . . x	648	P
Lehigh [Lehigh]	Clean-Up	. . x x	Overwrites	P,F
Vienna/648 (14) [Vienna]	Clean-Up	. . . . x	648	P
Jerusalem-B [Jeru]	Clean-Up	. . x . x x x . . .	1808	O,P
Alameda (2) [Alameda]	Clean-Up	. . x . . . . x . .	N/A	B
Friday 13th COM [Fri13]	Clean-Up	. . . . x	512	P
Jerusalem (9) [Jeru]	Clean-Up	. . x . x x x . . .	1808	O,P
SURIV03 [SurivB]	Clean-Up	. . x . x x x . . .		O,P
SURIV02 [SurivA]	Clean-Up	. . x . . x	1488	O,P
SURIV01 [SurivA]	Clean-Up	. . x . x	897	O,P
Brain (3) [Brain]	Clean-Up	. . x . . . . x . .	N/A	B

Total Known Viruses - 223

Legend:
* - Extinct Viruses (Viruses that are research only viruses, or have not been reported in the public domain for more than 12 months.)

Damage Fields -   B - Corrupts or overwrites Boot Sector

                 O - Affects system run-time operation

                 P - Corrupts program or overlay files

                 D - Corrupts data

                 F - Formats or erases all/part of disk

                 L - Directly or indirectly corrupts file linkage

Size Increase -   The length, in bytes, by which an infected program or overlay file will increase

Characteristics -   x - Yes

                 . - No

Disinfectors -   SCAN/D   - VIRUSCAN with /D option

                 SCAN/D/A   - VIRUSCAN with /D and /A options

                 MDISK/P   - MDISK with "P" option

                 All Others - The name of disinfecting program

Note: The SCAN /D option will overwrite and then delete the entire infected program. The program must then be replaced from the original program diskette. If you wish to try and recover an infected program, then use the named disinfector if available.

Can Your PC Get Sick?

Notice that this list shows various disinfecting possibilities. We'll discuss those in more detail later in this chapter. The point is that, although there are well over 200 known viri, plus mutations, if you practice safe computing there is very little likelihood that you will ever encounter one. However, there is a greater probability that you have encountered a far less intimidating, but equally vicious type of problem if you begin to have random PC problems.

Is It a Virus, or Just One of Those 24-Hour Bugs?

When a worm infected the Internet (a large international computer network with thousands of users) the damage caused was, in part, the result of an error. The designer of the worm claimed he created it to measure how long it would take to travel to all of the nodes (computers) on the network. It was intended to be benign (do no damage). However, a very slight error in writing the program caused it to do considerable damage. There is the lesson. Experts have said that the difference between a virus and a bug can be as little as a few bytes of code.

When you copy a program from a distribution disk (the one that the program comes to you on) to a backup disk, or, during the installation of the program on your PC, it is possible to *corrupt* (damage) the program. Depending on the nature of the corruption, the program may still appear to function. You might have no idea that your program is damaged until it starts doing strange things. It is true that one of the symptoms of virus infection is erratic, unexplained behavior of programs running on your PC. But those symptoms are equally typical of a corrupted program.

If you experience erratic behavior of a single program on your PC, don't immediately suspect a virus. Take these steps to isolate the problem. First, make a backup copy of any *data files* associated with your program. Next, make a new backup copy of the program from the distribution disks. What that means is that you will, per the suggestions of most software suppliers, create a second set of disks, copies of the originals, called *working disks*. You should usually avoid installing programs using the distribution disks.

When you make your working copy, use *diskcopy* instead of the DOS *copy* command. This will ensure that you have an accurate copy of the master disks. Put the master (distribution) disks away in a safe place. Now, reinstall your program from the new working disks. Your program should begin to work correctly. If it does not, there are some other possibilities.

The most likely possibility is that you have done something incorrectly during the installation procedure. Read your user's guide. You may need to increase the files or buffers statement in your Config.sys file. Or, you may have the DOS path set incorrectly. Another typical reason for erratic program behavior is lack of *environment space*. This is a special buffer that sets aside a portion of memory for managing commands. You can increase environment space by placing the following command in your Config.sys file:

shell=c:\command.com /e:512 /p

Obviously, if your Command.com is not on the C:> drive in the root (C:\) directory, you'll want to substitute the correct path. Also, it may be necessary to increase the 512 figure somewhat for complex environments. Your DOS user's manual will explain this a bit more, but this is a good starting point.

Any of these problems can make you think you have a virus infection. Actually, none of them has a thing to do with viri or worms. There is one other potential cause for erratic behavior. Occasionally, you'll encounter a bug (programming error) in a program. Bugs even occur in well-known commercial programs during the early stages of a product release. Usually these bugs don't show up until you use the program in an unusual manner. Since that won't be the common mode of operation, the problem will appear erratic.

The only thing you can do to isolate the problem is to attempt to reconstruct the circumstances under which the program misbehaved and contact the supplier's technical support. The important thing to remember is that you are far more likely to encounter these

Is It a Virus, or Just One of Those 24-Hour Bugs?

problems than a virus, unless, of course, you ask for trouble.

Safety First

There are, unfortunately, some surefire ways to contract a computer virus. Some of these unsafe computing practices can result in exposure to corrupted programs that, as we have discussed, act like, but aren't, viri. The best bet is to avoid these unsafe practices at all costs. The rule of thumb is, know where your program came from (not just the last person who used it, but where it *really* came from). Remember, when you install a program from an unknown source on your PC, you're potentially installing all of the problems on all of the PCs that used that program before you. There is a revealing story about a virus contamination at Lehigh University.

The story goes that computer users on campus started "sharing" copies of DOS. They were buying PCs that didn't come with DOS. (Some PC manufacturers a few years back made you buy your own copy of DOS separately from the PC. Today, most PCs come with DOS installed.) So, rather than buy DOS for each user they passed a copy around. That, of course, was a case of software piracy and, so the story continues, somewhere along the line Command.com became infected with a virus. The result was that most of the PCs on campus became infected.

Shareware

That story points out the first rule of safe computing. Never "share" software. Not only is it a copyright violation, it's dangerous. However, as we saw in Chapter 8, there is one perfectly legal case where software sharing occurs. That is when you use shareware. Shareware can come from several sources. There are stores that sell shareware, essentially for the price of the disk and copying services. This is similar to buying shrinkwrapped software in terms of being fairly safe.

However, shareware gets passed from user to user and is available on bulletin board systems. This is where the danger lies.

When you pass software around you should assume that it is either contaminated or corrupted and act accordingly. In the next section of this chapter, you'll learn about measures that you can take to check software for virus infection. The best bet, of course, is simply to avoid using suspect software.

Safety First

Should you not try shareware from your local BBS? There are some precautions you can take to help protect yourself while enjoying the fruits of low-cost software sources. First, if you frequent a BBS for the purpose of downloading software, get to know the BBS sysop. Does he or she check new software for infection before adding it to the library? Ask other users about their experiences. Have they ever seen virus contamination of this particular board? Get to know the uploaders.

You'll find that on most BBSs the bulk of the shareware is made available either by the sysop or by a few folks who like to add programs to the board's library. If you like a program, send your money to the developer. Often, you'll get another copy with more capability that you can be fairly sure is not contaminated. And, as we'll explain in the next section, test the program for contamination before you run it.

Even shrinkwrapped software from your local computer store may not be completely safe (although it's unlikely that you'll pick up a virus from them). Many stores sell software and then, if the user doesn't like it, the store will accept the return and reshrinkwrap it. Make sure you know your computer dealer. If they engage in this practice, do they test the program for possible damage or contamination before reselling it? Ask the store manager. If the answer is "no," don't buy your software there. However, by far the riskiest computing practice, both from the standpoint of virus infection and corrupted or damaged software, is software sharing. Get into the habit: don't share software!

We're Scanning the Alien, Captain Kirk

Kirk, Spock, Scottie, and the rest of the crew on Star Trek, had something important in common with the canny PC user. Before they plunged into the unknown, they would always use their scanners to attempt to detect danger. You as a PC user enter the unknown whenever you load a new piece of software on your PC. If you are a high-risk user (meaning that you get a lot of your software from BBSs or other shareware sources) you should know about the PC equivalent of the Star Ship Enterprise's scanners. These programs know the *signatures* of many PC viri and can inspect your new shareware program for infection.

Scanners

Antivirus programs fit into three broad categories. First are the scanners. Scanners inspect a program for virus contamination by looking for the virus. There is one major flaw to this approach. Viri are appearing at a faster rate than many of the scanner developers can keep up with them. Also, a minor mutation of a virus produces a different signature, making the virus undetectable until the new signature is added to the scanner. Mutations are produced by *virus cloners*. Cloners don't write their own virus programs—most aren't skilled enough at programming. Instead, they make a trivial modification to an existing virus, enabling it to pass undetected through the scanning process.

Among the best of the scanners is the McAfee Viruscan product. Viruscan is available on many bulletin boards, and from McAfee's own BBS (call (408) 988-4044 at 2400 bps). There's a word of warning here, though. If you get a virus scanner from a BBS, be sure you can establish the source of the software. There should be a note with the file that indicates that it was obtained from the developer and added directly to the board. Scanners are as subject to corruption as any other program. The good programs (like Viruscan) contain a method of verifying the integrity of the scanner itself before using it.

Validating Good Programs

The second method of identifying virus contamination doesn't depend on knowing the signature of the virus. Rather, it depends on knowing the signature of an *uninfected* program. This is one of the best approaches because it can also identify corruption of a file that has nothing to do with a virus. These programs, like McAfee's Validate, generate signatures for the programs on which you run them. Then you can check against a listing maintained by the developer for common programs, or build your own list from the programs known to be good on your own system. Run the validation program from time to time to ensure that none of your applications have been corrupted or infected.

We're Scanning the Alien, Captain Kirk

Containment

The third method combines validation with containment. That means that it watches any executable program for signs that it is performing a function that is considered dangerous. These functions include attempting to erase the entire hard disk, damaging the boot areas of your disk, attempting to alter other executable programs, or performing other "disallowed" functions. If the program detects such an activity, it intervenes, preventing the process, and warns the PC user that the activity was attempted. Probably the best example of this type of program is CERTUS from Certus Corporation in Cleveland, Ohio. If you are using your PC for business, and several people have access to the computer (another high-risk activity), you could benefit from a program like CERTUS.

The intention of this discussion has not been to overemphasize the danger of virus contamination. Rather, it is to emphasize that your data and programs deserve protection. How much they need depends on how much data you can afford to lose and how likely you are to lose it. If you have sensitive data (as in a business) and are at high risk of losing or damaging it, you might consider some of the measures we've discussed here. Remember, you are at higher risk of damage through misuse, accident, or computer (hardware or software) failure than you are from a virus.

However, there are many sick individuals who take pleasure in destroying or damaging other people's property. If you are using BBSs as a source for software (OK) or sharing software with friends or coworkers (not OK) you are exposing your PC to their mischief. If this is the case, take the appropriate precautions to ensure that you can continue to enjoy using your PC without the irritation of virus contamination.

Summary

- Most computer "illnesses" are the result of carelessness, bugs in a program, or hardware failure as opposed to virus infections. Even so, under some circumstances, viri are a real danger to some users.

- A virus is a program fragment that attaches itself to a legitimate program, usually for the purpose of doing damage.

- Most viri are designed to do their damage at some date in the future. Meanwhile, every time you execute the infected program, it, in turn, infects other programs, increasing the probability that you will execute an infected program at the time that the virus is set to do its damage.

- The program that brings a virus into your PC is called a vector or trojan horse.

- Worms are programs that do not need an executable program to function since they are, themselves, executable. They execute on their own—they don't need to have you run them. The usual intent of a worm is to steal system resources until the system can no longer function.

- The difference between a virus and a bug can be as little as a few bytes of code.

- Although one of the symptoms of virus infection is erratic, unexplained behavior of programs running on your PC, those symptoms are equally typical of a corrupted program.

- The only thing you can do to isolate an erratic problem in a PC program is to attempt to reconstruct the circumstances under which the program misbehaved and contact the supplier's technical support.

- Remember, when you install a program from an unknown

source on your PC, you're installing all of the problems from all of the PCs that used that program before you.

• The riskiest computing practice, both from the standpoint of virus infection and corrupted or damaged software, is software sharing.

PRACTICE WHAT YOU'VE LEARNED

1. What is the major difference between a virus and a worm?

2. What is a trojan horse?

3. What are other threats, besides viri and worms, to the security of your PC?

4. What is a mutation and why is it dangerous?

5. What software problems can cause the same types of erratic behavior symptomatic of a computer virus?

6. What are some high-risk computing practices?

7. What does a virus scanner do?

8. What is a validation program?

ANSWERS

1. A virus is a program fragment that must become part of an executable program in order to function. A worm can execute on its own. Also, a virus does some specific piece of damage. A worm, generally, uses up system resources in order to slow or incapacitate the computer.

2. A trojan horse, or vector, is a program within which a virus is hidden. Often a game or utility on a BBS will hide a virus. Virus builders select such high-use/interest programs as trojans because of the high likelihood that they will be selected for use and run often once they are part of the user's system.

3. Misuse, user error, and hardware or software malfunction

4. A mutation is a minor alteration to a virus by a virus cloner. It is dangerous because the mutation changes the virus's signature, without changing its potential for damage, making it more difficult to detect.

5. Corruption of the software program, incorrect installation of the program, too few files or buffers in your Config.sys file, an incorrect or incomplete DOS path command, and not enough environment space

6. Software sharing, allowing several people to use the same computer, obtaining software from unknown sources such as BBS systems

7. Virus scanners apply a process to a program that looks for the "signature" of a virus embedded in the program.

8. Validation programs apply a mathematical process to an executable program called a cyclic redundancy check (CRC) and compare the results with the known CRC signature of the "clean" (uninfected or uncorrupted) program.

10

Now, Let's Get Some Work Done

We've finally reached the reason that you purchased your PC: to do useful work. No book of this type would be complete without offering you some insight into the types of applications you might want to run on your computer. In this chapter you will learn about:

- ▲ **Word Processing**
- ▲ **Spreadsheets**
- ▲ **Databases**
- ▲ **Contact management programs**
- ▲ **Desktop publishing**
- ▲ **Drawing programs**
- ▲ **Business forms management**
- ▲ **Accounting programs**
- ▲ **Personal applications**
- ▲ **Utility programs**

Applications—Your PC's Working Tools

We have spent nine chapters learning about your PC itself. It's only right that we spend the last chapter learning about some of the types of programs that you can use on your PC. Before we get started, let's delve into a bit of applications philosophy. As a general rule, within any applications type (word processors, databases, etc.) you'll find that there is very little functional difference for the average user among the top contenders. Vendor hype and advertising claims aside, selecting an applications program comes down to a few very simple points:

1. How much are you willing to pay? Do you want a mainstream product, a low-end product, or shareware?

2. What are your particular needs? Do you need all the bells and whistles, or could you do very nicely with a workmanlike program that reliably produces fairly straightforward results without any exotica?

3. What environment are you going to use the application in? Do you need a special version for Windows, GEM, or a network?

4. How much technical support are you likely to need on the software?

Within the classification that emerges from your answers to these questions, you'll find that most programs are created pretty much equal. There is another issue. People become very emotional about programs that they either like or don't like. Thus, recommendations from other users must be viewed cautiously. When you ask the person at the next desk what word processor you should get, don't be surprised if the response is based on little except familiarity or emotional attachment to the product or supplier. If you are asking other users for recommendations (a good idea if done right), ask for specifics and try to weed out the emotional attachment.

AXIOM

Everyone's favorite software program is, unequivocally, the best on the market. Otherwise, why use it?

In the examples that follow, you'll get some idea of my own prejudices in this regard. However, for the most part, I've tried to stick with products that also reflect so-called "best seller" status. You won't find these examples obscure, by any means. They are typical of the kinds of programs that are available in the mainstream from your local computer store. In one or two cases I've picked an especially good or representative shareware program. However, remember that the screen illustrations in this chapter are meant to be representative or typical. Obviously, screens will vary from program to program, but they are reasonably consistent as to functionality, regardless of who the developer is.

Word Processing

The most-used programs in personal computing are probably word processors. In fact, as an office automation system, the popularity of PCs grew, at least in part, from early standalone word processing machines. The idea was that you needed more functionality for "power writing" than you could get in a simple typewriter. That led to a shopping list of things users wanted from their word processors. Like many types of programs, that list hasn't changed much over the years. Table 10.1 presents some of the things you should look for in a good word processing program. You can add or delete from this list depending on your particular needs.

Let's explore some of those terms so you'll know what you are looking for. We'll start with word wrap. Virtually all word processors today support word wrap. Word wrap is the function that watches your typing and, when you reach the end of a line, automatically moves you to the next line. Word wrap inserts a *soft return* at the end of every line. That means that the line has ended, but if you reformat the paragraph the soft return will automatically move to preserve effective word wrapping. A *hard return* is produced when you strike the [Enter] key. You generally use hard returns at the end of a paragraph.

A word processor without a spell checker is just about useless for most of us (Figure 10.1). There is simply no good reason to buy a word processing package without one. The more advanced products also add a thesaurus and the ability to create your own personal dictionary. Virtually all of them allow you to add new words to the program's dictionary.

Auto delete is the ability to easily delete characters, words, and whole lines of text. Unless you are specifically removing a character here or there, you should never have to remove a line or word a character at a time. Auto delete is a distant cousin of cut and paste. This is another "must have" function. Cut and paste lets you move or copy whole blocks of text within a document by marking the block and then moving it or copying it to some other location.

Special character effects, separate from font support, allow such elementary effects as boldface, underlining, and italics. Even the most primitive word processing requirements need this capability from time to time. Don't buy a word processor without it.

The idea of standard document support is a bit fuzzy. There are no real standards in this regard. There are several word processing programs that have gotten such wide use over the years that if you want to share documents on disk with other users, there is a good possibility that you'll run into one of them. Your word processor

---

▼ *Table 10.1. Typical Word Processor Capabilities*

• Word wrap	• Spell checking
• Auto delete	• Cut and paste
• Special character effects	• Standard document format
• Good printer support	• Paragraph formatting
• Large document support	• Format translation
• Column support	• Easy-to-use commands
• Search and replace	

▼ *Figure 10.1. A Typical Word Processing Screen (WordPerfect 5.1)*

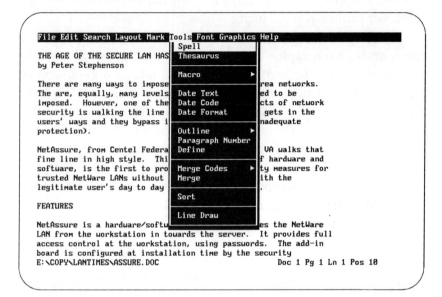

should be able to read and write document files in any of these formats or you won't be able to share. Here are a few of the best known formats.

- WordPerfect—all releases from 4.2 on
- Microsoft Word
- WordStar
- ASCII

There are others, of course, but these are the ones you'll run into most often.

Like standard formats, printer support is another area that is a bit unclear. There are hundreds, perhaps thousands, of different types and models of printers. No single program can possibly support them all on a model by model basis. However, the program should support a wide variety of common dot matrix printers such as Tally, Star Micronics, Epson, Diablo, and a few others. It should support all popular laser printers as well as PostScript (unless you never plan to use PostScript). And, of course, it should provide support, either directly or by supporting a workalike, for whatever printer you are using.

Paragraph formatting means that, in its simplest mode, a hard return ends a paragraph. Other features are automatic indent (both right-hand and left-hand) and adjustable tabs. An extension of paragraph formatting is the ability to manage *widows and orphans*. This is one of word processing's contributions to colorful computer phrases. Widows are the last lines of paragraphs that appear alone at the top of the next page. Orphans are the opposite: first lines of paragraphs that appear at the bottoms of pages.

Large document support is not usually a problem these days. But you should be sure that any limitations on the size of document files, maximum number of pages in a document, or the way the program handles large documents like books or large reports is consistent with the way you plan to use the application.

Format translation goes along with standard format support. The program should not only be able to use documents in other word processing formats, it should be able to save them to other formats. Column support is often important. Not all word processors are able to produce well-aligned columns in a multiple-column layout such as a newsletter. Your word processor should be able to produce smooth alignment whether your text is *right justified* (aligned against the right-hand side of the column), *left justified* (aligned against the left-hand edge of the column), or *ragged right* (justified against the left-hand edge but not the right). This should not change with the number of columns on the page.

In the easy-to-use commands department, there are many schools of thought. This is really a subjective decision. What is easy for you may not be easy for me. Part of this has to do with what you are used to. I prefer to use programs, such as WordPerfect, that make heavy use of function keys. However, if you type huge amounts of text without a lot of special formatting, you may prefer a program that uses combinations of [Ctrl], [Alt], and [Esc]ape with keyboard characters so that you don't have to take your fingers off the keyboard to touch the function keys. This may be the preference of many touch typists.

The last important feature of a good word processor is search

▼ *Table 10.2. Mainstream Word Processing Programs*

PROGRAM NAME	DEVELOPER
WordPerfect	WordPerfect Corp
Word	Microsoft Corp
Word for Windows	Microsoft Corp
WordStar	Micropro International
Multimate	Ashton-Tate
XyWrite	XyQuest

Applications— Your PC's Working Tools

and replace. This means that you can easily locate any combination of characters and, if you wish, replace it with other characters. We have (perhaps) spent an inordinate amount of time on the desirable features of word processors because they are the most commonly used of all applications. As you have seen, there is a lot that goes into them. We won't have quite as much to discuss with most of the other categories of software in this chapter. Table 10.2 lists some of the most popular word processor programs. All of these are mainstream programs.

Spreadsheets

Spreadsheets are programs that you mostly use for numeric (normally financial) analysis. They lay out numbers in a grid of *cells*. Each cell contains a number, text string, or a formula for making a calculation. The cells are identified on the grid by a combination of the number of a row and the letter of the column that intersects it. By placing formulas in some cells and numbers in others, you can calculate financial tables and reports including such things as balance sheets and profit and loss statements.

By extending the metaphor of the spreadsheet, you can produce an acceptable database format for collecting data, often numeric. Since this data is in a structured format, it is easy to extract and manipulate. Spreadsheets can be used for a variety of numeric reporting tasks. The two most popular spreadsheet programs are

1-2-3 produced by Lotus Development (Figure 10.2), and Quattro produced by Borland, International. For power users who need much more capability, including the ability to produce publishing quality printouts with several font styles, Microsoft Corporation produces Excel. Excel is available for both IBM-type PCs and Macintoshes.

If you need a spreadsheet program, for the most part, these are your choices. All have the same basic capabilities. They even accept data from Lotus 1-2-3 spreadsheets, the *defacto* standard. Also, many of the commands used by Quattro and Excel are the same as those used by 1-2-3. Quattro and Excel can produce spreadsheets that 1-2-3 can read. Even though 1-2-3 is the standard, you don't need to restrict your choice of a spreadsheet to the Lotus product. Quattro is a very commendable product and can cost less than 1-2-3. Excel is more expensive, requires Windows to run, and has significantly more capability than either Quattro or 1-2-3.

▼ *Figure 10.2. A Spreadsheet Screen (Lotus 1-2-3)*

```
A16:                                                                READY


          A        B        C        D        E        F        G        H
  1
  2                        MONTHLY SALES FIGURES
  3                        ---------------------
  4
  5
  6   DATE     VAL 1    VAL 2    VAL 3    VAL 4    VAL 5    SUM
  7   -------------------------------------------------------------------
  8   5/12/88     135     3948     6695    99843      553   111174
  9   6/15/88    4839     3498    45368     5637      453    59795
 10   7/13/88     763     5647    45327      679      345    52761
 11   8/14/88    4567     5768       80      456      790    11661
 12   9/15/88    3687     5789       45      890      324    10735
 13             -------- -------- -------- -------- -------- --------
 14   TOTALS    13991    24650    97515   107505     2465   246126
 15             ======== ======== ======== ======== ======== ========
 16
 17
 18
 19
 20
 18-Apr-91  05:24 PM                                               NUM
```

Database Management

Database management software is second in popularity to word processing software. It is also much more complex. There are two types of database management products: dedicated and nondedicated. Dedicated products are database management programs produced for a specific purpose. These are sometimes called *database applications*. Examples of these applications are phone list (Rolodex-type) programs, mailing list managers, and inventory control programs.

Nondedicated programs allow you to use a bare-bones database program for whatever task you wish. You use either a menu or you type commands to get the database to add records to a database file that you create, search the database for existing records, or create a database. Some of the more complete products are programmable. That means that you can write a database application for yourself, customized to your particular need. The prices of database management systems (sometimes called a *DBMS*) vary significantly from product to product. There are a few good shareware programs and there are complex programs costing thousands of dollars.

There is a lot of confusion in the database market about what the features of a database really mean. Due to the high level of advertising hype, novice users are very likely to make mistakes in the selection of a DBMS product. For example, many databases are advertised as being *relational*. For most database products all this really means is that you can use more than one database file at a time. For most beginning users, this is more than is needed. The typical new computer user needs little more than a simple way of organizing data and retrieving it systematically. The *single file* databases, generally the less expensive of the genre, are quite adequate for that.

There are literally hundreds of database products available. We certainly don't want to add to the confusion by discussing them all, so we'll stick with a few of the most representative. There are some *defacto* standards in the database world that you might want to consider, especially if you plan to exchange data with someone else. In terms of database formats, there are a few that you will run into more than others. The granddaddy of PC database management products is Ashton-Tate's dBASE line. The dBASE file format is considered almost a standard and many lesser products are designed to be compatible with it (Figure 10.3).

Borland's Paradox is also a very popular product, as is MicroRim's R:Base. Each of these products is programmable, sold as relational, and sports its own file format and programming language. They can also each be used without programming for *defacto queries. Defacto* queries are those that you make without writing a program. You simply make a choice from a menu or type a command or two. What the method of query is depends on the product. For example, you can use either a special menu (called the *command center*) or a command with dBASE. Paradox adds the ability to do *query by example*, a form of menuing, as does R:Base.

These three products are fairly expensive and complex, but they are also among the most complete DBMS programs available for your PC. Table 10.3 lists the typical programs, broken down by types.

▼ *Figure 10.3. A Database Management Program Screen (dBASE IV)*

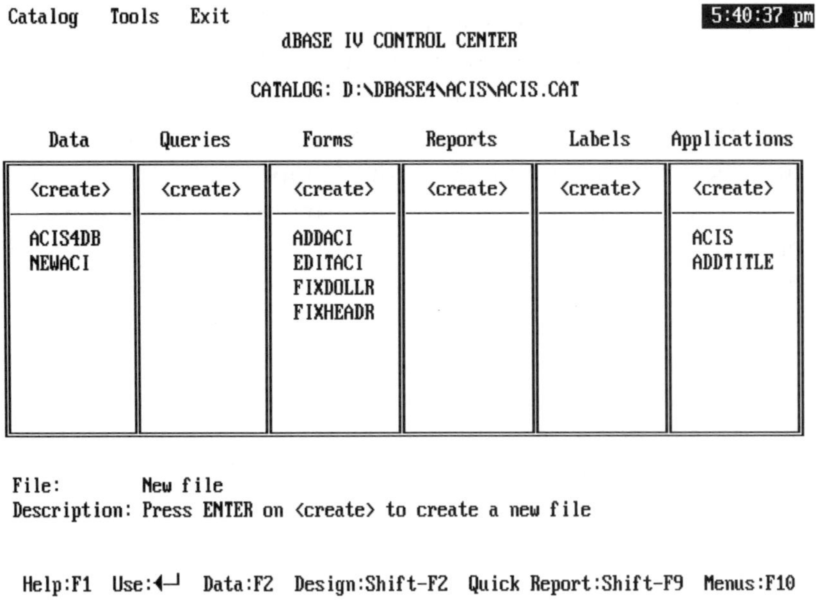

```
 Catalog   Tools   Exit                                       5:40:37 pm
                         dBASE IV CONTROL CENTER

                      CATALOG: D:\DBASE4\ACIS\ACIS.CAT

      Data       Queries      Forms      Reports     Labels    Applications
   ┌──────────┬──────────┬──────────┬──────────┬──────────┬──────────┐
   │ <create> │ <create> │ <create> │ <create> │ <create> │ <create> │
   ├──────────┼──────────┼──────────┼──────────┼──────────┼──────────┤
   │ ACIS4DB  │          │ ADDACI   │          │          │ ACIS     │
   │ NEWACI   │          │ EDITACI  │          │          │ ADDTITLE │
   │          │          │ FIXDOLLR │          │          │          │
   │          │          │ FIXHEADR │          │          │          │
   │          │          │          │          │          │          │
   │          │          │          │          │          │          │
   │          │          │          │          │          │          │
   └──────────┴──────────┴──────────┴──────────┴──────────┴──────────┘

 File:       New file
 Description: Press ENTER on <create> to create a new file

   Help:F1  Use:◄┘  Data:F2  Design:Shift-F2  Quick Report:Shift-F9  Menus:F10
```

There are, of course, a great many other products, but these are among the best known and easiest to locate in your computer store. They also contain the most representative of features. If you come across a product that you think you might like that is not on this list, simply find out how closely it resembles one of the example products.

Contact Management

Under this category I have included only those products that are designed specifically for contact management. These are professional products that you might use if you are a salesperson, for example. They are overkill if you simply want to keep track of a few dozen people on your Christmas card list. These products are high in functionality in those areas where professionals must manage a large list of contacts.

Capable contact management software products go far beyond being a database of names and addresses. They have the capability

▼ *Table 10.3. Typical Database Programs*

PRODUCT	DEVELOPER
SIMPLE, SINGLE FILE DATABASES	
PC File	Buttonware
Rapid File	Ashton-Tate
"RELATIONAL" DATABASES	
dBASE	Ashton-Tate
Paradox	Borland
R:Base	MicroRim
dBXL	WordTech Systems
FoxBase	Fox Software
TEXT DATABASES	
AskSam	AskSam Systems
Q & A	Symantic

of maintaining several phone numbers for each contact, lists of people associated with the contact, and even multiple addresses. They can organize contacts into groups based on a variety of criteria selected by you. For example, if you were an advertising salesperson, you might want to organize your client list by products, the frequency with which they advertise, or both.

Contact managers allow sorting geographically, by name, company, phone, or by any number of other criteria. They usually have built-in word processors that can create form letters addressed to contacts in the database according to whatever grouping you wish. Of course, they can print mail labels. These versatile programs keep track of your contact meetings, phone calls, and sales calls, and they notify when a followup is due. In short, they help you manage the entire sales process. There are only three of these products that have made serious inroads in mainstream business. They are The Maximizer, Telemagic, and Act.

Desktop Publishing

Desktop publishing adds a dimension to word processing: the dimension of graphics. Some advanced word processing programs, such as WordPerfect, contain elements of desktop publishing, but only a genuine DTP program provides all of the functionality you need (Figure 10.4). In addition to the usual word processing capabilities, DTP programs need extended font selection and control capability as well as the ability to control the spacing between characters (*kerning*) and the spacing between lines (*leading*). They need significant graphical controls so that pictures can be added easily. They also need advanced column controls along with a few typical graphics characters such as boxes.

DTP programs, as well as advanced word processors, make use of *style sheets*. Style sheets are layouts that you create that can be used over and over again to format text. By using style sheets, you don't have to set up the various type styles, spacings, and other design elements for a document each time you produce it. That means, for example, that you could have a style sheet for your company newsletter. Every time you produced the newsletter, the

▼ *Figure 10.4. A DTP Program Screen (Ventura Publisher)*

design would be exactly the same, and because of the style sheet you wouldn't have to set it up each time.

There are a number of desktop publishing systems available, but the two best known (and most competent) are Ventura Publisher and Aldus PageMaker. These are not trivial programs, nor are they inexpensive, but they contain everything you'd be likely to want in a desktop publishing program. Ventura Publisher is also available for the Macintosh (the Mac is the computer of choice for many desktop publishing practitioners because of its superior graphics handling capability). Another DTP program, available only for the Macintosh, is Quark Xpress. Any of these programs can range from the simple (uncomplicated brochures, manuals, newsletters, flyers) to the complex (four-color prepress designs, complex brochures, advertisements). They require significant computer resources, but if you need this type of computer power they are the best of the bunch.

Drawing Software

Drawing software is an extension of desktop publishing software. Its purpose, as the name implies, is to produce drawings. To augment drawing and desktop publishing software, you can purchase ready-made drawings called clip art. Clip art consists of pictures of almost all kinds in computer-usable format. By using clip art and your imagination you can modify the pictures to fit into your application, whether it is a newsletter, advertising piece, or a book like this one. The illustrations in this book were produced using clip art from a Canadian company called Art Right and modified to meet our needs using a drawing package called Corel Draw, also from Canada (Figure 10.5). There are dozens of other drawing packages, but they all share common characteristics.

A good drawing package must be able to fully manipulate pictures. That means not just drawing them, but rotating, stretching, and *scaling* them (adjusting them to fit in a space different from the one for which they were drawn originally). It must accept drawings in a variety of file formats because there is no single standard for file types in desktop publishing. You should be able to manage pictures in color and produce color separations for four-color reproduction if necessary and the package should support a wide variety of printers.

Business Forms Management

All businesses, large and small, use a variety of forms. In large companies these forms can run into the thousands. Many computer users depend on desktop publishing or word processing to create forms. However, there are some functions that are awkward to perform on these packages. Thus there is a relatively new class of software called *forms management software* (Figure 10.6). These products allow you to produce the kinds of boxes and lines typical of forms and, like database management systems, give the forms intelligence that allows users to fill them in easily on a PC.

There are two basic types of forms packages. One type, generally inexpensive, creates text-only forms. These simple, low-cost

Applications—Your PC's Working Tools

▼ *Figure 10.5. A Drawing Program Screen (Corel Draw)*

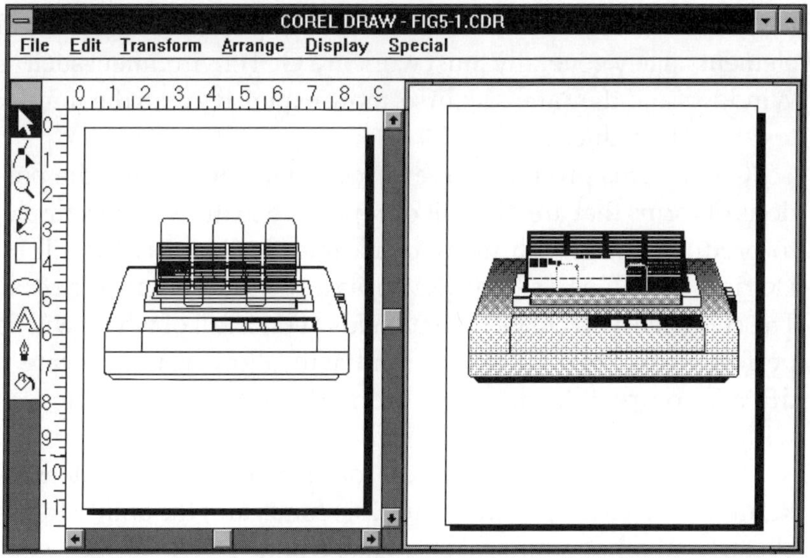

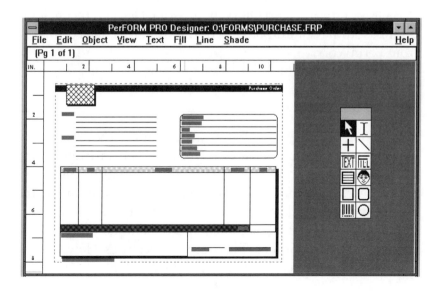

▼ *Figure 10.6. A Forms Management Program Screen (PerFORM Pro)*

programs cannot produce graphics or incorporate pictures in the forms. The other type, the graphical form processor, can create forms that are identical in look to the WYSIWYG forms produced by graphic artists. They can include logos and other graphical elements. They generally must work in a GUI environment such as Windows and they are, of course, more expensive than the simpler text-based products.

Good forms products have special tools for creating the portions of forms that are difficult or repetitive to draw. For example, to produce forms with many blank lines (called *fields*) to fill in, Delrina Technology's PerFORM uses a special tool called a *comb*. The comb lets you create several fields at once, all of which will be perfectly aligned and spaced and will allow you to create a dBASE-compatible database from the information filled in within them.

Like DTP packages, graphical forms products have extensive kerning and leading control, multiple fonts, and the ability to use clip art and other graphical elements. Unlike DTP packages, your ability to modify drawing in the forms package is limited. You must do that in a drawing package and import the finished drawing into the form. You can also support databases in forms packages. That means that you can fill in a form on your PC and save the data in a database. Good forms programs support industry standard databases such as dBASE. The major packages on the market are PerFORM Pro and PerFORM, both from Delrina Technology, FormBase from Ventura Software (formerly Xerox), and FormWorx from FormWorx.

Accounting

Accounting packages are all pretty much alike. They all contain accounts payable and receivable, payroll, and general ledger. Some also include sales order entry and inventory control. The differences are in the completeness of the packages. For example, the more expensive packages include support for multiple types of currencies, several bank accounts, more than one profit or cost center, and a host of other "big company" features. However, for most small businesses these functions are overkill.

Also, many of the more comprehensive (as well as more expensive and complicated to use and set up) packages come as separate *modules*. That means that, instead of buying a single accounting package, you buy the pieces you need and connect them together. If that sounds a bit complex to you, you're right. If you need something that extensive, I suggest that you find a computer literate accountant or a consultant who specializes in accounting applications and let them install your system for you.

If, on the other hand, you need only a small system (typical of small businesses and individual professionals such as doctors, lawyers, and consultants) you should go for the simplest package you can find (Figure 10.7). These packages tend to emulate your checkbook with the addition that they allow you to group your checks and deposits into categories called a *chart of accounts*. These categories, such as Travel, Advertising, and Taxes, are necessary for filling out your annual income tax return if you are in business. Probably the most popular of the simple "checkbook" packages is Quicken. It is also very inexpensive and available universally.

*Applications—
Your PC's
Working Tools*

▼ *Figure 10.7. A Very Simple Accounting Program Screen (Quicken)*

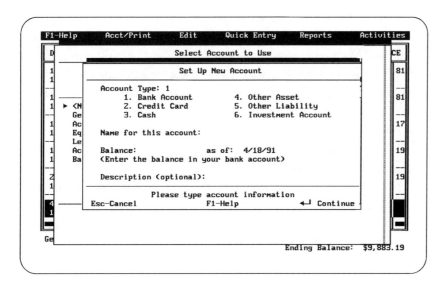

Personal Applications

This category takes in a number of different types of programs, such as personal organizers, desktop accessories, and information managers. Personal organizers follow the metaphor of the popular "Daytimer" time notebooks. These are calendars that leave space to schedule appointments, keep notes of meetings, collect phone numbers, and so forth. One of the best of these, with over 3,000,000 copies sold since the dawn of PC popularity, is SideKick from Borland. SideKick adds a calculator and other accessories to the calendaring.

Desktop accessories, like SideKick, are usually "pop-up" programs. They sit in your PC's memory and pop up when you strike a combination of keys called a "hot key." Desktop accessories usually include some type of notepad, a card file, a calculator, and some kind of calendaring. Windows includes an excellent set of desk accessories. There are many others, most of which are not from mainstream software companies. However, an inquiry to your computer dealer will certainly produce one or two alternatives. What to watch for with these products? Does it have the accessories you need? If it is a pop-up, how much memory does it consume? If you have expansion memory, can it use it?

Information Managers are little more than freeform text databases. You enter notes randomly, much as you would on a notepad or on the little yellow "stickies" called Post-it notes from 3M. Then the information manager (sometimes called a *PIM*—Personal Information Manager) organizes your notes so that you can retrieve the information in a variety of ways. Look for keyword searches in any PIM you buy; if you forget how you made your entry, you can still find the information if you can remember any key word or phrase in it.

The best of the low-cost PIMs in terms of popularity and availability is InfoSelect (formerly called Tornado Notes) from MicroLogic (Figure 10.8). Like the desktop pop-ups, InfoSelect can be installed as a pop-up so that you can hot key it onto your screen as you do something else, make your note or do a search, and return it to memory so that you can continue your task.

Utility Programs

Utility programs encompass those programs that perform some small useful function, usually related to the PC itself. There are many of these programs and quite a few are available as shareware. It seems that, of all the categories of software, utilities is the broadest and most difficult to define. This is because many programmers write these small programs to assist themselves in some task and then decide that the utility might have commercial possibilities.

There are a few things to look for in utility programs. First, because most of these programs have some purpose relating directly to your PC, they must be safe. Before you use a new utility, be sure that you have a good, current backup of any information on your hard disk. Second, ask as many people who have used the utility as you can find if they have had any difficulties with it. You can also refer to published reviews if there are any. Again, your

---

▼ *Figure 10.8. A Simple PIM Screen (InfoSelect)*

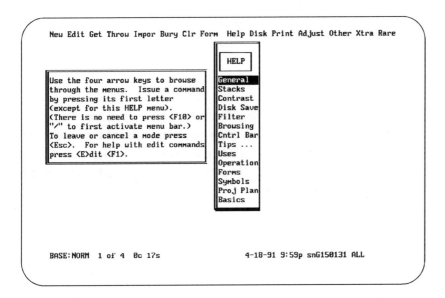

computer dealer can help you. Finally, most utilities are pretty easy to use. Many, like the Norton Utilities or PC Tools, come in collections. Here are some of the most common types of PC utilities.

File Recovery

"Oops. . .." It's the most dreaded word in the PC user's vocabulary. It usually means that he or she has just done something to lose a file or, worse, several files. Sometimes it comes right after the [Enter] following a del *.* command. It means data is gone. Data that may have taken months or years to accumulate. Fortunately, at this point the data is not really gone. As you learned when we talked about hard disks, the directory entry has simply been altered so that you can no longer see the file(s) and DOS can write new files over it (them).

If there were only a way to change the directory entry back. . .. There is. It's called a file recovery utility and the first and most popular is the unerase utility in the Norton Utilities from Peter Norton Computing. As long as you haven't saved anything to the disk, by using the Norton Utilities, PC Tools, or the Mace Utilities (among others) you should be able to resurrect your "deleted" file(s) from the dead and gone.

The file recovery utilities are the most useful of all of this class of software. Every PC user should have one.

AXIOM

Every PC user will, at some time in their career, experience a lost file, either through a problem with an errant program, or due to carelessness. The value of that one file, even if it is only a word processing document that you have been working on for a day or so, will more than justify the purchase of a file recovery utility.

Defragmenters

We briefly discussed defragmenters and why they are needed in Chapter 4. However, we didn't make any specific recommendations at that time. This is another class of software utility that belongs in every PC user's kit. However, this one requires careful selection because it is directly modifying the data on your hard disk.

Defragmenters read files, even if they are fragmented, and then they rewrite the files to a contiguous area on the hard disk. That means that the utility is constantly reading and writing data. Of necessity, it writes data from one part of the disk to another part, perhaps containing other data. If this process is not carefully controlled by the utility, you could lose a lot of data. For this reason, be sure that you have a current backup before you use a "defragger." Also, before you settle on a defragmenting utility, check the trade magazines for reviews and talk to your computer dealer.

Defraggers are very useful utilities. They can materially improve the performance of your hard disk, especially as it begins to fill with data. They require care to use and there are not very many good ones. Three of the best are Speed Disk, included with the Norton Utilities, FastTrax, and SpinRight. These have all been proven safe and effective.

File Transfer

There are times when you might want to transfer several files from one PC to another. One of those times is when you use a laptop PC and you want to put files on it from a desktop PC. This is the time to use a file transfer utility. These utilities don't let two computers *share* files, as in a local area network. They simply let you *move* files from one computer to another through a cable connecting the two PCs. There are two very good file transfer utilities. The most popular is LapLink from Traveling Software (Figure 10.9). The other program, also excellent, is called the Brooklyn Bridge.

Zippers

The last class of utility software we're going to discuss is called *file compression software*, or "zippers." The purpose of a zipper is to compress a large file for storage so that it doesn't take as much disk space. The slang term comes from the utility by Phil Katz called

▼ *Figure 10.9. A File Transfer Software Screen (LapLink)*

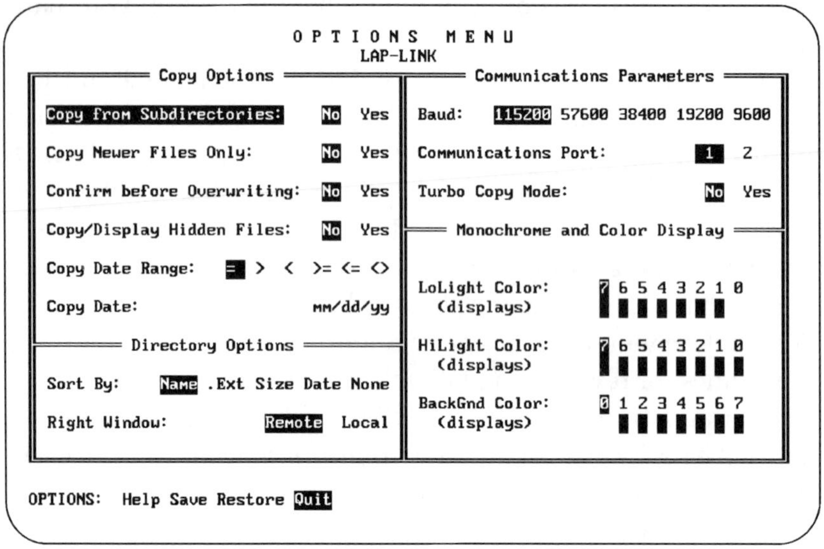

```
                    O P T I O N S   M E N U
                         LAP-LINK
═════ Copy Options ═════      ═══ Communications Parameters ═══

Copy from Subdirectories:  No  Yes   Baud:  115200 57600 38400 19200 9600

Copy Newer Files Only:     No  Yes   Communications Port:      1  2

Confirm before Overwriting: No Yes   Turbo Copy Mode:          No Yes

Copy/Display Hidden Files:  No  Yes  ═══ Monochrome and Color Display ═══

Copy Date Range:    = > < >= <= <>   LoLight Color:   7 6 5 4 3 2 1 0
Copy Date:              mm/dd/yy      (displays)

═════ Directory Options ═════        HiLight Color:   7 6 5 4 3 2 1 0
                                       (displays)
Sort By:    Name .Ext Size Date None
                                     BackGnd Color:   0 1 2 3 4 5 6 7
Right Window:      Remote  Local       (displays)

OPTIONS:  Help Save Restore Quit
```

Pkzip. Pkzip produces a compressed copy of a file that takes up much less space on a disk than the original.

You can't use a compressed file without *uncompressing* it first. Logically, for every "zipper" there is an "unzipper." In the case of Pkzip, not surprisingly, it is Pkunzip. Pkzip is a fairly recent product. Prior to Pkzip, Phil Katz produced Pkarc (an archiving program that performed the same task). However, another company controlled the term "arc" when referring to an archiving program, and Katz had to create a new program with a new name.

Pkzip, for single users, is in the public domain. As you have already learned, that means you don't need to purchase it to use it. If you are a corporation or if you are including the program in your own product, however, you will need to pay a license fee. Pkzip is readily available on virtually every bulletin board system in the country. You will need it if you are downloading programs from BBS systems since almost all such programs are zipped to save space and combine several programs into a single file. When you unzip the file, Pkunzip not only uncompresses the file, it separates the several files included in the "zip-file" into their original states. You won't need this one unless you need to unzip zipped files or if you want a way of compressing files that you no longer use, but wish to save.

Summary

- As a general rule, within any applications type (word processors, databases, etc.) you'll find that there is very little functional difference for the average user among the top contenders.

- If you are asking other users for recommendations, ask for specifics and try to weed out the emotional attachment.

- A word processor without a spell checker is just about useless for most of us.

- Spreadsheets are programs that you usually use for numeric (normally financial) analysis. They lay out numbers in a grid of *cells*.

- There are two types of database management products: dedicated and nondedicated. Dedicated products are database management programs produced for a specific purpose. Nondedicated programs allow you to use a bare-bones database program for whatever task you wish.

- For most database products all being relational really means is that you can use more than one database file at a time.

- Desktop publishing adds the dimension of graphics to word processing. Some advanced word processing programs contain elements of desktop publishing, but only a genuine DTP program provides all of the functionality you need.

- Forms processors allow you to produce the kinds of boxes and lines typical of forms and, like database management systems, give the forms intelligence that allows users to fill them in easily on a PC.

PRACTICE WHAT YOU'VE LEARNED

1. What are some of the criteria that you can use to determine what software package you purchase?

2. What are the two most-used types of software applications?

3. What is word wrap?

4. What is the difference between right justified, left justified, and ragged right in word processing?

5. What can contact managers do for you?

6. What are style sheets?

7. What differentiates forms management software from DTP or word processing software?

8. What is a PIM?

9. Name an important precaution to take prior to defragmenting your hard disk.

ANSWERS

1. How much are you willing to pay? What are your particular needs? What environment are you going to use the application in? How much technical support are you likely to need on the software?

2. Word processors and database management systems

3. Word wrap is the function that watches your typing and, when you reach the end of a line, automatically moves you to the next line.

4. Left justified aligns the text with the left-hand side of the column.Right justified aligns it with the right column edge and ragged right justifies left and leaves the right-hand side unjustified.

5. They have the capability of maintaining several phone numbers for each contact, lists of people associated with the contact, and multiple addresses. They organize contacts into

groups based on a variety of criteria selected by you. They allow sorting geographically, by name, company, phone, or by any number of other criteria. They have built-in word processors that can create form letters and can print mail labels. They keep track of your contacts and notify when a followup is due.

6. Style sheets are layouts that you create that can be used over and over again to format text.

7. Good forms products have special tools for creating the portions of forms that are difficult or repetitive to draw.

8. Personal Information Manager

9. Back up your disk

Index

A

Accessories, described, 14–15. See also
    Peripherals; *entries under specific
    equipment*
Accounting programs, selection of,
    232–233
Add-in cards, ports and, 59, 60
Adobe Corporation, 35, 131
Aldus PageMaker, 229
American Standard Code for Informa-
    tion Interchange. *See* ASCII
ANSI, terminal program and, 156–157
Apple Computer. *See also* Macintosh
    DOS and, 29
    graphical work surface menus and,
        170
    operating system of, 11–12
    processors and, 36
Application programs. *See also* Software;
    Utility programs
    accounting, 232–233
    business forms management,
        230–232

bytes and, 25
    contact management, 227–228
    database management, 225–227
    described, 17, 22–23
    desktop publishing, 228–229
    drawing software, 230
    personal applications, 233–234
    selection of, 218–219
Application programs (*continued*)
    spreadsheets, 223–224
    word processing, 219–223
Argument, command syntax and, 76
Art Right, 230
ASCII (American Standard Code for
    Information Interchange)
    defined, 23
    printers and, 121–122
    text file, batch file and, 89
Ashton-Tate dBASE line, described, 38,
    226
Assistance, information resources, 21–22
AT command set. *See* Commands:
    modems

Autoexec.bat file
  described, 24, 92–94
  file organization and, 107, 109

B

Backup, 112–115
  defined, 23–24
  DOS and, 29
  grandfathering, 113–115
  importance of, 112
  techniques of, 112–113
Backup command, described, 77–78
Bad block error, terminal program and, 151
Baseline, backups and, 114
Basic Input/Output System (BIOS). *See* BIOS
Batch files
  described, 24, 89
  file organization and, 108
BAT directory, creation of, 108
Battery, CMOS memory and, 71
BBS programs. *See* Bulletin board systems (BBSs)
BIOS
  command.com and, 26
  described, 25, 72–73
  purpose of, 70
Bit, byte and, 25
BIX system, 156
Boot files. *See* Autoexec.bat file; Config.sys file
Borland, International, 223–224
Braces ({}), command syntax and, 76
Brackets ([]), command syntax and, 76
Buffers
  Config.sys file and, 90–91
  erratic program behavior and, 209

Bugs, viri contrasted, 209–210
Bulletin board systems (BBSs)
  described, 154–157
  shareware viri and, 193, 211
  virus scanners from, 212–213
  zipper programs and, 238–239
Business forms management programs, selection of, 230–232
BusinessLand, evaluation of, 20
Bus mouse, 34, 62
Bus width, speed and, 44–45
Button, Jim, 191
Byte, defined, 25–26

C

Call command, described, 94
Cartridges. *See* Toner cartridges
Cd or chdir command, described, 78
CD-ROM, defined, 34
Central processor unit. *See* Processor(s)
Centronics connector, 60, 124
CERTUS program, 213
Chain stores, evaluation of, 20
Character sets, 121–122, 127
Chdir or cd command, described, 78
Checkbook, buying decision and, 3–4
Chips, processor types and, 36, 43
Chkdsk command, described, 78–79
Clip art
  drawing software and, 230
  laser printer and, 128
Clones
  cost of, 12
  risk in buying, 12–14
Cls command, described, 79–80
CMOS
  BIOS contrasted, 72
  described, 71–72

purpose of, 70
Color displays, 51–53. *See also* Displays
Color Graphics Adapter (CGA), 51–52
    described, 28
    Enhanced Graphics Adapter (EGA), 52
    Microsoft Windows and, 173
    Video Graphics Array (VGA), 52–53
Color Graphics Adapter (CGA), 28, 51–52
Command.com
    defined, 26
    DOS and, 29, 73–74
    file organization and, 107
Commands
    backup, 77–78
    chdir or cd, 78
    chkdsk, 78–79
    cls, 79–80
    date, 80
    del, 80
    dir, 81–82
    diskcomp, 82–83
    diskcopy, 83
    fdisk, 83–84
    format, 84–85
    mkdir or md, 85
    modems and, 146, 151–154
    ren, 85
    restore, 85–86
    rmdir or rd, 86
    syntax overview of, 76–77
    time, 86–87
    type, 87
    ver, 87
    xcopy, 87–88
COMM ports
    described, 37, 58–60

modems and, 140–144, 148
    printers and, 124
Communication. *See* Modems
Communication ports. *See* COMM ports
Compatibility
    BIOS and, 72–73
    modems and, 146, 151–52
CompuServe system, 156
Computer bulletin board systems (BBSs). *See* Bulletin board systems (BBSs)
ComputerLand, evaluation of, 20
Computer paper. *See* Paper
Config.sys file
    described, 24, 90–91
    erratic program behavior and, 209
    file organization and, 107, 109
Conflicts, I/O or interrupt request (IRQ) conflicts, 64, 142–143
Contact management programs, selection of, 227–228
Containment, virus protection through, 213–214
Contiguous memory. *See* ExTended memory
Continuous feed, printers and, 122
Control characters, printers and, 133–135
Controller card, disks drives and, 57
Corel Draw, 230
Corona wire, laser printer maintenance, 130–131
Corruption, viri and, 208
Costs
    clones, 12
    hard disk drives, 58
    low-cost software, 187–200
CPU. *See* Processor(s)
Cursor
    defined, 26

mouse and, 62
Cut sheet feeder, described, 122
Cyclic redundancy check, terminal
    program and, 150
Cylinder, defined, 56

D

Daisy wheel printer, 32, 120–121, 125
Database, described, 17–18
Database management systems
    graphical work surface menus and,
        170
    selection of, 225–227
    system software and, 38
Data bits, terminal program and, 148
Date command, described, 80
dBASE IV, described, 38, 226
Defacto queries, database management,
    226
Defragmenter utility programs
    described, 110–111
    selection of, 236–237
Del command, described, 80
Delimeter characters, command syntax
    and, 76
Delrina Technology, 232
Density, floppy disk drives, 53
Desktop accessory programs, described,
    233–234
Desktop (graphical work surface)
    menus, described, 162, 166, 169–172
Desktop publishing programs
    defined, 26–27
    laser printer and, 31, 127
    selection of, 228–229
Device drivers. *See also* Driver software
    Config.sys file and, 91

file organization and, 108
Digitizer puck, 62
Dir command, described, 81–82
Directories
    key directories, 108–109
    menu shells and, 168–169
    other directories, 109
    structure of, hard disk and, 102–103
Diskcomp command, described, 82–83
Diskcopy command
    backup and, 113
    described, 83
Disk drive(s), 53–58
    defined, 27–28. *See also* Floppy
        disk(s); Floppy disk drive(s);
        Hard disk(s); Hard disk drive(s)
Disk manager utility, described, 111–112
Disk Operating System (DOS). *See* DOS
Display adapter, described, 28
Displays, 50–53
    color, 51–53
        Color Graphics Adapter (CGA),
          51–52
        Enhanced Graphics Adapter
          (EGA), 52
        Video Graphics Array (VGA),
          52–53
    described, 14, 28
    desktop publishing and, 27
    GEM desktop menu system and,
        170–171
    Microsoft Windows and, 173
    monochrome, 28, 50–51
DOS
    ASCII and, 23
    backup and recovery by, 23–24
    COMM ports and, 58, 142
    described, 29, 73–76

menu shells and, 167, 168
purpose of, 70
DOS commands. *See* Commands
DOS directory, creation of, 108
DOS formatting, hard disk, 106–107. *See also* Formatting
DOS memory, described, 61, 94–95
DOS prompt
interfacing at, 163
menu shells and, 169
DOS prompt commands, described, 93–94
Dot matrix printer(s), 29–30, 120, 123–125. *See also* Laser printer(s); PostScript laser printers and language; Printer(s)
Downloading, terminal program and, 150–151
Drawing software programs, selection of, 230
Driver software. *See also* Device drivers
mouse, 63
printer drivers, 134–135
scanners and games, 64
Drop-down menu, described, 166
Drums, laser printer maintenance, 130–131

E
Egghead Discount Software, evaluation of, 20
Electronic mail, described, 155–156
Electronic printers, described, 122. *See also* Laser printers; Printers
Enhanced Graphics Adapter (EGA), 28, 52
Enhanced keyboard, 49–50

Enter key, functions of, 48
Erasable optical disk, defined, 35
ESDI, described, 57
Excel program, 224
ExPanded memory, described, 61, 94, 95–96
Expansion memory, described, 94, 95–96
ExTended memory
described, 94, 95–96
RAM and, 61

F
FastTrax program, 237
FAT (File Allocation Table), creation of, 106
Fdisk
described, 83–84
hard disk partitioning, 106
File Allocation Table (FAT), creation of, 106
File compression software (zippers), selection of, 237–239
File management and organization, 107–109
backing up and, 112–115
disk manager utility, 111–112
fragmented files, 110–111
key directories, 108–109
other directories, 109
overview of, 107
File recovery
defined, 23–24
DOS and, 29
File recovery utility programs, selection of, 236
Files. *See* System files
Files statement, erratic program

behavior and, 209
File transfers, terminal program and, 150–151
File transfer utility programs, selection of, 237
Fixed disk drives. *See* Hard disk drive(s)
Floppy disk(s). *See also* Disk drive(s); Hard disk(s); Hard disk drive(s)
    $3\frac{1}{2}$" disks, 54–55
    $5\frac{1}{4}$" disks, 53–54
    defined, 27
Floppy disk drive(s), described, 14, 27, 53–55
Fluegelman, Andrew, 191
Fonts
    defined, 30
    laser printer and, 31, 127
    selection of, 128
Format command, described, 84–85
Formatting
    floppy disks, 53–54
    hard disk, 57
    DOS formatting of, 106–107
    low-level formatting of, 104–105
FormBase program, 232
Forms management programs, selection of, 230–232
FormWorx, 232
Forward slash (/), command syntax and, 76
Foxbase program, 170
Fragmented files
    defragging, 110–111
    defragmenter utility program selection, 236–237
Free software, 194–195
Freeware, described, 194–195
Full page monitor. *See* Paper-white

graphics display
Function keys, use of, 48

G
Game port, described, 63
Games, described, 18
GEM desktop menu system, described, 170–172
Grandfathering, backing up, 113–115
Graphical user interface (GUI), 163
    described, 166
    Microsoft Windows, 172–182
Graphical work surface. See Desktop (graphical work surface) menus
Graphics
    defined, 30
    graphical user interface (GUI) and, 166
    laser printer and, 127
Graphics monitors, described, 50–51
Gray-scale displays, described, 51
GUI. *See* Graphical user interface (GUI)

H
Handbooks, information resources, 19–20
Handshaking, terminal program and, 151
Hard disk(s). See also Disk drive(s); Floppy disk(s); Floppy disk drive(s)
    defined, 27
    directory structure and, 102–103
    disk manager utility, 111–112
    DOS formatting of, 106–107
    file organization and, 107
    low-level formatting of, 104–105

partitioning of (FDISK program),
106
Hard disk drive(s), 55–58
described, 14, 27, 55–56
preparation for use of, 56–57
speed of, 57–58
Hard return, word wrap and, 220
Hardware, software matching and, 4–5.
See also Displays; Mouse; Peripherals;
Printer(s); Processor(s)
Hayes Microcomputer Products, 146,
151–152
Hercules graphic card, 28, 50
Hewlett-Packard Company, 31, 32, 35
laser printer standards, 127
PostScript printers compared, 131,
132
Hierarchical menus, described, 167
High memory, described, 61, 96–97
HOLD directory, creation of, 108
Hot keys
desktop accessory programs, 233,
234
pop-ups and, 97

I
IBM
DOS and, 29, 74–75
operating system of, 11–12
processors and, 36
Ibmbios.com, DOS and, 73
Ibmdos.com, DOS and, 73
IBM extended characters, printers and,
121–122
Icons, Macintosh and, 170
Incremental backup, described, 114
Information Manager program,

described, 234
Information resources, 18–22
assistance and, 21–22
magazines and handbooks, 19–20
salespeople, 20–21
Info Select program, 234
Ink jet printer, described, 121
Intel Corporation, processors and, 43
Internal word size, processing speed
and, 45
Interrupt request (IRQ)
COMM ports and, 142–143
conflicts and, 64
ports and, 59
I/O address
COMM ports and, 142–143
conflicts and, 64
ports and, 59
IRQ. *See* Interrupt request (IRQ)

J
Jargon, 22
Joystick, described, 63

K
Katz, Phil, 195, 238
Keyboard, 47–50
Kilobyte, defined, 25–26

L
LAN, defined, 30–31
Laser printer(s), 126–133. *See also*
PostScript laser printers and
language; Printer(s)
clip art and, 128

described, 31–32, 121
fonts for, 128
memory requirements for, 128–129
paper and toner for, 129–131
PostScript printers, 131–133
selection of, 129
speeds of, 128
standards of, 127
Letter quality printer(s), 32, 120–121,
    125. *See also* Printer(s)
Licensing, of software, 196–198
Light bar menus, described, 162
Line printers, described, 122
Local Area Network (LAN), defined,
    30–31
Logic bomb, defined, 202
Lotus 1-2-3 program, 223–224
Lotus Development, 223
Lotus menu, described, 165–166
Low-cost software, 187–200
    free software, 194–195
    overview of, 187–188
    piracy, 196–198
    pricing games and, 188–191
    shareware, 191–194
Low-level formatting, hard disk, 56,
    104–105
LPT1
    defined, 37
    ports and, 60
    printers and, 123, 124
LPT4, defined, 37

M
Mace Utilities, 236
Macintosh. *See also* Apple Computer
    desktop publishing and, 229

graphical work surface menus, 170
    processors and, 36
Magazines, information resources, 19–20
Magnetic tape storage, defined, 32
Mail-order buying, assembly require-
    ments, 13–14
Mass storage, defined, 32
McAfee and Associates, 203, 204
McAfee Validate, 213
McAfee Viruscan, 212
MCIMail, described, 155–156
Md or mkdir command, described, 85
Megabyte, defined, 25
Memory
    defined, 32–33
    DOS memory, 94–95
    expansion of, 95–96
    high memory, 96–97
    laser printer requirements of,
        128–129
    menu shells and, 167, 168
    overview of, 61–62
    processor and, 36, 44, 46
    RAM, defined, 32–33
    RAM resident programs and, 37
    recommended requirements for, 97
    ROM, defined, 37
    types of, 94
Menu(s), 162–172
    defined, 33
    desktop (graphical work surface),
        169–172
    menu shells, 167–169
    overview of, 162
    selection of, 163
    types of, 164–166
MFM hard disk drive, described, 57
MicroLogic, 234

Microsoft Corporation, 224
Microsoft DOS, 74
Microsoft Windows, 172–182
    applications of, 173–174
    files in, 175–181
    GEM interface and, 171
    modes of, 173
    non-Windows applications,
      174–175
    overview of, 172–173
    simplification of, 181–182
Mkdir or md command, described, 85
Modems, 139–159
    BBS programs and, 154–157
    commands for, 151–154
    described, 15, 143–144
    ports and, 60, 140–143
    speed of, 145
    terminal program and, 145–151
Monitor. *See* Displays
Monochrome displays, described, 28,
    50–51
Mother board, processor types and, 43
Mouse
    described, 33–34, 62–63
    driver of, 63
Mouse.com file, 63
Mouse pad, described, 62
Mouse.sys file, 63
Moving bar menu, described, 164–166
MS-DOS, defined, 29. See also entries
    under DOS

N
Near letter quality printer, described, 29,
    123, 125
Nesting, Microsoft Windows and,
    181–182
Norton Utilities, 236, 237
Numeric keypad, functions of, 48–49
Num Lock key, functions of, 49

O
One byte at a time port, defined, 37
Operating systems. *See also entries under*
  DOS
    computer types and, 5, 11–12
    DOS and, 29
Optical disk, 34–35
Optical storage, 32
Options, command syntax and, 76

P
Page definition language, 32, 35
Page frame, exPanded memory and, 96
PageMaker (Aldus), 229
Page printers, described, 122
Paper
    dot matrix printers and, 122–123
    laser printers and, 130
Paper-white graphics display, 28, 50–51
Parallel dot matrix printers, described,
    123, 124
Parallel ports, 37, 59–60
Parity, terminal program and, 148
Parity check, terminal program and, 149
Partitioning, hard disk, 56–57
PATH statement
    menu shells and, 168–169
    program installation and, 109
Payload, defined, 202
PC-DOS, defined, 29
PerFORM program, 232

Peripherals
 Config.sys file and, 91
 described, 15, 35
 mouse, 62–63
 ports and, 58
 RS-232 and, 37
Personal applications programs, selection of, 233–234
Personal computer
 accessories for, 14–15
 buying decision, 3–5
 information resources for, 18–22
 operating system types of, 11–12
 types of, 5–11
 upgrading of, 10–11
Personal Information Manager programs, described, 234
Personal organizer programs, described, 233–234
Peter Norton Computing, 236
Pins, dot matrix printer and, 123
Piracy, 196–198
Pixels
 defined, 52
 displays and, 52–53
Pkarc program, 238
Pkunzip program, 193, 238–239
Pkzip program, 193, 195, 238
Platter, defined, 55–56
Pointing devices
 digitizer puck, 62
 mouse, 62–63
Pop-ups. See RAM resident memory
Ports
 described, 58–60
 modems and, 140–143
 printers and, 123, 124
 RS-232 and, 37

PostScript laser printers and language
 control characters for, 133
 described, 32, 35, 131–133
 fonts for, 128
 laser printer standards, 127
 word processing programs and, 221
Printer(s), 119–138. See also Dot matrix printer(s); Laser printer(s); PostScript laser printers and language
 basic concepts of, 120–121
 control of, 133–135
 described, 15, 16
 desktop publishing and, 27
 dot matrix printers, 29–30, 123–125
 driving of, 134–135
 laser printers, 31–32, 126–133
 letter quality printer, 32
 PostScript and, 35
 theory behind, 121–123
 word processing programs and, 221–222
Printer driver. See Device drivers; Driver software
Printer ports, described, 58–60
Processing speed
 bus width and, 44–45
 hard disk drives and, 57–58
 processor and, 44, 45–46
Processor(s), 42–46
 bus width and, 44–45
 defined, 35–36
 functions of, 43–44
 Microsoft Windows and, 173
 overview of, 42–43
 types of, 9, 10, 45–46
  8088 processor, 36
  80286 processor, 36
   described, 45

speed and, 44
80386 processor, 36
    described, 46
    Microsoft Windows and, 173
    speed and, 44
80386SX processor, 36
    described, 46
    Microsoft Windows and, 173
80486 processor, 36
    described, 46
    Microsoft Windows and, 173
Program Information Files (PIFs), 175
Programming language software,
    described, 17
Prompt commands, described, 93–94
Pull-down menu, 165, 166

Q
QuarkXpress program, 229
Quattro program, 223–224

R
Radio Shack (Tandy), evaluation of, 20
RAM
    defined, 32–33
    divisions of, 61
RAM resident program (terminate and
    stay resident program)
    defined, 37
    high memory and, 96–97
    mouse and, 63
Rd or rmdir command, described, 86
Recovery. *See* File recovery
Ren command, described, 85
Resolution, monitors and, 28
Restore command, described, 85–86. *See*

also File recovery
Ribbon cables, disks drives and, 57
RLL hard disk drive, described, 57
Rmdir or rd command, described, 86
ROM
    BIOS and, 72
    defined, 37
RS-232, defined, 37

S
Safety. *See* Backup; Viruses
Salespeople, information resources,
    20–21
Scanners
    described, 30, 63–64
    virus protection by, 212–213
Screen. *See* Displays
SCSI, described, 58
Sector, defined, 56
Separator characters, command syntax
    and, 76
Serial dot matrix printers, described,
    123, 124
Serial mouse, 34, 62
Serial ports, 37, 59–60
Setup program, CMOS and, 71
Shareware
    described, 191–194
    viri and, 210–212
Shelling, explained, 167
Soft fonts
    defined, 31
    laser printer standards and, 127
    selection of, 128
Soft return, word wrap and, 219–220
Software. *See also* Application programs;
    Utility programs

BBS programs and, 155
buying decision and, 4
described, 17–18, 22–23
hardware matching and, 4–5
low-cost software, 187–200
piracy of, 196–198
system software, defined, 38
SoftWareHouse, evaluation of, 20
Software Publishers Association, 198
Speed. *See* Processing speed
Speed Disk program, 237
Spell checker, 220
SpinRight program, 237
Spreadsheet programs, selection of,
223–224
Startup, information resources for, 21–22
Stop bits, terminal program and, 149
Storage, mass storage, defined, 32. *See
also* Memory
Submenus, described, 167
Super VGA, defined, 28
Switches, command syntax and, 76
Syntax, defined, 76
System files
Config.sys file and, 90–91
DOS and, 73
System.ini file, described, 175–176, 179
System level programs, 70–100
Autoexec.bat file, 92–94
batch file, 89
BIOS, 72–73
CMOS and setup, 71–72
commands in, 76–88
Config.sys file, 90–91
DOS, 73–76
overview of, 70
System software, defined, 38. *See also*
Software

Sytem clock, speed and, 44, 45

T
Tandy (Radio Shack), evaluation of, 20
Telephone. *See* Modems
TEMP directory, creation of, 108
Terminal program, 146–151
ANSI and, 156–157
file transfers and, 150–151
purposes of, 146–147
setup of, 148–150
Terminate and Stay Resident (TSR). *See*
RAM resident program
Text files
ASCII and, 23
bytes and, 25
Thesaurus, 220
Time command, described, 86–87
Timeout error, terminal program and,
151
Toner cartridges
described, 129–131
refilling of, 130
Tractor, printers and, 122
Trojan horse, viri and, 203
TSRs. See RAM resident program
Type command, described, 87

U
Unzipper, shareware and, 193
Uploading, terminal program and,
150–151
User interfaces, 161–185
menus, 162–172
Microsoft Windows, 17–182
Utilities

backup and recovery by, 23–24
described, 17
disk manager utility, 111–112
DOS and, 73–74
Utility programs, 235–239. *See also*
   Application programs; Software
      defragmenters, 236–237
      file recovery, 236
      file transfer, 237
      overview of, 235–236
      zippers, 237–239
UTILS directory, creation of, 108

V
Vector, viri and, 203
Ventura Publisher, 229
Ventura Software, 232
Ver command, described, 87
Video display terminal (VDT). *See*
   Displays
Video Graphics Array (VGA), 28, 52–53
Video memory, described, 61
Viri, 201–216
      action of, 202–203
      classification of, 203–208
      definitions in, 202
      diagnosis of, 208–210

methods of identifying, 212–214
shareware and, 192–193, 210–212
worms contrasted, 203

W
Windows. *See* Microsoft Windows
Win.ini file, described, 175–176
Word processing documents, bytes and,
   25
Word processing programs
      ASCII and, 23
      selection of, 219–223
Word size (internal), processing speed
   and, 45
Word wrap, described, 219–220
Worms, described, 203
WORMs (optical disk), defined, 34
WYSIWYG, defined, 38

X
Xcopy command, described, 87–88

Z
Zipper utility programs, selection of,
   237–239